Anti-Avoidance Legislation

R. K. Ashton
Ph.D, ACA,
Barrister of Lincoln's Inn

London
Butterworths
1981

England Butterworth & Co (Publishers) Ltd
London 88 Kingsway, WC2B 6AB

Australia Butterworths Pty Ltd
Sydney 271–273 Lane Cove Road, North Ryde, NSW 2113
Also at Melbourne, Brisbane, Adelaide and Perth

Canada Butterworth & Co (Canada) Ltd
Toronto 2265 Midland Avenue, Scarborough, M1P 4S1

New Zealand Butterworths of New Zealand Ltd
Wellington 33–35 Cumberland Place

South Africa Butterworth & Co (South Africa) (Pty) Ltd
Durban 152–154 Gale Street

USA Butterworth (Publishers) Inc
Boston 10 Tower Office Park, Woburn, Mass 01801

ISBN 0 406 11140 5

Photoset by Butterworths Litho Preparation Department
Printed and bound in Great Britain
by Billing and Sons Limited
Guildford, London, Oxford, Worcester

Preface

The motivation for writing this book was twofold: one – the increasing use made by the Revenue of Part XVII of the Taxes Act, and two – the lack of a comprehensive guide to the legislation and related tax law. In the last few years there has been a significant increase in tax planning and the Revenue have sought to use these sections wherever they think there is scope for their application, irrespective of the 'mischief' originally arrived at by the legislation. For example, recently the Revenue have sought to apply the provisions of TA 1970, ss. 471–475 to merchant banks dealing in Eurobonds; hitherto these provisions were thought to be of more restricted application.

The attitude of successive Governments to tax avoidance as reflected by the legislation has been to legislate on a piecemeal basis, as and when a scheme was either brought to the attention of the Revenue or after litigation in the courts. The hostility of the Revenue referred to above has demonstrated itself in two ways: the introduction of retrospective legislation to counter a scheme once it has become 'publicised' in the press, e.g. the partnership commodity straddle arrangements, and the zeal with which it has conducted recent litigation; no document has been unimportant enough not to pursue with tenacity that has often bordered on harassment and an abrogation of civil rights.

This hostility has led a number of people to think that in the next few years widely drawn anti-avoidance legislation of a general nature will be introduced, the effect of which will be to set aside arrangements where the principal motive and benefit is the avoidance of tax. Such legislation is difficult to draft but does exist in the United States, South Africa and Australia. This may come with a change of government but it must be doubted, given the assurances by the Conservative party in opposition that schemes would be legislated on as and when they were brought to the attention of the Revenue, that such legislation will be introduced in the immediate future. In addition the Revenue may now feel they have sufficient ammunition to counter all tax arrangements as a result of the *Ramsay* decision.

It follows from this discussion that until general anti-avoidance legislation is introduced there is a need for a book which provides professional advisers and their clients with a comprehensive review of the legislation and related case law, together with some useful pointers as to how arrangements can be structured which are outside the clutches of the relevant section or sections of the Taxes Act.

This book will be of assistance to accountants and solicitors in practice and to any businessman who is contemplating a transaction which might fall within these sections. It will also be of use to students studying Revenue Law at both undergraduate and graduate levels.

Finally, I would like to thank my wife and family who have become accustomed to my being locked away in my study for many hours in preparation of this book.

The law is as stated at 1 August 1981.

R. K. Ashton
3 Verulam Buildings
Gray's Inn
London WC1

September 1981

Contents

Table of statutes

Paragraph numbers printed in bold type indicate where the section of an Act is set out in part or in full.

Table of cases

1 Transactions in securities

1.1 Introduction

The provisions of TA 1970, ss. 460–468 are often very important in relation to the reconstruction and reorganisation of family controlled companies. Indeed, until recently, most of the litigation relating to these sections involved family controlled companies. An example of a potential 's. 460' situation is where a subsidiary of a family controlled company is liquidated with a substantial balance standing to the credit of the profit and loss account etc., and the assets are sold for a nominal sum to another company in the group. Clearly the subsidiary has profits available for distribution which it is distributing in a non-taxable form by selling the assets for a nominal sum. In practice the Revenue have not taken the point that this situation is a potential 's. 460' case but it does highlight the pitfalls of this section for the unwary.

This chapter will examine the legislation (TA 1970, ss. 460–468) and the related case law. Most of the substantial issues are dealt with in ss. 460 (1)–(3), 461, 466 and 467: these are examined in sections 1.2–1.5 below. Section 1.6 will review the procedural provisions (TA 1970, ss. 460, 462–464).

1.2 TA 1970, s. 460 (1)–(3), ss. 461, 466 and 467

Section 460 (1)–(3) reads as follows:—

CANCELLATION OF TAX ADVANTAGES FROM CERTAIN TRANSACTIONS IN SECURITIES

460 Cancellation of tax advantage

(1) Where:—

(a) in any such circumstances as are mentioned in s. 461 below, and

(b) in consequence of a transaction in securities or of the combined effect of two or more such transactions,

a person is in a position to obtain, or has obtained, a tax advantage, then unless he shows that the transaction or transactions were carried out either for bona fide commercial reasons or in the ordinary course of making or managing investments, and that none of them had as their main object, or one of their main objects, to enable tax advantages to be obtained, this section shall apply to him in respect of that transaction or those transactions:

Provided that this section shall not apply to him if:—

(i) the transaction or transactions in securities were carried out, and

(ii) any change in the nature of any activities carried on by a person, being a change necessary in order that the tax advantage should be obtainable, was effected,

before 5 April 1960.

(2) Subject to s. 468 (3) below, for the purposes of this Chapter a tax advantage obtained or obtainable by a person shall be deemed to be obtained or obtainable by him in consequence of a transaction in securities or of the combined effect of two or more such transactions, if it is obtained or obtainable in consequence of the combined effect of the transaction or transactions and of the liquidation of a company.

(3) Where this section applies to a person in respect of any transaction or transactions, the tax advantage obtained or obtainable by him in consequence thereof shall be counteracted by such of the following adjustments, that is to say an assessment, the nullifying of a right to repayment or the requiring of the return of a repayment already made (the amount to be returned being chargeable under Case VI of Sch. D and recoverable accordingly), or the computation or recomputation of profits or gains, or liability to tax, on such basis as the Board may specify by notice in writing served on him as being requisite for counteracting the tax advantage so obtained or obtainable.

TA 1970, ss. 461, 466 and 467 read as follows:—

461 The prescribed circumstances

The circumstances mentioned in s. 460 (1) above are:—

A. That in connection with the distribution of profits of a

company, or in connection with the sale or purchase of securities being a sale or purchase followed by the purchase or sale of the same or other securities, the person in question receives an abnormal amount by way of dividend, and the amount so received is taken into account for any of the following purposes:—

(a) any exemption from tax, or
(b) the setting-off of losses against profits or income, or
(c) the giving of group relief, or
(d) the application of franked investment income in calculating a company's liability to pay advance corporation tax, or
(e) the application of a surplus of franked investment income under s. 254 or s. 255 of this Act, or
(f) the computation of profits or gains out of which are made payments falling within s. 52 or s. 53 of this Act, or
(g) the deduction from or set-off against income of interest under s. 75 of the Finance Act 1972.

OR

B. (1) That in connection with the distribution of profits of a company, or in connection with the sale or purchase of securities being a sale or purchase followed by the purchase or sale of the same or other securities, the person in question becomes entitled:—

(a) in respect of securities held or sold by him, or
(b) subject to s. 468 (3) below, in respect of securities formerly held by him (whether sold by him or not),

to a deduction in computing profits or gains by reason of a fall in the value of the securities resulting from the payment of a dividend thereon or from any other dealing with any assets of a company.

(2) Where a company in the circumstances mentioned in sub-para. (1) above becomes entitled to a deduction as there mentioned, s. 460 above shall apply in relation to any tax advantage obtained or obtainable in consequence of that deduction by another company by way of group relief as if obtained or obtainable by the other company in circumstances falling within sub-para. (1) above.

OR

C. (1) That the person in question receives, in consequence of a transaction whereby any other person:—

(a) subsequently receives, or has received, an abnormal amount by way of dividend; or

(b) subsequently becomes entitled, or has become entitled, to a deduction as mentioned in para. B (1) above,

a consideration which either:—

(i) is, or represents the value of, assets which are (or apart from anything done by the company in question would have been) available for distribution by way of dividend, or

(ii) is received in respect of future receipts of the company, or

(iii) is, or represents the value of, trading stock of the company,

and the said person so receives the consideration that he does not pay or bear tax on it as income.

(2) The assets mentioned in sub-para. (1) above do not include assets which (while of a description which under the law of the country in which the company is incorporated is available for distribution by way of dividend) are shown to represent a return of sums paid by subscribers on the issue of securities.

OR

D. (1) That in connection with the distribution of profits of a company to which this paragraph applies, the person in question so receives as is mentioned in para. C (1) above such a consideration as is therein mentioned.

(2) The companies to which this paragraph applies are:—

(a) any company under the control of not more than five persons, and

(b) any other company which does not satisfy the condition that its shares or stocks or some class thereof (disregarding debenture stock, preferred shares or preferred stock), are authorised to be dealt in on a stock exchange in the United Kingdom, and are so dealt in (regularly or from time to time),

so, however, that this paragraph does not apply to a

company under the control of one or more companies to which this paragraph does not apply.

(3) Subsections (2) to (6) of s. 302 of this Act (definition of control) shall apply for the purposes of this paragraph.

OR

E. (1) That in connection with the transfer directly or indirectly of assets of a company to which para. D above applies to another such company, or in connection with any transaction in securities in which two or more companies to which para. D above applies are concerned, the person in question receives non-taxable consideration which is or represents the value of assets available for distribution by such a company, and which consists of any share capital or any security (as defined by s. 237 (5) of this Act) issued by such a company.

(2) So far as sub-para. (1) above relates to share capital other than redeemable share capital, it shall not apply unless and except to the extent that the share capital is repaid (in a winding-up or otherwise), and where s. 460 above applies to a person by virtue of sub-para. (1) above on the repayment of any share capital any assessment to tax under subs. (3) of the said s. 460 shall be an assessment to tax for the year in which the share capital is repaid.

(3) In this paragraph:—

"assets available for distribution" means assets which are, or apart from anything done by the company in question would have been, available for distribution by way of dividend, or trading stock of the company,

"non-taxable", in relation to a person receiving consideration, means that the recipient does not pay or bear tax on it as income (apart from the provisions of this Chapter),

"share" includes stock and any other interest of a member in a company,

and the references in sub-para. (2) above to the repayment of share capital include references to any distribution made in respect of any shares in a winding-up or dissolution of the company.

(4) This paragraph has effect subject to s. 468 (3) below.

466 Meaning of "tax advantage"

(1) In this Chapter "tax advantage" means relief or increased relief from, or repayment or increased repayment of, tax, or the avoidance or reduction of a charge to tax or an assessment to tax or the avoidance of a possible assessment thereto, whether the avoidance or reduction is effected by receipts accruing in such a way that the recipient does not pay or bear tax on them, or by a deduction in computing profits or gains.

467 Further interpretation

(1) In this Chapter:—
"company" includes any body corporate,
references to dividends include references to other qualifying distributions (as defined in s. 84 (4) of the Finance Act 1972) and to interest,
"securities":—
(a) includes shares and stock, and
(b) subject to s. 468 (3) below, in relation to a company not limited by shares (whether or not it has a share capital) includes also a reference to the interest of a member of the company as such, whatever the form of that interest,
"trading stock" has the same meaning as in s. 137 of this Act,
"transaction in securities" includes transactions, of whatever description, relating to securities, and in particular:—
(i) the purchase, sale or exchange of securities,
(ii) the issuing or securing the issue of, or applying or subscribing for, new securities,
(iii) the altering, or securing the alteration of, the rights attached to securities.

(2) In s. 461 above:—
(a) references to profits include references to income, reserves or other assets,
(b) references to distribution include references to transfer or realisation (including application in discharge of liabilities), and
(c) references to the receipt of consideration include references to the receipt of any money or money's worth.

(3) For the purposes of s. 461 above an amount received by way of dividend shall be treated as abnormal if the Board, the Special Commissioners or the tribunal, as the case may be, are satisfied:—

(a) in the case of a dividend at a fixed rate, that it substantially exceeds the amount which the recipient would have received if the dividend had accrued from day to day and he had been entitled only to so much of the dividend as accrued while he held the securities, so however that an amount shall not be treated as abnormal by virtue only of this paragraph if during the six months beginning with the purchase of the securities the recipient does not sell or otherwise dispose of, or acquire an option to sell, any of those securities or any securities similar to those securities, or

(b) in any case, that it substantially exceeds a normal return on the consideration provided by the recipient for the relevant securities, that is to say, the securities in respect of which the dividend was received and, if those securities are derived from securities previously acquired by the recipient, the securities which were previously acquired; and for the purposes of this paragraph:—

(i) if the consideration provided by the recipient for any of the relevant securities was in excess of their market value at the time he acquired them, or if no consideration was provided by him for any of the relevant securities, the recipient shall be taken to have provided for those securities consideration equal to their market value at the time he acquired them; and

(ii) in determining whether an amount received by way of dividend exceeds a normal return, regard shall be had to the length of time previous to the receipt of that amount that the recipient first acquired any of the relevant securities and to any dividends and other distributions made in respect of them during that time:

Provided that there shall be disregarded any amount received by a company before 30 April 1969 by way of dividend from an associated company in so far as the dividend is paid out of income arising to the company paying it since the two companies became associated companies, and Sch. 17 to the Finance Act 1965 shall with the necessary modifications apply for determining the extent to which the dividend was so paid.

In this proviso references to an associated company or companies shall be construed in accordance with paras. (c) and (d) of s. 486 (4) of this Act.

(4) For the purposes of subs. (3) (a) above securities shall be deemed to be similar if they entitle their holders to the same rights against the same persons as to capital and interest and the same remedies for the enforcement of those rights, notwithstanding any difference in the total nominal amounts of the respective securities or in the form in which they are held or the manner in which they can be transferred, and for those purposes rights *guaranteed by the Treasury* shall be treated as rights against the Treasury.

1.3 The general scope of the provisions

1.3.1 Introduction

The provisions of TA 1970, ss. 460–468 were first enacted as FA 1960, s. 28 to counteract tax advantages obtained by 'a device' referred to as 'dividend stripping'. However, the courts' interpretation of TA 1970, ss. 460–468 has not been restricted to the 'mischief' aimed at and the courts have sought to give a much wider meaning to the provisions.

Section 460 (1) sets out three conditions which must be satisfied before the provisions of ss. 460–468 can be invoked against the taxpayer. These are:—

(a) a transaction in securities or the combined effect of two or more such transactions; and
(b) as a result of (a) the taxpayer obtains, or is in a position to obtain, a tax advantage; and
(c) any one of the five circumstances set out in s. 461 are present.

Where these conditions are satisfied the Revenue can counteract the tax advantage by:—

(a) nullifying a right to repayment;
(b) issuing a Sch. D Case VI assessment to recover the repayment;
(c) computing or recomputing the profits or gains, or liability to tax, on such basis as the Board may specify.

1.3.2 A transaction in securities or the combined effect of two or more such transactions

Securities are defined widely and non-exhaustively in TA 1970, s. 467 (1) and include shares and stock and in the case of a company not limited by shares, the interest of a member of such a company, whatever the form of that interest. The most thorough judicial consideration of this term can be found in the judgment of Ungoed-Thomas J in *IRC v Parker* (1966) 43 TC 396 at 408. He thought the term was wide enough to also include:—

(a) a secured debt;
(b) a document acknowledging personal liability without a charge being created on property.

This dictum was also supported by the House of Lords in the same case.

The phrase 'transaction in securities' is also defined in non-exhaustive terms as including the purchase, sale or exchange of securities, the issuing or securing the issue of, or applying for or subscribing for, new securities and the altering or securing the alteration of the rights attached to securities.

The all embracing nature of his definition was confirmed by Lord Guest in *IRC v Parker* (1966) 43 TC 396 at 437, where it was held that the redemption of a debenture was a transaction in securities. More recently, the House of Lords in *Williams v IRC* [1980] STC 535 have confirmed this view by holding that loans received by shareholders without paying or bearing tax and which were repayable to a company under their control were 'transactions in securities'.

The term 'transaction' has also been given a wide meaning. In *Greenberg v IRC* (1971) 47 TC 240 at 271–272 Lord Reid stated that although the word normally denoted some bilateral activity this was not essential and that the declaration of a dividend and the payment of the purchase price due on the sale of securities could be regarded as transactions relating to securities.

During the late 1960s and early 1970s there was considerable discussion about whether the liquidation of a company could, by itself, be regarded as a transaction in securities. This question was examined in *IRC v Joiner* [1975] STC 200. In the Court of Appeal it was held that a liquidation was a transaction in securities. This view was decisively rejected in the House of Lords. The Lords held that to be within the section (TA 1970, s. 460 (2)) there had to be a transaction in securities other than the mere liquidation of a company. Having said this it should be pointed out that in a number of liquidations, particularly where a reorganisation is being effected, there is both a transaction in securities and a liquidation. Where such transactions are being contemplated, it is essential for the adviser to consider the implications of TA 1970, s. 460. Shortly before the *Joiner* case was heard at first instance, Mr. John Nott, then Treasury Minister of State, assured the House of Commons that the Inland Revenue had not, and would not, apply the provisions of TA 1970, s. 460 to ordinary liquidations. (See HC Debate Vol cols 136 and 137.) 'Ordinary' in this context means the winding up of a distinct entity, irrespective of whether the business with its goodwill comes to an end and is taken over by some other concern which is under different control. After the decision at first instance, he was asked to clarify the Revenue's position which he reiterated in the terms outlined in the previous sentence (HC Debate Vol cols 159 and 160) but added that the Revenue would not regard as 'ordinary' a liquidation which is part of a scheme of reconstruction that enables the old business to be carried on as before with substantially, either directly or indirectly, the same shareholders' control.

1.3.3 Tax advantage

By this is meant one of the following:—
(a) relief or increased relief from tax;
(b) repayment or increased repayment of tax;
(c) avoidance or reduction of tax;
(d) avoidance or possible avoidance of an assessment to tax.
The scope of (c) and (d) includes the situation where the avoidance or reduction is effected by receipts accruing in such a way that the taxpayer does not pay or bear tax on them, or by a deduction in computing his profits or gains.

This expression has been further elucidated by Lord Wilberforce in *IRC v Parker* (1966) 43 TC 396 at 441 in the form of a test. There must be a contrast between the actual receipts where these accrue in a non-taxable form and the way in which they might accrue in a taxable form. Unless this contrast was established a tax advantage would not arise. Prior to *IRC v Wiggins* [1979] STC 244 it had been thought that the Revenue had to show that what had been received in a capital or non-taxable form could have been received from the same person in a form subject to income tax. The author has never held this restricted view and is in total agreement with Walton's view, as expressed in the *Wiggins* case, that, in establishing a tax advantage, it is only necessary to look for another possible way in which the sum could have reached the shareholders and then make the comparison. Whilst Walton's decisions have given rise to some controversy in tax litigation, it is submitted that this view is correct. For instance, in a recent case *Anysz v IRC* [1978] STC 297 it was held that a taxpayer had received a tax advantage as a result of a share exchange. The advantage arose because the shares received in exchange could have been purchased by the company in which he originally held shares and then distributed in specie by that company to the taxpayer.

The other judicial embellishments on this term relate to:—

(a) the tests that will be applied in determining whether one of the main objectives of a transaction was to obtain a tax advantage;
(b) the scope of the words 'avoidance or possible assessment thereto';
(c) the meaning of the word 'receipt'.

The tests referred to in (a) were considered in *Addy v IRC* [1975] STC 601 where it was held that it was necessary to consider the subjective intention of those in control of the company, or the transaction, in deciding as a matter of fact whether there had been an intention to obtain a tax advantage. It was not open to the taxpayer, who had not been intimately involved in the scheme, to raise the defence that he had relied on those in control of the company (or transactions) as evidence that he had not intended to obtain a tax advantage. This decision accords with the general principle of law that ignorance of the law is no defence. The scope of the words 'avoidance or possible assessment' was considered by Lord Upjohn in *IRC v Cleary* (1967) 44 TC 399 at 428: he held that the term was not limited to a reduction of physical assets available for that purpose. The scope of the word 'receipt' was considered by Lord Guest in *IRC v Parker* (1965) 43 TC 396 at 437. 'Receipt' in his view was a deliberately wide term (this statement is very much in line with the wide interpretation policy which has been followed in s. 460 cases) and that accruing did not necessarily mean payment.

The final part in this section relates to the question of which taxes fall within the ambit of the phrase 'tax advantage'. The word 'tax', for the purposes of the Taxes Acts, means either income tax or corporation tax. The term, however, is not actually defined. This means that capital gains tax is not within this definition and further support for this view can be found in TA 1970, s. 461 which makes reference to 'profits or gains' – the latter being outside the scope of the capital gains tax legislation (see CGTA 1979, s. 155 (5)). Certainly the Revenue, to the author's knowledge, have not taken the point that capital gains tax might be within the scope of the expression. It is submitted that the above view is correct.

1.3.4 The five circumstances (TA 1970, s. 461)

These circumstances are set out in five paragraphs A to E and whilst each paragraph will be reviewed in some detail, most litigation has related to transactions falling within para. D, even though the majority of cases have been decided on different grounds, e.g. whether or not the main intention was to obtain a tax advantage or whether the exemption in respect of bona fide commercial transactions applied. For most practical purposes this paragraph is the one most likely to be encountered by practitioners and the section covering para. D reflects this. Until recently, about one case per year was brought before the courts, but this trend has now changed. Over the last two years, a number of cases have come before the courts. In two cases, *IRC v Garvin* [1981] STC 344 and *IRC v Williams* [1980] STC 535 (both schemes involved a well-known personality in the field of 'tax schemes', a Mr. Godfrey Bradman) it is likely that the Revenue's attitude has been partly influenced by the provocative tax avoidance nature of the schemes. In most of the other cases it is difficult to identify a policy.

1.4 The five circumstances (TA 1970, s. 461)

1.4.1 Paragraph A

For this paragraph to be applicable there must either be a distribution of profits by a company, or a sale or purchase of securities followed by a purchase or sale of the same securities and as a result the person concerned receives an abnormal dividend which is taken into account for any of the following:—

(a) an exemption from tax, or
(b) the setting off of losses against profits or income,
(c) the giving of group relief, or
(d) the application of franked investment income in calculating a company's liability to pay advance corporation tax, or
(e) the application of a surplus of franked investment income under TA 1970, s. 254 or s. 255, or
(f) the computation of profits or gains out of which annual payments are made within TA 1970, ss. 52–53, or
(g) by deduction from or set off against interest under s. 75 FA 1972.

This paragraph is aimed at the classic 'dividend stripping' scheme whereby a person received an abnormal amount by way of dividend which was exempt from tax, or was able to reclaim the tax on the dividend as a result of losses or other reliefs. The particular 'mischief' was abnormal in the sense that it represented several years' accumulated profits. The expression 'abnormal dividend' is defined in TA 1970, s. 467 (3) by reference to the amount of dividend or interest received in relation to the consideration paid for the securities (or the market value where the consideration is in excess of or below the market value) after taking into account the length of time the securities have been owned by the person who receives the dividend or interest. No cases have arisen under this section to date and it is rarely met in practice as the paragraph has successfully covered a 'loophole' in the earlier legislation.

1.4.2 Paragraph B

This paragraph will apply where either a company distributes a dividend, or a person sells or purchases securities, and this is followed by a purchase or sale of the same securities and the person in question becomes entitled in respect of the securities held by him, or formerly held by him, to a deduction against his profits or gains which must arise from a fall in the value of the securities as a result of a dividend payment or from any other dealing with any assets of the company.

This section was enacted to counter the 'mischief' whereby a dealer in securities would claim a trading loss as a result of acquiring shares at a price which reflected an imminent dividend or interest payment and selling them at a much lower price shortly after the dividend or interest payment. For historical reasons the dividend or interest was not brought into the dealer's taxable profit or loss computation.

In *IRC v Kleinwort Benson* (1969) 45 TC 369, the Revenue sought to apply this paragraph to a bank which had incurred a trading loss as a result of the purchase and redemption of certain debenture stock. The stock was acquired at a time when the interest due on the stock was substantially in arrears; subsequently both the capital and arrears of interest were paid in full. A loss arose because the bank were entitled to exclude the interest from its taxable profit. It was held that the transaction was not within para. B. Cross J held that there was never any fall in the value of the stock by reason of the payment of interest. Principal premium and arrears of interest were paid off on the same day (see *IRC v Kleinwort Benson* (1969) 45 TC 369 at 381. Cross J also held that the commercial exemption applied).

For the same reasons as set out in para. A the circumstances posited in this paragraph are rarely met in practice.

1.4.3 Paragraph C

This paragraph deals with the other party to the dividend stripping transactions and will come into operation where one party to a transaction receives a *consideration* which represents:—

(a) the value of assets available for distribution, or
(b) future receipts of the company, or
(c) the value of trading stock,

and the other party to the transaction receives or has received an *abnormal dividend* or a deduction from profits or gains.

The words in italics are defined in TA 1970, s. 467 (2) and (3) and readers are referred to **1.4.1** above where the definition of an abnormal dividend was referred to. Consideration includes the receipt of any money or money's worth. The term 'assets available for distribution' was held by Megarry J in *IRC v Brown* (1971) 47 TC 217 to be profits legally available for distribution and not those that might be commercially available. The reason for this seems to have been the arbitrary and uncertain nature of the latter as compared to the former. This decision was followed in *Addy v IRC* [1975] STC 601 where it was held that the section was not limited to distributions from revenue reserves and the test adopted in the *Brown* case was followed. The question of distributable profits was also considered in *Green v IRC* [1975] STC 633; this case turns on the peculiarities of the income tax system as it related to companies prior to 1966. However, it was held that in determining distributable profits, depreciation of plant and depletion of land values should not be taken into account. The author is of the view that this case can be distinguished from those of *IRC v Brown* and *Addy v IRC* on the rather special facts of the case. It is further submitted that a depreciation provision is a proper deduction if the directors take the view, providing it is bona fide, that it is in the interests of the company as a going concern.

It was stated above that para. C is intended to cover situations where one party to the transaction receives a capital sum and the other party receives an abnormal dividend and/or a loss deduction. It has been suggested that this paragraph could apply where shareholders in a family company sell out to a company which then extracts the assets of the company by way of group dividend. This author's view is that the Revenue will only be able to succeed if they can establish a causal connection between the share purchase and the subsequent abnormal dividend. This follows the House of

Lords' decision in *IRC v Garvin* [1981] STC 344. In the leading judgment Lord Wilberforce did not think that the word 'transaction' could be limited to the immediate cause of the dividend being received. The word must be capable of including some anterior step in the scheme which led to the declaration of the dividend. The connection between that step and the dividend is denoted by the word 'whereby' which he thought was equivalent to the words 'by which' and must connote some causal connection, although this might be quite loose. On the facts it was held that even if the word 'whereby' were given a wide meaning the necessary causality was not present. A similar finding was expressed by Lord Russell who expressed the view that to establish the causality more than the 'causa sine qua non' was required. Lord Bridge also stressed the causal connection and held that it was not possible to construe the word 'transaction' as a series of transactions. Whilst it may be easier in some cases than in others to establish a connection the unwary should take note of Templeman J's dissenting judgment in the Court of Appeal and the relative ease with which the Revenue's arguments were accepted.

A recent example of this can be seen in the case of *Emery v IRC* [1981] STC 150. In the court at first instance it was held that the phrase 'a transaction whereby any other person . . . subsequently receives . . . an abnormal amount by way of dividend' should be given a wide meaning both as a whole and in regard to its individual components. The word 'transaction' covered the entire series of transactions up to and including the payment of the dividend, notwithstanding that the taxpayer did not participate in every transaction.

It should also be pointed out that whilst the other party can claim the bona fide commercial exemption, or that the transaction was in the ordinary course of making or managing investments, this relief is not available to the party in receipt of the capital sum. This paragraph also covers the device known as 'forward shipping': this occurred when the holder of shares in a company, which was about to make large profits, created a special share that carried a high dividend for a few years and then sold them to an exempt person or dealer for a capital sum, the latter after being satisfied in instalments pro tanto with the dividend payments (see *IRC v Tunnicliffe* (1971) 47 TC 240).

1.4.4 Paragraph D

This paragraph will apply where in connection with a distribution of profit of a company a person receives a consideration which represents the assets of the company available for distribution, or the value of its trading stock, or which is received in respect of future receipts of the company. As we shall see, the effect of these words is that this paragraph extends the coverage of para. C as it does not require either an abnormal dividend to be paid or a deduction in computing profits or gains. In another sense, however, it is narrower than para. C in that para. D only applies to a certain class of company. However, the paragraph will only apply to companies under the control of five or fewer persons or where the shares or stock of the company are not dealt in on a regular basis on the Stock Exchange. It follows that a quoted company can be within para. D but a company under the control of a non-para. D company is not subject to para. D. In determining control the rules set out in TA 1970, s. 302 (2)–(6) are applied. These subsections define control in terms of the persons who control the voting power or who would receive the greater part of the profits or losses available for distribution by way of dividend or on a liquidation.

The expression 'consideration' has already been referred to in **1.4.3** above. A distribution is defined in s. 467 (2) and includes a transfer or realisation and the discharge of liabilities. In *Emery v IRC* [1981] STC 150 it was held that the words 'in connection with' were satisfied by a less definite causal link than the expression 'whereby' in para. C and in *Anysz v IRC* [1978] STC 296 it was held that there must be a clear connection between the receipt of the consideration and the subsequent dividend.

The expressions 'consideration' and 'distribution' have already been defined above in connection with para. C (see **1.4.3**). Profits are defined in s. 464 and include references to income, reserves or other assets. It seems that the parliamentary draftsman thought that income and reserves were shown on the same side of the balance sheet as assets, a point which was judicially acknowledged by Lord Upjohn in *IRC v Cleary* (1967) 44 TC 399 at 428.

This paragraph is intended to cover almost any form of distribution of a company's assets and would include a distribution of capital profits and a reduction in capital over and above the stated nominal value. This reasoning was accepted in *Hague v IRC* (1968) 44 TC 619 where a capitalisation of undistributed profits followed by a reduction of capital was held to be within para. D and in *IRC v Horrocks* (1968) 44 TC 645 where a reduction preceded a capitalisation.

The two leading cases on this paragraph are *IRC v Parker* (1966) 43 TC 396 and *IRC v Cleary* (1967) 44 TC 399. In the former, accumulated profits were capitalised and shareholders received a bonus issue of interest free redeemable debentures. Some years later these were redeemed and the Revenue argued that the taxpayer had received a tax advantage within para. D. The House of Lords by a majority of three to two held that the redemption of the debentures was in connection with the distribution of profits and therefore within para. D. The other question raised by the case was the date the tax advantage arose – the date of the bonus issue – 1953 or the date the debentures were redeemed – 1961? It was held by the majority that a tax advantage had been obtained in 1961 when the debentures were redeemed, not in 1953, as no part of the company's profits were distributed to the taxpayer at that date.

In *IRC v Cleary* (1967) 44 TC 399 two sisters, who owned all the shares in two companies, sold their shares in one of the companies to the other for a cash consideration at market value. In a unanimous judgment it was held by the House of Lords that the transaction was within para. D because there was a transfer and application of the company's profits and assets in discharge of a liability it had incurred by agreeing to purchase the other company's shares. One of the arguments put forward by Counsel for the two sisters was that there could not be a distribution of profits without a diminution of the amount available for distribution. Viscount Dilhorne rejected this argument on the grounds that it involved ignoring the definition of the words 'distribution' and 'profits' and it required reading into the section a qualification which was not there. The other issue concerned the question of whether there was a tax advantage. This was more easily resolved: a unanimous House held that the money received by the sisters for their shares could have been received in a taxable form, i.e. as a dividend. It was also acknowledged by the Lords that their decision could give rise to double taxation if the purchasing company distributed by way of dividend the value of the shares it had bought. Since these two cases there have been two further cases which have so far reached the House of Lords. In *Williams v IRC* [1980] STC 535, it was held that loans received by shareholders, from a company under their control, without paying or bearing tax were received by them in connection with a distribution of profits within para. D and represented assets available for distribution. In *IRC v Garvin* [1981] STC 344 the House of Lords held that the relevant date for determining whether a company is within this paragraph (in colloquial terms, 'a D company') was not the date when the taxpayers receive the special kind of money consideration referred to in para. C (in this case it was the proceeds from the sale of shares) but the date when the profits were distributed. Lord Wilberforce was of the opinion that the language of the paragraph was plain. The words 'in connection with the distribution of profits' must contemplate a distribution by the company and so a state of control at that date; it was impossible to relate the question of control to the receipt of the consideration or to any other transaction.

Paragraph D is a sweeping up provision designed to cover cases where, without the help of a third party, the shareholders of a company obtain funds in a non-taxable form which might otherwise have been used to pay dividends.

1.4.5 Paragraph E

This paragraph will apply where there is either:—

(a) a transfer of assets (either directly or indirectly) between two para. D companies; or

(b) a transaction in securities involving two or more such companies; and

a person receives, in the form of share capital or any security, a non-taxable consideration which is, or represents, the value of assets available for distribution of a para. D company.

However, it is also provided that this proviso will only apply where the person receives redeemable share capital or where he receives irredeemable share capital which is subsequently repaid, either as a result of a winding up or a capital reduction. In the latter cases the assessment under s. 460 (3) will be deferred until the year in which the capital is repaid.

This paragraph will be relevant where one para. D company acquires another D company by means of a share exchange. This circumstance appears to have been drafted with the *Cleary* case in mind but will obviously cover other situations. For instance, where a person receives shares or other securities (or the proceeds of their redemption) in a D company without having acquired them for full consideration, it will be necessary to ascertain whether the shares or securities represent assets of the company available for distribution. On a disposal of such shares or securities it will be advisable to obtain clearance under TA 1970, s. 464 (this topic will be discussed in more detail below) in order to avoid both a capital gains and income tax liability. To date there has only been one case where the question of para. E liability has arisen, *Williams v IRC* [1979] STC 598. The facts involved a complicated tax avoidance system promoted by a well-known personality in this field, Mr. G Bradman. Bridge LJ noted in *Williams v IRC* [1979] STC 598 at 608, that if all the relevant definitions and cross-references were applied to the companies falling within the first limb of para. E the circumstances also fell within para. D. The main finding in this case was to the effect that the taxpayers were entitled to a deferment of their liability under para. E (2) of TA 1970, s. 461 (but not under para. C) notwithstanding that they also fell within para. D because para. E (2) prevailed over para. D; for the underlying reason see *Williams v IRC* [1979] STC 598 at 608. In the House of Lords the appeal by the Revenue was dismissed and the case was decided on other grounds.

1.5 Bona fide commercial transactions

Where the taxpayer shows that the transactions were carried out for bona fide commercial reasons or in the ordinary course of making or managing investments and that none of them had as their main object, or one of their main objects, a tax advantage, the transactions will not give rise to a liability under TA 1970, s. 460.

The question of whether a transaction satisfies the commercial criteria is one of subjective intention. As this is a question of fact a determination of the Special Commissioners can only be upset if it can be shown that no body of commissioners acting judicially and properly instructed as to the relevant law could come to the conclusion they did (see *Addy v IRC* [1975] STC 601 and *IRC v Goodwin* [1976] STC 28). The leading case on this question is *IRC v Brebner* (1967) 43 TC 705: the directors wished to resist a take-over bid and together with some of the other shareholders made a counter offer that was accepted by nearly all the shareholders. The funds for enabling the directors and their friends to make this offer were provided by a bank. To enable the directors and their associates to repay the bank a scheme of reorganisation was effected whereby the capital of the company was increased and then subsequently reduced, as a result of which £75,000 was returned to the shareholders as a return of capital. It was agreed that the first transaction (the offer to purchase the shares from the other shareholders) was a commercial decision and that the main object of the second transaction was the obtaining of a tax advantage. However, the House of Lords agreed that the transactions should not be taken in isolation but together as the first part of the transaction had committed them to the second. The importance of the commissioners' findings was also discussed; Lord Pearce recognised that the commissioners 'could have reached a contrary conclusion, which would have been equally unassailable'. The scope of this exemption has also been considered in *IRC v Brown* (1971) 47 TC 217; *Hasloch v IRC* (1971) 47 TC 50 and, more recently, in *IRC v Goodwin* [1976] STC 28 and *Clark v IRC* [1978] STC 614.

In *IRC v Brown* (1971) 47 TC 217 the taxpayer sold securities for full consideration to a company owned by himself. Russell LJ held that the evidence amounted to no more than saying that the taxpayer and his wife wanted some money and entered into a transaction to get it. As such the case did not fall within the scope of the exemption.

In *Hasloch v IRC* (1971) 47 TC 50 the company capitalised undistributed profits and made a bonus issue of ordinary and redeemable preference shares. Some years later the preference shares were redeemed at par. One of the main reasons for the bonus issue was to bring the company's issued share capital into line with the capital likely to be needed after its projected expansion. The subsequent redemption of the preference shares was with a view to removing the annual liability to pay a preference dividend in view of the then current corporation tax proposals. Another, but subsidiary, reason was that the redemption of the shares would facilitate a public flotation should this be in the interests of the company. However, it was also admitted by the Board that one of the main objects of the redemption was to put money into the hands of the preference shareholders. The commissioners held that whilst all the transactions were bona fide commercial the main object of the Board in redeeming the shares was to put money into the shareholders' hands in a non-taxable form. The taxpayer's claim was unsuccessful as he had failed to show that the scheme had not, as one of its main objects, the obtaining of a tax advantage. This was upheld at first instance and highlights the importance of not only being able to show that the transactions were commercial but also that they had not as one of their main objects the obtaining of a tax advantage.

A more recent case, *IRC v Goodwin* [1976] STC 28 and one which was eventually heard by the House of Lords, concerned a family controlled company which capitalised a certain proportion of its profits in 1951 and applied the sum in making a bonus issue of redeemable preference shares. In 1958, shortly before the company's shares were offered to the public, the company again capitalised part of its accumulated profits and distributed to the family shareholders a bonus issue of redeemable preference shares and deferred ordinary shares. The bonus shares issued in 1951 were redeemed in 1963. The reason for issuing the redeemable preference shares was to provide funds for the payment of estate duty in order to retain control within the family. It was common ground that a tax advantage had been obtained but not that it was one of the main objects of the scheme. The substantive question was whether the transactions were carried out for bona fide commercial reasons. The House of Lords held that the transactions were for bona fide commercial reasons as retention of family control was important for company–customer and employer–employee relations, and the transactions facilitated easier access to the money market.

The importance of the commissioners' findings was also stressed by Lord Edmund-Davies (*IRC v Goodwin* [1976] STC 28) who reiterated the point established by earlier cases that findings of the commissioners to the contrary would have been equally unassailable.

The most recent case that has been considered, albeit at first instance only, was that of *Clark v IRC* [1978] STC 614. The taxpayer was a farmer who learned of an opportunity to purchase a substantial farm which adjoined his own. He considered that the acquisition of the farm would be of commercial advantage as it could be efficiently combined with his own. The taxpayer proposed to finance the purchase by selling his 50% interest in a family-owned investment company known as 'Highland', the principal asset of which was a holding of shares in a quoted company. The taxpayer also had an interest with other members of his family in another company, 'Equity', which carried on business as an investment trust. To obtain the best possible price for his shares the taxpayer asked his brother (who owned the other 50% of Highland) to sell his shares at the same time. The taxpayer's father opposed the sale as it would involve losing control of the quoted company in which Highland had an interest and he eventually persuaded his son to sell the Highland shares to Equity at net asset value. The commissioners found that the sale of the Highland shares to raise money was not sufficient reason to justify a finding that the transaction was for bona fide commercial reasons. In their view, to satisfy this exemption the commercial reasons had to be connected with the vendor's interest in the company concerned in, or affected by the transaction. On appeal, Fox J held that the commissioners had misdirected themselves as their approach to the 'bona fide commercial' test was too narrow. Whilst it was not in dispute that the transaction was bona fide the question was whether the reasons were commercial. This question had to be considered in the context of all the relevant circumstances. It followed that the sale of the shares should not be considered in isolation. The sole purpose of the sale was to enable the taxpayer to purchase the farm and as there were sound commercial reasons for the purchase the transaction was held to be within the bona fide commercial exemption.

1.6 Procedural aspects of TA 1970, s. 460

1.6.1 Introduction

Where the Board consider that a tax advantage has been obtained they must, in accordance with TA 1970, s. 460 (6), serve notice on the taxpayer to the effect that they have reason to believe that the section may apply to him in respect of the transaction(s) specified in the notice. The taxpayer may then reply within 30 days by way of statutory declaration setting out the relevant facts and the reasons why in his view the section cannot apply to him. The Board, after considering the statutory declaration can, if they see reason to take the matter further, send to the Tribunal (set up under the provisions of s. 463, see below) a certificate to that effect, together with the statutory declaration and any counter-statement they feel appropriate. The Tribunal then considers these statements to determine whether there is a prima facie case for proceeding further. If it determines that there is no case no further action can be taken by the Revenue in relation to the particular transaction. If it decides that a prima facie case exists the Board will then serve notice under TA 1970, s. 460 (3) specifying the method by which they intend to counteract the alleged tax advantage. It should be noted that the taxpayer has no right to see counter-statements or to be heard by the Tribunal (*Wiseman v Borneman* (1967) 45 TC 540 and *Balen v IRC* [1978] STC 420).

It is provided in TA 1970, s. 463 that the Tribunal shall consist of the chairman, who shall either be the chairman of the Board of Referees or a person appointed by the Lord Chancellor and two or more persons appointed by the Lord Chancellor as having special knowledge of and experience in financial or commercial matters. It was held by the House of Lords in *Howard v Borneman (No 2)*, [1975] STC 327 that the chairman, together with two or more appointees, was a validly constituted Tribunal and so it was not necessary for all the appointees (there were four at the time) to consider the particular case.

The person served with the notice may, within 30 days, appeal to the Special Commissioners on the grounds that the section does not apply to him in respect of the transaction(s) in question, or that the adjustments being proposed are inappropriate (TA 1970, s. 462 (1)). If either the taxpayer or the Board is dissatisfied with the decision of the Special Commissioners they can, within 30 days of the decision, require the appeal to be reheard by the Tribunal. There is no necessity to appeal to the Tribunal on a point of law, as a direct appeal can be made from the Special Commissioners. An appeal on a point of law can also be made from the Tribunal (TA 1970, s. 462 (3)).

1.6.2 Clearance under TA 1970, s. 464

Under this section a person can submit details of a proposed or completed transaction to the Revenue and within 30 days, unless they ask for further information, the Revenue must notify the person whether or not a notice should be given in respect of the transaction(s). If the Revenue are satisfied that a notice is not applicable to the transaction(s) no further action can be taken unless the particulars submitted did not make a full and accurate disclosure of all the facts. In the absence of such non-disclosure further action may be taken in respect of the transaction(s) if another *undisclosed* transaction takes place which is combined with the first transaction(s) (this would appear to be within the scope of TA 1970, s. 460 (1)).

Clearance applications are made to the Board of Inland Revenue, Technical Division, Melbourne House, Aldwych, London WC2B 4LL. In the application the tax and reference number of the applicant and other affected parties should be stated. The letter should set out all the salient facts and supporting documentation should be attached such as accounts, contracts and minutes. Where clearance is refused, the Revenue are under no statutory obligation to give reasons, but in June 1978 they announced that for a trial period they intended to:—

(a) give reasons in appropriate cases why clearance had been refused; and
(b) grant an interview in order to clarify the position.

The text of the letter to the Consultative Committee of Accountancy Bodies setting out these new procedures is contained in Appendix I. This was followed up by a statement in the Chancellor's 1979 Budget speech, which reiterated the Board's new policy and added that in future the Board will only refuse clearance if, on the information available to them, they would actually expect to counteract the transactions contemplated. Whilst many accountants have an abhorrence, in many cases for justifiable reasons, of clearance procedures, the author has found that under the new procedures the Revenue have been very helpful. However, the author must concede that most of his experience has been in connection with either the reconstruction or reorganisation of family controlled companies. He has found that even if clearance is refused it is possible from the nature of the replies to amend the scheme in such a way that it becomes acceptable to the Revenue. In one case brought to the author's attention, the accountant who had proposed the scheme said that the Revenue had shown him how to do it! Whilst all this may give rise to a euphoric state it should be pointed out that all these schemes had one ingredient missing – a tax avoidance nature. Without exception all the schemes had a 'strong' commercial flavour and were necessitated by either individual members of the family wanting to trade on their own account or some members wanting to take a more active part than others, or it was necessary to provide an incentive for younger generations of the family who were working full time in the family business. It follows that the new procedure is not appropriate for the professional tax avoider, although in a number of cases the decision whether to obtain a clearance may be borderline.

1.7 Conclusions

In practice, advisers are only likely to meet the circumstances falling within either para. D or E. It is therefore crucial that advisers fully appreciate the scope of these two paragraphs. The conclusions can be divided into two categories: firstly, those which relate to the canons of statutory interpretation which have been applied to this section and secondly, the types of transactions that are likely to go unchallenged.

In respect of the former, two points can be made. Firstly, although as a normal rule in interpreting taxing statutes the subject is not liable to tax unless he is brought clearly within the legislation, the courts have applied, and the House of Lords in particular, a different method of interpretation to this section. Secondly, although it is essential to consider the transactions at which the legislation was directed in order to understand the various provisions, the courts (again on the highest authority) have consistently refused to restrict the scope of the legislation by reference to the alleged mischief that it was intended to cover. In *IRC v Parker* (1965) 43 TC 396 both Viscount Dilhorne and Lord Wilberforce declined to take a narrow view of the section and stated that the section was directed at tax avoidance and that the courts must decide whether in any particular case the provisions of TA 1970, s. 460 were applicable. These two points are dealt with in Lord Wilberforce's speech in *IRC v Joiner* [1975] STC 657 where he stated:—

> 'On the enactment of the original s. 28 of the Finance Act 1960 it was possible to contend, and it was contended, that this section (and its associated sections) was directed against a particular type of tax avoidance known generally under such descriptions as dividend stripping, asset stripping and bond washing, and that the sections and particular expressions used in them, amongst other 'transactions in securities', should be interpreted in the light of this supposed purpose. But this line of argument became unmaintainable after the decisions of this House in *IRC v Parker* and *Greenberg v IRC*. It is clear that all the members of this House who decided those cases were of the opinion that a wide interpretation must be given to the sections and to the expressions used in them. More than this, it appeared from the opinion of Lord Reid in *Greenberg v IRC* that the sections called for a different method of interpretation from that traditionally used in Taxing Acts. For whereas it is generally the rule that clear words are required to impose a tax, so that the taxpayer has the benefit of doubts or ambiguities, Lord Reid made it clear that the scheme of the sections introducing as they did a wide and general attack on tax avoidance, required that expressions which might otherwise have been cut down in the interest of precision were to be given the wide meaning evidently intended, even though they led to a conclusion short of which judges would normally desire to stop. If we are to follow this path, and I see no other open to us, we must continue to give "transactions in securities" and "transactions relating to securities" the widest meaning: we can neither confine these expressions to instances given in TA 1970, s. 467 (1), nor can we deduce from that enumeration any limitation on their scope.'

This method of interpretation has generally been adopted and has recently been followed by the Court of Appeal in *Williams v IRC* [1979] STC 598 at 613. Taxpayers should therefore be wary of the company purchase schemes which are marketed from time to time. Whilst the scheme might be technically sound based on normal canons of interpretation the above discussion has shown that in relation to this section these canons have not been applied. This point is frequently overlooked by advisers.

The second category of conclusions relates to the types of transaction which the Revenue are unlikely to challenge. These will have a 'strong commercial flavour' and whilst the way the transactions are structured may give rise to tax advantages, it must be shown that they can be justified on a sound business basis quite independent of the tax implications. Support for this view can be found in Lord Upjohn's speech in *IRC v Brebner* (1966) 43 TC 705 at 718 where he stated:—

> 'My Lords, I would only conclude my judgment by saying, when the question of carrying out a genuine commercial transaction, as this was, is considered, the fact that there are two ways of carrying it out – one by paying the maximum amount of tax, the other by paying no, or much less, tax – it would be quite wrong as a *necessary* consequence to draw the inference that in adopting the latter course one of the main objects is, for the purposes of the section, avoidance of tax. No commercial man in his senses is going to carry out commercial transactions except upon the footing of paying the smallest amount of tax involved.'

By contrast the type of transaction that is likely to be challenged is one where in the words (although stated in the context of a capital gain tax case) of Templeman LJ (*W T Ramsay Ltd v IRC* [1979] STC 582):—

> 'The taxpayer company and the consultants revolved and exchanged money through companies controlled by them or their directors and thereby at negligible cost to the taxpayer company and without earning a gain or suffering a loss, created for the taxpayer company a claim for a non-taxable gain and for a tax deductible loss, thus achieving no result save a manufactured claim to entitlement to tax relief.'

One question which arose in an acute form in *IRC v Garvin* [1981] STC 344 which has not been discussed above concerns the possibility of a double charge to tax where shares are sold and the Revenue raise both a capital gains tax assessment and one under s. 460. As it was held that the transactions were outside the scope of para. D this point was not decided. Lord Wilberforce pointed out that s. 460 was drafted prior to the introduction of capital gains tax and obviously without regard to the possible cumulation of both taxes. He noted that the Crown had agreed that if their appeal was successful they would credit the capital gains tax paid by the taxpayers against the s. 460 liability. Lord Wilberforce thought this concession was fair but unsatisfactory and similar views were expressed by Lords Scarman and Bridge. The government should remove the doubt which still exists and clarify the position. It is surely inequitable to impose two taxes on the same receipt and the uncertainty which arises from the *Garvin* case is surely unacceptable in a democratic society.

1.8 Appendix I
Text of letter to the Consultative Committee of Accountancy Bodies (CCAB)

As you are aware, s. 460 and the succeeding sections (which provide for the cancellation of tax advantages from certain transactions in securities) contain extensive safeguards against counteraction being taken unwarrantedly in respect of transactions which a taxpayer has carried out. Section 464 provides also a procedure for him to be told in advance whether the Revenue are satisfied that proposed transactions, as described to us, would, if carried out, not invoke counteraction.

Where we cannot give clearance under s. 464 we are not – for good reasons – obliged to say why and our practice has been to decline to do so. The Revenue cannot divert costly resources to helping taxpayers work out their plans nor can we enter into discussions which effectively help them to find ways round anti-avoidance provisions. It seems however that some genuine misunderstanding exists about the scope of s. 460 in relation to transactions with a commercial element and we have therefore been reviewing the working of the clearance procedure.

Where there is a tax advantage, s. 460 applies unless the taxpayer shows that both of the two conditions set out in subs. (1) are satisfied. When applicants set out a full and, so far as possible substantiated, account of each major part of their proposed transactions and relate this to both conditions, they sometimes realise for themselves why clearances must be refused, and a more general practice of doing so might help understanding of the section.

For our part, we have decided to modify the practice set out above where the applicant has given full reasons for his transactions. If, in such cases we have to refuse clearance, where possible we shall in future indicate the main grounds for doing so. Naturally we cannot undertake always to do so. Furthermore, in appropriate cases where we did not think it right to give reasons, we shall invite the principals themselves, as well as their advisers, to an interview so that we can be certain we have fully appreciated the position.

2 Bond washing and dividend stripping

2.1 Introduction

This chapter will discuss the avoidance provisions which have been enacted to counter two devices which have become known as 'bond washing' and 'dividend stripping', which were very popular in the 1950s and early 1960s before a comprehensive capital gains tax was introduced. Two examples of the activities towards which the legislation is directed are as follows:—

(a) A higher rate taxpayer would sell his rights to dividends/interest on his securities for a capital sum to a non-taxpaying body, such as a charity or pension fund. The capital sum would not be taxable in the hands of the taxpayer and the non-taxpaying body could reclaim the tax deducted from the dividends/interest.

(b) A share-dealer would purchase the share capital of a company with substantial reserves and from these reserves pay a large dividend. Shortly after the dividend payment the shares would be sold and the loss on the shares offset against the tax deducted from the dividend payment.

Obviously numerous variations of these two arrangements were effected by taxpayers, and to counter these abuses comprehensive legislation has had to be introduced. The relevant provisions which will be considered in this chapter are TA 1970, ss. 30, 281, 469–477 and 486. The 'bond washing' provisions are set out in TA 1970, ss. 469–471 and 477 and the 'dividend stripping' provisions in TA 1970, ss. 281, 476 and 486. The procedural aspects of both bond washing and dividend stripping are contained in TA 1970, ss. 472–475.

Prior to the introduction of this legislation most of the schemes were challenged on the basis that the relevant transactions were not trading transactions but could be more appropriately described as 'planned raids on the Inland Revenue' (see the remarks of Lord Donovan in *Lupton v FA & AB Ltd* (1971) 47 TC 580 at 629). Thus this chapter will also discuss the litigation to which bond washing and dividend stripping have given rise. In this connection the success or failure of the arrangements has depended on whether the transactions could be classified as share-dealing transactions forming part of a trade.

This chapter, therefore, will review both the litigation (see **2.2**) and also the legislation which has largely supplemented and superseded the litigation (see **2.3**).

2.2 The litigation

2.2.1 Introduction

The relevant cases in connection with 'bond washing' and 'dividend stripping' are *J P Harrison (Watford) Ltd v Griffiths* (1962) 40 TC 281; *Finsbury Securities Ltd v Bishop* (1965) 43 TC 591; *Lupton v FA & AB Ltd* (1971) 47 TC 580; *Thomson v Gurneville Securities* (1969) 47 TC 633. In all these cases the question arose as to whether the purchase and sale of securities were trading transactions when concomitantly there were dividend payments and income tax repayment claims. Also all four cases were taken, not surprisingly, to the House of Lords. As the term trade is not defined comprehensively in TA 1970 it follows that questions relating to transactions which might fall into the category of trade are questions of fact for determination by the Special Commissioners. It is only if their findings are erroneous in law (see *Edwards v Bairstow* (1955) 36 TC 207 for the criteria as to this requirement) that a higher court can reverse the Commissioners' decision. Whilst findings of fact will not normally be questioned by the higher courts the facts of the 'dividend stripping cases' as they have become known have been so complicated that their decisions have been reversed. One such case was *J P Harrison (Watford) Ltd v Griffiths* (1962) 40 TC 281.

2.2.2 *J P Harrison (Watford) Ltd v Griffiths* (1962) 40 TC 281

Very briefly the facts of the case were that a company trading in merchandise changed its Memorandum in order to allow dealing in shares. The company had incurred substantial losses as merchants and purchased the shares of a company with large accumulated profits. These profits were subsequently distributed in the form of dividends and the shares sold at a loss. The company then reclaimed the tax deducted from the dividend on the basis that the gross dividends were less than the losses from share dealing and trading as merchants. In the House of Lords a majority of three to two held that the Commissioners could not have reasonably come to the conclusion that the transaction was not a share-dealing transaction. The majority took the view that the fiscal motives were irrelevant to the question of whether the transactions were of a trading nature. Lord Morris, one of the majority, made the following points:—

(a) on the facts, the transaction amounted to share-dealing;
(b) the inherent nature of the transactions was unaltered by the object of entering into those transactions to secure a tax advantage;
(c) the objects and intentions may be relevant in some circumstances;
(d) trading transactions can be the prelude to the recovery of tax but the recovery is made in the capacity as a taxpayer and not as a trader.

Lord Guest, another of the majority, examined the Crown's contention that a transaction entered into with the intention of making a loss but which was expected to be less than the tax recovered, could not be classified as trading. He pointed out that this confused 'trading' with the 'results of trading'. The intention of making a profit was important in determining whether the transaction was an adventure in the nature of trade but the converse did not follow. The test to be applied was objective and he cited Lord Clyde's speech in *IRC v Livingston* (1927) 11 TC 538 in order to support this view:—

> 'are the operations involved . . . of the same kind and carried on in the same way, as those which are characteristic of ordinary trading in the line of business in which the venture was made'.

The other majority view, Viscount Simmonds, did not add anything to the above speeches. However, the two dissenters, Lord Reid and Lord Denning, were of the view that the Commissioners' findings were not unreasonable. Lord Denning expressed a view not too dissimilar to that of Lord Guest (see above). He made the point that an isolated transaction not effected with the object of making a profit provided some grounds for thinking the transaction did not amount to trading. Counsel for the company advanced the argument that only the transaction should be examined and not the object or result of it. Lord Denning rejected this as he said it was like looking at half the transaction and he did not believe there was a rule of law which required the Commissioners to do this. This approach amounts to saying that the totality of the transactions should be examined and this has been adopted in later cases (*Finsbury Securities Ltd v Bishop* (1965) 43 TC 591; *Lupton v FA & AB Ltd* (1971) 47 TC 580 and *Thomson v Gurneville Securities* (1969) 47 TC 633).

2.2.3 *Finsbury Securities Ltd v Bishop* (1965) 43 TC 591

In this case a company created and issued shares which carried the right to most of the dividends that might be paid over the following five years. The shares were then sold by the person to whom they were issued on the following terms:—

(a) the sale price was only ascertainable after five years;
(b) the purchaser could not sell the shares until after the five-year period;
(c) the vendors were to share any tax which was recovered in respect of the dividends to be paid on the shares.

At the end of the five-year period the purchaser sold the shares at a loss and claimed a trading loss on the basis that he was a share-dealer. The House of Lords unanimously held that, distinguishing the *Harrison* case (see **2.2.2**), there were no elements of trading present in the transactions. Their judgment, delivered by Lord Morris, was based on the following grounds:—

(a) the vendors in the *Harrison* case retained no interest in the shares after the sale and, in particular, there was no expectation that they would share any tax subsequently recovered;
(b) in the *Harrison* case shares were acquired, a dividend declared and the shares then sold;
(c) in the *Finsbury* case the future interests of the vendors were safeguarded as they retained the full benefits which would have accrued had there been no scheme;
(d) the purchasers in the *Harrison* case were free to dispose of their shares, whilst in the *Finsbury* case a sale would breach the original agreement for sale: it followed that the shares could not be dealt in but had to be retained and so had the characteristics of a fixed asset rather than stock-in-trade.

2.2.4 *Lupton v FA & AB Ltd* (1971) 47 TC 580

A share-dealing company specialising in dividend stripping purchased the shares of a company with a substantial accumulated profit and investments of about £700,000. It was agreed that if the share-dealing company recovered any tax on the reduction in value of the shares acquired as the result of a subsequent dividend payment, the tax recovered would be divided by the vendors and purchasers on a 50:50 basis. The House of Lords unanimously rejected the claim by holding that the transaction was not carried out in the course of the appellant's trade as share-dealers.

The leading judgment was again delivered by Lord Morris and he distinguished both the *Harrison* case and the *Finsbury* case. Referring to the distinguishing features of the *Harrison* case he reiterated his view that where a tax advantage might arise a transaction was not necessarily trading. In the *Harrison* case no fiscal arrangement entered into the bargain whilst in the *Finsbury* case the fiscal considerations were an inherent part of the transactions and were of such an order as to change the nature of the transactions. Lord Morris also approved the opinion of Megarry J, at first instance, to the effect that the transactions he had in mind were equivocal when considered separately from the motives of the participators, in that it could not be clearly determined whether or not they were trading transactions. After stating that the *Harrison* case and the *Finsbury* case are at opposite ends of the spectrum he went on to say ((1971) 47 TC 580 at 621):—

> 'The question is, whether viewed as a whole, the transaction is one which can fairly be regarded as a trading transaction. If it is, then it will not be denatured merely because it was entered into with motives of reaping a fiscal advantage. Neither fiscal elements nor fiscal motives will prevent what in substance is a trading transaction from ranking as such. On the other hand, if the greater part of the transaction is explicable only on fiscal grounds, the mere presence of elements of trading will not suffice to translate the transaction into the realms of trading. In particular, if what is erected is predominantly an artificial structure, remote from trading and fashioned so as to secure a tax advantage, the mere presence in that structure of certain elements which by themselves could fairly be described as trading will not cast the cloak of trade over the whole structure.'

It is this author's view that this statement is not consistent with the general case-law on what is trading. The cases clearly establish that motives can be important in determining the nature of a transaction. The above speech indicates that when a transaction is not in a form which is clearly a trading transaction its objects are material, whilst they are not when the form is clearly defined as trading.

Lord Morris felt that, on the facts, the transactions in the case were not those normally undertaken by a share-dealer and that it was a delusion to regard them as share-dealing transactions. Lord Guest agreed with Lord Morris and stated that there was no inconsistency between the two earlier decisions and the *Harrison* case. Although the transactions realised a loss, the fiscal motive did not prevent them from being trading transactions; by contrast the various transactions in the *Finsbury* case were clearly not in the nature of trading. Lord Donovan took a bold view and declared that the transaction constituted:—

> 'the . . . execution of a raid on the Treasury using the technicalities of revenue law and company law as the necessary weapon.'

Lord Donovan also distinguished the *Harrison* and *Finsbury* cases on the basis that in the former the component parts of the transaction were examined, that is, the purchase of the shares, the receipt of the dividends and the subsequent sale of the shares – these were transactions normally associated with share-dealers and it was irrelevant that the trader also had a tax advantage in view; the minority view, which was accepted in the *Finsbury* case, was to look at the totality of transactions. He felt that the different approach in the *Finsbury* case was the correct one. Viscount Dilhorne thought that both cases were indistinguishable but faced with a choice he expressed that he would follow the *Finsbury* case. Like Lord Donovan he felt the correct approach was to look at the transaction as a whole, that is, not only at its inception but also at the manner in which it is implemented. On this basis he concluded that the transactions were entered into with a view to establishing a claim against the Inland Revenue and as a result the transactions could not be classified as trading.

The speech of Lord Simon provides probably the best analysis of the two cases. He felt that the decision in the *Harrison* case was a very narrow view and added ((1971) 47 TC 580 at 631–632):—

> 'In my view, the two cases, taken as a binary system, establish the following propositions: (1) the question in every case is whether the relevant loss has been incurred in the course of trade (of dealing in shares); (2) dividend stripping (or any other transaction to secure a fiscal advantage) is not in itself part of the trade of dealing in shares (cf. also *IRC v Dowdall O'Mahoney & Co Ltd* [1952] AC 401); (3) share-dealings and other business transactions vary almost infinitely; and to

> determine whether the transaction is, on the one hand, a share-dealing which is part of the trade of dealing in shares or, on the other, merely a device to secure a fiscal advantage, all the circumstances of the particular case must be considered; (4) a share-dealing which is palpably part of the trade of dealing in shares will not cease to be so merely because there is inherent in it an intention to obtain a fiscal advantage, or even if that intention conditions the form which such share-dealing takes; (5) what is in reality merely a device to secure a fiscal advantage will not become part of the trade of dealing in shares just because it is given the trappings normally associated with a share-dealing within the trade of dealing in shares; (6) if the appearance of the transaction leaves the matter in doubt, an examination of its paramount object will always be relevant and will generally be decisive.'

He went on to conclude:—

> 'My Lords, this is not share-dealing within the trade of dealing in shares. It is plainly a joint venture of the appellants and the vendors of the shares, by taking advantage of quirks of revenue and company law, to obtain money out of the public purse and share it between them. Even if the transaction were equivocal, its true nature would, in my view, be resolved by investigation of its paramount object: since, on the findings of the Special Commissioners, the transaction would produce a loss to the appellants unless repayment of income tax were obtained, I conclude that the paramount object of the transaction was to procure such repayment of income tax: it was, in other words, a tax-recovery device.'

2.2.5 *Thomson v Gurneville Securities Ltd* (1969) 47 TC 633

In the last case the substance of the transaction was that a share-dealing company would incur a loss as a result of writing down the value of its shareholding in another company, as a result of dividends paid by that other company. This case differed from the *Lupton* case in as much as a small commercial profit was included in the arrangements but this was only about one-fifth of the loss claim in respect of the dividend stripping transactions. Again, the House of Lords unanimously held that the transactions were not trading transactions of a share-dealer.

Lords Morris and Guest and Viscount Simmonds thought that the transactions were mainly designed to provide a basis for claims against the Revenue. Lord Donovan dismissed the company's claim that a commercial profit was realised on the transactions on two grounds:—

(a) the commercial profit element was part of the scheme;
(b) any assessment of the profit on a commercial transaction is by nature a speculative estimate; in this case it was agreed on before the transactions were implemented.

As in the *Lupton* case, Lord Donovan thought that, looking at the scheme as a whole, the transactions were designed to exploit the fiscal system and not within the scope of trading as share-dealers.

Lord Simon expressed the view that the presence of tax advantages in share transactions did not necessarily mean that the shares had not been acquired by the taxpayer company as part of their stock-in-trade and that all the circumstances surrounding the transactions had to be examined. In the context of the case he felt the commercial profit was of a very curious nature and commented as follows ((1969) 47 TC 633 at 679):—

> 'As for the respondents' argument based on the "commercial profit", this was a commercial profit of a very curious nature. It was built into the scheme from the outset by the stipulation that the price to be paid should be fixed at 95% (later 94%) of the value of the underlying assets as subsequently ascertained. The result was that on resale the respondents were *bound* to make a profit . . . the 5% to 6% cut giving rise to the "commercial profit" can be regarded either as a reward to the respondents for putting up a tax avoidance scheme (and so not a commercial profit earned by the respondents on their trade of dealing in shares); or, being an integral part of the entire scheme, as a colourable device to make a mere expedient for extracting money from the public purse appear to be a bona fide dealing in shares, by assuming the semblance of a "commercial profit" arising from the transaction; or partly the one, partly the other. On no view was it true "commercial profit".'

On the question raised by the case he concluded ((1969) 47 TC 633 at 679):—

> 'In the instant case the question can be narrowed: looking at the transaction as a whole, it was, on the one hand, one whereby a true commercial profit was taken in a fiscally advantageous way or, on the other, one in which a "commercial profit" was merely a by-product of, or a disguise for, what was really a tax recovery device? Whichever way the question

is put, I have no doubt that, judged both qualitatively and quantitatively, the transaction falls into the latter category in each case.'

2.2.6 Conclusions

The four cases discussed in **2.2.2–2.2.5** give rise to a number of points.

The *Harrison* decision is a very narrow one and has been superseded by a wider approach which views the transactions as a whole. Examining the transactions as a whole comes very close to abrogating the rule established in the *Duke of Westminster v IRC* (1935) 19 TC 490 case that it is the legal form of the transaction and not the substance which determines its status. In the case of a share-dealer, or for that matter any other trader, the expected commercial profits must be realistic in relation to any inherent tax advantages: this will obviously be a question for the Commissioners to decide: inevitably the cases will involve analysing very complicated facts and the weight given to any one fact will depend very much on the circumstances of the case.

2.3 The statutory provisions

2.3.1 Introduction

This section reviews the legislation which has been enacted to counter the mischiefs known as bond washing and dividend stripping. The order in which these provisions will be discussed is set out below:—

Nature of Transaction	Main Provisions
'BOND WASHING'	
Sale and repurchase of securities	TA 1970, s. 469
Sale of interest on securities without selling the securities	TA 1970, s. 470
Bond washing by purchase and resale	TA 1970, ss. 471–475
Bond washing by creating interest and dividend payments	TA 1970, s. 477

'DIVIDEND STRIPPING'

Individuals

Sales cum dividend	TA 1970, s. 30

Companies

Dividend stripping	TA 1970, s. 281
Distribution materially reducing value of holding	TA 1970, s. 476
Transactions between a dealing company and an associated non-dealing company	TA 1970, s. 486

2.3.2 Sale and repurchase of securities (TA 1970, s. 469)

TA 1970, s. 469 reads as follows:—

469 Sale and repurchase of securities

(1) Where the owner of any securities (in this subsection and subs. (3) below referred to as "the owner") agrees to sell or transfer those securities and by the same or any collateral agreement:—

(a) agrees to buy back or re-acquire the securities, or

(b) acquires an option, which he subsequently exercises, to buy back or re-acquire the securities,

then, if the result of the transaction is that any interest becoming payable in respect of the securities is receivable otherwise than by the owner, the following provisions shall have effect:—

(i) the interest payable as aforesaid shall, whether it would or would not have been chargeable to tax apart from the provisions of this section, be deemed for all the purposes of the Tax Acts to be the income of the owner and not to be the income of any other person; and

(ii) if the securities are of such a character that the interest payable in respect thereof may be paid without deduction of tax, the owner shall be chargeable to tax under Case VI of Sch. D in respect of the interest which is deemed to be his income as aforesaid, but shall be entitled to credit for any tax which that income is shown to have borne.

(2) In relation to corporation tax:—

(a) subject to the provisions of the Tax Acts about distributions, interest deemed under subs. (1) (i) above to be the income of the owner shall be chargeable under Case VI of Sch. D, and

(b) subs. (1) (ii) above shall not apply.

(3) The references in subs. (1) above to buying back or re-acquiring the securities shall be deemed to include references to buying or acquiring similar securities, so, however, that where similar securities are bought or acquired, the owner shall be under no greater liability to tax than he would have been under if the original securities had been bought back or re-acquired.

(4) Where any person carrying on a trade which consists wholly or partly in dealing in securities agrees to buy or acquire any securities, and by the same or any collateral agreement:—

(a) agrees to sell back or re-transfer the securities, or

(b) acquires an option, which he subsequently exercises, to sell back or re-transfer the securities,

then, if the result of the transaction is that any interest becoming payable in respect of the securities is receivable by him, no account shall be taken of the transaction in computing for any of the purposes of the Tax Acts the profits arising from or loss sustained in the trade.

(5) Subsection (4) above shall have effect, subject to any necessary modifications, as if references to selling back or re-transferring the securities included references to selling or transferring similar securities.

(6) This section shall not apply to any income to which s. 496 (3) of this Act (transactions associated with loans or credit) applies.

(7) For the purposes of this section:—

(a) "interest" includes a dividend,

(b) "securities" includes stocks and shares,

(c) securities shall be deemed to be similar if they entitle their holders to the same rights against the same persons as to capital and interest and the same remedies for the enforcement of those rights, notwithstanding any difference in the total nominal amounts of the respective securities or in the form in which they are held or the manner in which they can be transferred.

(8) The Board may by notice in writing require any person to furnish them within such time as they may direct (not being less than twenty-eight days), in respect of all securities of which he was the owner at any time during the period specified in the notice, such particulars as they consider necessary for the purposes of this section and for the purpose of discovering whether tax has been borne in respect of the interest on all those securities.

Two examples of the type of transaction at which this section is directed are set out in **2.1**. This type of transaction first came under attack in FA 1937 and all the relevant provisions have since been consolidated in TA 1970, s. 469; before the Revenue can invoke the section two conditions must be satisfied:—

(a) the owner of any securities must agree to sell or transfer them and by the same or collateral agreement agrees to buy back or re-acquire the securities, or acquire an option, which he subsequently exercises, to buy back or re-acquire the securities; and

(b) as a result of the transaction interest is payable to someone other than the 'owner'.

The interest paid is then deemed to be income of the owner and the income, whether received by an individual or company, is chargeable to tax under Sch. D, Case VI, but subject to a credit for any tax which that income is shown to have borne.

Share-dealing purchasers are affected by subss. (4) and (5) which are wider. For instance there is no justification for limiting collateral agreements to agreements made at the same time or by the same parties. It is only necessary that a person dealing in securities agrees to acquire securities within subs. (4) (a) or (b) and as a result of such an acquisition interest is receivable by him, in which case no account will be taken of the transaction in computing his profit or losses from share-dealing.

It should be noted that where one party to a transaction falls within either subs. (1) or (4), the other party to it will not necessarily be within the other subsection.

EXAMPLE 2.01

X, the owner of securities, agrees to sell them to Y, a share-dealer, and Y takes an option, by collateral agreement, to sell the securities back to X. If the option is subsequently exercised Y appears to be within subs. (4) but X will be outside subs. (1), if interest on those securities becomes payable to X.

The words 're-acquire' and 're-transfer' are not necessarily limited to a re-acquisition from the original purchaser or to a re-transfer from the original vendor. There is, however, very little authority on the meaning to be attributed to the word collateral. In one case (*Re Athill, Athill v Athill* (1880) 16 ChD 211 at 222) it was held to mean parallel or additional. It should also be noted that it is the agreement, rather than the actual transfer, which brings the section into operation. This can be contrasted with options which must be exercised.

Subsection (6) provides that the section is not to apply to transactions associated with loans or credit. Where a transaction falls within both TA 1970, ss. 469 (4) and (5) and 472, the former prevails and as we shall see in **2.3.4** (c) these two subsections impose a greater burden.

Subsection (8) is procedural and defines the scope of the Revenue's information gathering powers; as is usual with anti-avoidance legislation the Revenue are given very wide investigative powers.

2.3.3 Sale of interest on securities without selling the securities (TA 1970, s. 470)

TA 1970, s. 470 reads as follows:—

470 Transfers of income arising from securities

(1) Where in any chargeable period the owner of any securities (in this section referred to as "the owner") sells or transfers the right to receive any interest payable (whether before or after the sale or transfer) in respect of the securities without selling or transferring the securities, then, for all the purposes of the Tax Acts, that interest, whether it would or would not be chargeable to tax apart from the provisions of this section:—

(a) shall be deemed to be the income of the owner or, in a case where the owner is not the beneficial owner of the securities and some other person (hereafter in this section referred to as "a beneficiary") is beneficially entitled to the income arising from the securities, the income of the beneficiary, and

(b) shall be deemed to be the income of the owner or beneficiary for that chargeable period, and

(c) shall not be deemed to be the income of any other person:

Provided that, in the case of a sale or other realisation the proceeds whereof are chargeable to tax under Sch. C or under 159 (3) of this Act (foreign dividends, etc.), the interest so deemed to be the income of the owner or beneficiary shall be deemed to be equal in amount to the amount of those proceeds.

(2) Nothing in subs. (1) of this section shall affect any provision of this Act authorising or requiring the deduction of income tax from any interest which is deemed to be the income of the owner or beneficiary as aforesaid or from the proceeds of any subsequent sale or other realisation of the right to receive that interest:

Provided that the proceeds of any such subsequent sale or other realisation shall not, for any of the purposes of the Tax Acts, be deemed to be to the income of the seller or the person on whose behalf the right is otherwise realised.

(3) Where the securities are of such a character that the interest payable in respect thereof may be paid without deduction of income tax, the owner or beneficiary, unless he shows that the proceeds of any sale or other realisation of the right to receive the interest which is deemed to be his income by virtue of this section have been charged to tax under Sch. C or under s. 159 (3) of this Act, shall be chargeable to tax under Case VI of Sch. D in respect of that interest, but shall be entitled to credit for any tax which that interest is shown to have borne.

Provided that, in any case where if the interest had been chargeable under Case IV or Case V of Sch. D, the computation of tax would have been made by reference to the amount received in the United Kingdom, the tax under Case VI shall be computed on the full amount of the sums which have been or will be received in the United Kingdom in the year of assessment or any subsequent year in which the owner remains the owner of the securities.

(4) In relation to corporation tax subs. (3) above shall not apply and the following provisions of this subsection shall have effect.

Subject to the provisions of the Tax Acts about distributions, the owner or beneficiary shall, in respect of any interest which is deemed to be his income by virtue of this section, be chargeable to corporation tax under Case VI of

Sch. D unless he shows that the proceeds of any sale or other realisation of the right to receive that interest have been charged to tax under Sch. C or under s. 159 (3) of this Act.

(5) In this section:—
"interest" includes dividends, annuities and shares of annuities, and
"securities" includes stocks and shares.

(6) The Board may by notice in writing require any person to furnish them within such time as they may direct (not being less than twenty-eight days), in respect of all securities of which he was the owner at any time during the period specified in the notice, with such particulars as they consider necessary for the purposes of this section and for the purpose of discovering whether:—
(a) tax has been borne in respect of the interest on all those securities; or
(b) the proceeds of any sale or other realisation of the right to receive the interest on the securities have been charged to tax under Sch. C or s. 159 (3) of this Act.

TA 1970, s. 470 covers the position where a person (the 'owner') transfers or sells the right to receive any interest payable, whether before or after the sale/transfer, without selling or transferring the securities. In such a case the interest payable is deemed to be that of the owner and not that of the person to whom the right was sold. This rule applies regardless of whether the interest would be chargeable to tax. If the right to more than one year's interest is sold, the interest for all the years covered by the disposal is treated as income of the year of assessment in which the sale is made. In the case of a sale or other realisation chargeable to tax under Sch. C or under TA 1970, s. 159 (3) (foreign dividends etc), the interest that will be imputed to the owner, or beneficiary, will be the realisation proceeds.

Subsection (2) provides that tax must be deducted from the interest (or from the proceeds of a subsequent sale or realisation) in the usual way, irrespective of whether the income is deemed to be that of the owner. The proceeds of a subsequent sale are not treated as income of the subsequent seller.

Subsection (3) covers the mechanism of assessment and charges the owner to tax under Sch. D, Case VI on the income imputed to him subject to a credit for any tax which the deemed income has borne. An exception to this rule is where the proceeds of any realisation of the right to receive that income has been charged to tax under Sch. C or under TA 1970, s. 159 (3). Where the interest would be chargeable under Sch. D, Cases VI or V on the amount received in the United Kingdom, the tax chargeable under Sch. D, Case VI is computed on the full amount which has been, or will be remitted to the United Kingdom in a year of assessment. What is not clear from TA 1970, s. 470 is how the 'sums received in the United Kingdom' are to be computed. The owner, after selling the right, has no control over the interest and so cannot supply the necessary data. Furthermore, there are no provisions which compel the purchaser to disclose his intentions and so the assessment must be based on guess-work or be issued after the income becomes known. If it is based on the former, it must be in accordance with the constitutional principles set out in *Vestey v IRC* (No 2) [1980] STC 10. It follows that if such assessment did not satisfy these principles the assessment would be void.

The Revenue's powers of gathering information are the same as those set out in TA 1970, s. 469 (8) (see **2.3.2**).

2.3.4 Bond washing by purchase and resale (TA 1970, ss. 471–475)

(a) Introduction

TA 1970, ss. 471–475 form a connected group and are directed at transactions which are the reverse of 'bond washing' transactions. Usually they consist of a purchase cum interest, followed by a receipt of interest and a sale ex-interest. The sale price would inevitably be less than the purchase price and if the transaction was effected by a share-dealer the difference would be treated as a trading loss. As a result any tax deducted from the interest received could be recovered from the Revenue.

In essence the provisions apply to the purchase and sale of the same, or similar securities, within one month of each other, or in certain circumstances, within six months of each other. The effect of the provisions is to reduce the purchase price of the securities by the 'appropriate amount in respect of the interest'. This figure is computed on a time apportionment basis.

(b) Bond washing: purchase and resale of securities (TA 1970, s. 471)

TA 1970, s. 471 reads as follows:—

471 Application of following sections

(1) Subject as hereinafter provided ss. 472, 473 and 474 below relate to cases of a purchase by a person (in those sections referred to as "the first buyer") of any securities and their subsequent sale by him, the result of the transaction being that interest becoming payable in respect of the securities (in those sections referred to as "the interest") is receivable by the first buyer.

(2) The said sections do not relate to cases where:—

(a) the time elapsing between the purchase by the first buyer and his taking steps to dispose of the securities exceeded six months, or

(b) that time exceeded one month and it is shown to the satisfaction of the Board that the purchase and sale were each effected at the current market price, and that the sale was not effected in pursuance of an agreement or arrangement made before or at the time of the purchase.

The jurisdiction of the General Commissioners or Special Commissioners on any appeal shall include jurisdiction to review any relevant decision taken by the Board in the exercise of their functions under this subsection.

(3) The reference in subs. (2) above to the first buyer taking steps to dispose of the securities shall be construed:—

(a) if he sold them in the exercise of an option he had acquired, as a reference to his acquisition of the option,

(b) in any other case, as a reference to his selling them.

(4) For the purposes of this and the said three sections a sale of securities similar to, and of the like nominal amount as, securities previously bought (hereinafter referred to as "the original securities") shall be equivalent to a sale of original securities, and subs. (3) above shall apply accordingly; and where the first buyer bought parcels of similar securities at different times a subsequent sale of any of the securities shall so far as may be related to the last to be bought of the parcels, and then to the last but one, and so on:

Provided that a person shall be under no greater liability to tax by virtue of this subsection than he would have been under if instead of selling the similar securities he had sold the original securities.

(5) Where at the time when a trade is, or is deemed to be, set up and commenced any securities form part of the trading

stock belonging to the trade, those securities shall be treated for the purposes of this section as having been sold at that time in the open market by the person to whom they belonged immediately before that time and as having been purchased at that time in the open market by the person thereafter engaged in carrying on the trade; and, subject to the preceding provisions of this subsection, where there is a change in the persons engaged in carrying on a trade which is not a change on which the trade is deemed to be discontinued the provisions of this section shall apply in relation to the person so engaged after the change as if anything done to or by his predecessor had been done to or by him.

(6) For the purposes of this and the said three sections:—

(a) "interest" includes a qualifying distribution and any dividend which is not a qualifying distribution, and in applying references to interest in relation to a qualifying distribution "gross interest" means the qualifying distribution together with the tax credit to which the recipient of the distribution is entitled in respect of it and "net interest" means the qualifying distribution exclusive of any such tax credit;

(b) "person" includes any body of persons, and references to a person entitled to any exemption from tax include, in a case of an exemption expressed to apply to income of a trust or fund, references to the persons entitled to make claims for the granting of that exemption;

(c) "securities" includes stocks and shares;

(d) securities shall be deemed to be similar if they entitle their holders to the same rights against the same persons as to capital and interest and the same remedies for the enforcement of those rights, notwithstanding any difference in the total nominal amounts of the respective securities or in the form in which they are held or the manner in which they can be transferred, and for the purposes of this paragraph rights guaranteed by the Treasury shall be treated as rights against the Treasury;

and in para. (a) above "qualifying distribution" and "tax credit" have the same meanings as in Part V of the Finance Act 1972.

This section is procedural and defines the scope of the terms used in TA 1970, ss. 472–475. The term 'the first buyer' is widely defined in subs. (3) to include the acquisition of an option to sell. Subsection (4) defines the rules for identifying securities purchased and resold. The securities first acquired are referred to as 'the original securities' and a sale of 'similar securities' of the like nominal amount is equivalent to a sale of the original securities. Where there are purchases of several parcels of 'similar securities' the sales are identified on a last-in-first-out basis. However, it is provided that a person's tax liability should not be increased as a result of this identification process rather than if he had sold the 'original securities' and not the 'similar securities'.

Where a trade is, or is deemed to be, set up or commenced, any securities forming part of the person's trading stock are treated as having been sold at that time in the open market by the person to whom they belonged before that time and as having been purchased by the person who subsequently carried on the trade. Where there is a change in the persons carrying on the trade, which does not give rise to a discontinuance and a new trade, the persons who carry on the trade are treated as if the acts done to or by their predecessors were their own (see subs. (5)).

(c) Dealers in securities (TA 1970, ss. 472 and 475)

TA 1970, ss. 472 and 475 read as follows:—

472 Dealers in securities

(1) Subject to the provisions of this section, if the first buyer is engaged in carrying on a trade which consists of or comprises dealings in securities, then in computing for any of the purposes of the Tax Acts the profits arising from or loss sustained in the trade the price paid by him for the securities shall be reduced by the appropriate amount in respect of the interest, as determined in accordance with s. 475 below.

(2) Subsection (1) of this section shall not apply if the first buyer:—

(a) is in the opinion of the Board bona fide carrying on the business of a discount house in the United Kingdom, or

(b) is a member of The Stock Exchange who is recognised by the Council thereof as carrying on the business of a jobber,

and the securities were bought in the ordinary course of his said business.

(3) Subsection (1) of this section shall not apply if the purchase of the securities by the first buyer and their resale, or as the case may be the subsequent sale of similar securities, constitute a transaction which is to be left out of account in computing profits or losses by virtue of s. 469 (4) above.

(4) Subsection (1) of this section shall not apply if the securities are overseas securities bought by the first buyer on a stock exchange outside the United Kingdom in the ordinary course of his trade as a dealer in securities and the following conditions are satisfied, namely:—

(a) the interest is brought into account in computing for the purposes of the Tax Acts the profits arising from or loss sustained in the trade, and

(b) where credit against tax would fall to be allowed in respect of the interest under s. 497 or s. 498 of this Act (double taxation relief), the first buyer elects that credit shall not be so allowed.

In this subsection "overseas securities" means securities of the government of, or of a body of persons resident in, any country or territory outside the United Kingdom and the Republic of Ireland.

475 Meaning of "appropriate amount in respect of" interest

(1) For the purposes of s. 472 above the appropriate amount in respect of the interest is the appropriate proportion of the net interest receivable by the first buyer.

(2) For the purposes of ss. 473 and 474 above the appropriate amount in respect of the interest is the gross amount corresponding with the appropriate proportion of the net interest receivable by the first buyer.

(3) For the purposes of this section the appropriate proportion is the proportion which:—

(a) the period beginning with the date on which the securities were first listed in The Stock Exchange Daily Official List at a price excluding the value of the interest payment last payable before the interest receivable by the first buyer, and ending with the day before the day on which the first buyer bought the securities, bears to:—

(b) the period beginning with the said date and ending with the day before the first date after the purchase by the first buyer on which the securities are quoted in the said list at a price excluding the value of the interest receivable by the first buyer.

(4) Where the interest receivable by the first buyer was the first interest payment payable in respect of the securities, paras. (a) and (b) of subs. (3) above shall have effect with the substitution, for references to the date on which the securities were first quoted as mentioned in the said para. (a), of the beginning of the period for which the interest was payable:

Provided that where the capital amount of the securities was not fully paid at the beginning of the said period and one or more instalments of capital were paid during that period:—

(a) the interest shall be treated as divided into parts, calculated by reference to the amount of the interest attributable to the capital paid at or before the beginning of the said period and the amount thereof attributable to each such instalment, and

(b) treating each of the said parts as interest payable for the said period or, where the part was calculated by reference to any such instalment, as interest payable for the part of the said period beginning with the payment of the instalment, there shall be calculated, in accordance with the preceding provisions of this section, the amount constituting the appropriate proportion of each part, and

(c) the appropriate proportion of the interest for the purposes of this section shall be the proportion thereof constituted by the sum of the said amounts.

(5) In relation to securities not listed in The Stock Exchange Daily Official List, subs. (3) above shall have effect with the substitution for the periods therein mentioned of such periods as in the opinion of the Commissioners having jurisdiction in the matter, correspond therewith in the case of the securities in question.

(6) Where the securities are of a description such that under the rules of the London Stock Exchange the bargain price is increased, where interest is receivable by the buyer, by reference to gross interest accruing before the bargain date, the preceding subsections shall not apply but for the

> purposes of ss. 472, 473 and 474 above the appropriate amount in respect of the interest shall be the amount of the increase in the bargain price.

These two sections cover the purchase and sale of securities where 'the first buyer' is a dealer in securities. In computing the profit/losses of that person the price paid by him for the securities is reduced by the 'appropriate amount in respect of the interest'. The 'appropriate proportion' can be defined more simply as the period which has elapsed prior to ownership by the 'first buyer' since the securities were last quoted ex-dividend divided by the period between the ex-dividend dates.

EXAMPLE 2.02

Suppose the ordinary shares of X are quoted ex-dividend on the Stock Exchange on 1 January and 30 June respectively and that shares in X were acquired by a taxpayer dealing in securities on 16 June 1980; the appropriate proportion for the purposes of TA 1970, s. 475 (3) would be:—

1 January–15 June	= 166 days
1 January–29 June	= 180 days
Appropriate proportion	= $\frac{166}{180}$

If the dealer paid £40,000 for the shares on 16 June 1980 and subsequently sold them within one month on 7 July 1980 for £39,000 after receiving a dividend of £1,400 net, the apparent loss would be £1,000 (£40,000 – £39,000). The adjusted loss, taking into account TA 1970, s. 475 (3), would be:—

	£000's	*£000's*
Disposal proceeds		39
Less: Cost	40	
Less: Appropriate proportion of net dividend $\frac{166}{180} \times £1,400$	1.3	38.7
Sch. D, Case I Loss		0.3

It is important to note that TA 1970, s. 472 (2)–(4) sets out three exceptions to the general provisions. Firstly, TA 1970, s. 472 (2) states that subs. (1) will not apply where the first buyer is a UK discount house, or a recognised jobber on the Stock Exchange. Secondly, under TA 1970, s. 472 (3) the transaction is not within TA 1970, s. 472 (1) if the purchase and resale by the first buyer is not brought into account in computing his profits/losses by virtue of TA 1970, s. 469 (4). The third exemption relates to overseas securities where the first buyer brings the interest into the computation of his profits from trade and elects not to claim any double tax relief he may otherwise be entitled to under TA 1970, ss. 497 or 498.

Where the securities are new issues the beginning of the period from which the interest is payable is substituted for the ex-dividend date. In cases where the securities are not fully paid at the beginning of the period the formula prescribed in TA 1970. s. 472 (4) must be applied. In effect the formula is based on a division of the interest into parts corresponding to the periods between the payment of one capital instalment and the next.

(d) Persons entitled to exemptions (TA 1970, s. 473)

TA 1970, s. 473 reads as follows:—

> If the first buyer is entitled under any enactment to an exemption from tax which, apart from this subsection, would extend to the interest, then the exemption shall not extend to an amount equal to the appropriate amount in respect of the interest, as determined in accordance with s. 475 below:
>
> Provided that if the first buyer is entitled as aforesaid and any annual payment is payable by him out of the interest, the annual payment shall be deemed as to the whole thereof to be paid out of profits or gains not brought into charge to income tax, and s. 53 of this Act shall apply accordingly.

Under this section the exempt taxpayer is not exempt from tax on an amount equal to the 'appropriate amount in respect of the interest'. This sum is calculated by reference to the gross interest; and otherwise in accordance with the provisions of TA 1970, s. 475.

EXAMPLE 2.03

Suppose in Example **2.02** a charity acquired the shares on 16 June 1980 and after receiving the dividend on 1 July 1980, disposed of the shares within one month of their acquisition. By virtue of this subsection the gross dividend of £2,000 will not be exempt from tax and the charity will only be able to reclaim a proportion of the tax on the dividend.

	Gross	*Tax*	*Net*
	£	£	£
Dividend	2,000	600	1,400
Not exempt × $\frac{166}{180}$	1,844	553	1,291
Amount exempt	£ 156	£47	£ 109

If the exempt first buyer has to make any annual payments these are treated as not having been paid out of profits chargeable to tax. The tax deducted from these payments will be accountable for under the provisions of TA 1970, s. 53.

(e) Persons other than dealers in securities (TA 1970, s. 474)

TA 1970, s. 474 reads as follows:—

(1) If the first buyer carries on a trade not falling within s. 472 above, then in ascertaining whether any or what repayment of income tax is to be made to him under s. 168 of this Act by reference to any loss sustained in the trade and the amount of his income for the year of assessment his income for which includes the interest, there shall be left out of account:—

(a) the appropriate amount in respect of the interest, as determined in accordance with s. 475 below, and

(b) any tax paid on that amount.

(2) Where the first buyer is a company which does not carry on a trade falling within s. 472 above, the appropriate amount in respect of the interest, as determined in accordance with s. 475 below, and any tax paid in respect of or deducted from that amount shall be disregarded except that, for the purposes of corporation tax on chargeable gains:—

(a) where that appropriate amount is determined in accordance with s. 475 (2) below, the appropriate proportion of the net interest receivable by the first buyer as mentioned in that subsection, and

(b) where that appropriate amount is determined in accordance with s. 475 (6) below, the net amount of interest corresponding to the gross interest referred to in that subsection,

shall be treated as if it were a capital distribution within the meaning of s. 72 (5) (b) of the Capital Gains Tax Act 1979 received in respect of the holding of the securities concerned.

This subsection applies to any interest received after 29 April 1969.

(3) In applying references in this section to interest in relation to a qualifying distribution, references to any tax paid on or in respect of an amount shall be construed as references to so much of any related tax credit as is attributable to that amount; and for this purpose "related tax credit", in relation to an amount, means the tax credit to which, under s. 86 of the Finance Act 1972, the recipient of the distribution of which that amount is a proportion is entitled.

TA 1970, s. 474 applies to a trader who has trading losses (other than from share-dealing) but no income against which he can set those losses. By purchasing cum interest securities he could offset the trading losses against the interest on the securities and reclaim any tax which had been deducted from the interest. This section provides that in ascertaining any repayments of tax which might be due to the first buyer under TA 1970, s. 168 the gross amount of interest and the tax on that interest should not be brought into account.

This provision also applies where the first buyer is a company. In addition, however, a part of the appropriate amount is treated as a capital distribution. It follows that if the value of the securities becomes less as a result of a distribution there will be an allowable loss if the securities are subsequently sold by the first buyer. This will be offset by the capital distribution, the amount of which will depend on the computation of the appropriate amount. If the security is purchased very shortly before the interest payment and market conditions remain stable the allowable loss will be completely offset by the capital distribution in the form of the interest payment.

2.3.5 Bond washing by creating interest or dividend payments (TA 1970, s. 477)

TA 1970, s. 477 reads as follows:—

(1) Subject to the provisions of this section, where:—

(a) under a contract for the sale of securities the seller is required to pay to the purchaser the amount of a periodical payment of interest on the securities, and

(b) the seller does not satisfy the following condition, that is to say that he is entitled to that payment of interest either as the registered holder of the securities or from a person from whom the seller purchased them,

s. 53 (2) of this Act and Sch. 20 to the Finance Act 1972 (which both impose a liability to account for income tax deducted) shall apply as if the payment by the seller were an annual payment made, after due deduction of tax, wholly out of a source other than profits or gains brought into charge to income tax.

(2) Subsection (1) of this section shall not apply where the interest in question is payable without deduction of tax or where, under the rules of the stock exchange governing the transaction, the payment required to be made in respect of the interest is of the amount of the interest before deduction of tax.

(3) If for any chargeable period the liability to tax of a jobber is determined on the footing that any excess of his payments in respect of interest on securities over his receipts in respect thereof, being payments made or receipts accrued in pursuance of a contract for the sale or purchase of the securities, is to be treated for all the purposes of the Tax Acts as an annual payment made by him, then as respects that chargeable period subs. (1) of this section shall not apply to him if he sold the securities in the ordinary course of his business as a jobber.

(4) Where the seller is resident in the United Kingdom and purchased the securities (otherwise than through a broker) from a person not so resident, then para. (b) of subs. (1) of this section shall have effect as if after the word "say" there were inserted the word "either" and as if for the words from "either as" to the end of the paragraph there were inserted the words "as the registered holder of the securities or that he shows that he acquired the securities, directly or indirectly, from a person who was so entitled to the payment".

(5) Where the seller under such a contract as is mentioned in para. (a) of subs. (1) of this section is not resident in the United Kingdom, and the sale is effected through a broker, that subsection shall not apply but unless the broker shows either that the seller was entitled to the

payment of interest as the registered holder of the securities or that the seller acquired the securities, directly or indirectly, from a person who was so entitled to the payment, the said s. 53 (2) of this Act shall apply as if the payment through the broker of the amount of the payment of interest were an annual payment by the broker made, after due deduction of tax, wholly out of such source as is mentioned in subs. (1) of this section.

(6) In this section:—

"broker" means a member of The Stock Exchange who carries on his business in the United Kingdom and is not a jobber,

"dealing broker", in relation to any sale of securities, means a member of a stock exchange in the United Kingdom, other than the London Stock Exchange, who is recognised by the committee of his exchange as carrying on the business of a dealer and authorised by them to deal in those securities,

"jobber" means a member of The Stock Exchange who is recognised by the Council thereof as carrying on the business of a jobber,

"securities" includes shares and stock,

and references to a periodical payment of interest include references to a qualifying distribution, as defined in s. 84 (4) of the Finance Act 1972, and any dividend which does not fall within that definition.

(6A) In the application of this section in a case where the references in subs. (1) above to a periodical payment of interest are construed as references to a qualifying distribution, subs. (2) above shall be omitted,

(7) Where it appears to the Board that by reason of any transaction or transactions a person may by virtue of this section have incurred any liability to tax, the Board may by notice in writing served on him require him, within such time not less than twenty-eight days as may be specified in the notice, to furnish information in his possession with respect to the transaction or any of the transactions, being information as to matters, specified in the notice, which are relevant to the question whether he has incurred such a liability as aforesaid.

TA 1970, s. 477 was introduced to counter a specific mischief. A stock exchange trader (T) would sell securities when they were 'cum-dividend' to a purchaser (A) and would cover this transaction by a subsequent purchase of an equivalent number of the same securities from another person (B), when they had gone 'ex-dividend'. B was entitled to the dividend (as an ex-dividend seller) on the securities but A was also entitled to be paid a sum equal to the net dividend (as a cum-dividend purchaser). T would pay an equivalent sum to A, in addition to transferring the shares to A and if the difference between the buying and selling price was more than the net dividend T made a profit. If A and B were exempt bodies or otherwise in a non-taxpaying position the Revenue were faced with two repayment claims. B would produce his dividend voucher and A, under the practice of the Exchange, received another on settlement with his broker. T had therefore created a dividend available for relief which had never in fact existed (see, for example, *Multipar Syndicate Ltd v Devitt* (1945) 26 TC 359).

TA 1970, s. 477 provides that where, under a contract of sale of securities, the seller is required to pay the purchaser the amount of a periodical payment of interest on the securities and is not entitled to that interest as a registered holder of the securities or from a person he purchased them from, the payment by the seller is treated as an annual payment not paid out of chargeable profits so that he is liable to pay the tax deducted to the Revenue. If the interest is paid gross the section does not apply.

Special provisions apply to jobbers and where:—

(a) a UK resident seller buys shares from a non-resident person, otherwise than through a broker, and
(b) the seller is a non-resident and the sale is effected through a broker.

In case (a) the seller will not be chargeable if he acquired the securities directly, or indirectly, from a person who was entitled to the dividend. Where the sale is through a broker, as in case (b), providing the condition referred to in the last sentence is satisfied, the payment by the broker will be treated as an annual payment under TA 1970, s. 53 (2) and made wholly out of profits or gains brought into charge to income tax.

2.3.6 Sales cum dividend (TA 1970, individuals s. 30)

TA 1970, s. 30 reads as follows:—

> (1) Any individual upon whom notice is served by the Board requiring him to furnish a statement of and particulars relating to any assets in which, at any time during the

period specified in the notice, he has had any beneficial interest, and in respect of which, within such period, either no income was received by him or the income received by him was less than the sum to which the income would have amounted if the income from such assets had accrued from day to day and been apportioned accordingly, shall furnish such a statement and such particulars in the form and within the time (not being less than twenty-eight days) required by the notice.

(2) The Board may serve further notices whenever they consider it necessary for the purposes of this section until complete particulars have been furnished to their satisfaction.

(3) If it appears to the Board by reference to all the circumstances in relation to the assets of any such individual (including circumstances with respect to sales, purchases, dealings, contracts, arrangements, transfers or any other transactions relating to such assets) that the individual has thereby avoided, or would avoid, more than 10% of what would have been his excess liability for any year if the income from those assets had been deemed to accrue from day to day and had been apportioned accordingly and the income so deemed to have been apportioned to him had been treated as part of his total income, then those assets shall be deemed to be assets to which subs. (4) below applies.

In this subsection "excess liability" means the excess of liability to income tax over what it would be if all income tax were charged at the basic rate to the exclusion of any higher or additional rate.

(4) For the purpose of assessing any individual to tax in pursuance of this section, the income from any assets to which this subsection applies shall be deemed to accrue from day to day and, in the case of the sale or transfer of any such assets by or to him, shall be deemed to have been received as and when it is deemed to have accrued:

Provided that an individual shall not be liable to be assessed to tax under this section in respect of any such income if he proves to the satisfaction of the Board that the avoidance of tax was exceptional and not systematic, and that there was not in his case in any of the three next preceding years any such avoidance of tax as is described in the provisions of subs. (3) above.

(5) If any individual fails to furnish any statement or particulars required under this section, or if the Board are not satisfied with any statement of particulars furnished under this section, they may make an estimate of the amount of the income which, under the preceding provisions of this section, is to be deemed to form part of his total income.

(6) For the purposes of this section "assets" means:—

(a) stocks or securities entitled to interest or dividend at a fixed rate only, not being stocks or securities the interest or dividend on which is dependent on the earnings of a company, and

(b) any other stocks or securities and any shares, if transactions in relation thereto have been effected by the individual otherwise than through a stock exchange in the United Kingdom and by a transfer on which ad valorem duty has been paid under the heading "Conveyance or Transfer on Sale" in Sch. 1 to the Stamp Act 1891.

TA 1970, s. 30 covers the situation where a taxpayer sells, for a capital sum, securities which are about to pay a dividend/interest and the purchaser acquires both the right to the latter and ownership of the securities. It is customary for companies quoted on the UK Stock Exchange to announce in advance the dates on which dividends or interest will be paid. Up to a certain date the securities will carry the rights to dividends and interest and will be quoted on the Stock Exchange as 'cum dividend'. After that date and for some time after, the security will not carry any rights to dividends or interest and will be quoted 'ex-dividend'. Ignoring market fluctuations, the price will gradually increase up to the date the securities go 'ex-dividend' and will then fall by the amount of dividend/interest paid. Prior to the introduction of TA 1970, s. 30 a higher rate taxpayer would find it profitable to sell securities just before they were 'ex-dividend', as the price of the security would reflect the dividend after taking into account basic rate tax. The capital sum, if received prior to 6 April 1965, was not chargeable to tax and if after that date, only to capital gains tax at a maximum rate of 30%. This contrasts with post-war income tax rates which have been as high as 98%. Often the taxpayer would subsequently re-acquire the securities when they were quoted ex-dividend.

To deal with this and other similar devices TA 1970, s. 30 was introduced. The section provides that if it appears to the Revenue that by reference to an individual taxpayer's circumstances (including sales, purchases, dealings, contracts, arrangements, transfer or any other transactions relating to such assets) he has reduced or would reduce his higher rate tax liability by more than 10% for any year of assessment, as a result of not treating the income from those assets as if it had accrued from day to day, then such income will be apportioned to him for the purposes of computing his liability to higher rate tax. No charge to tax will arise where an individual can prove that avoidance was exceptional and unsystematic and that no such avoidance was effected in any of the three years preceding the year in question. As with the other sections discussed in this chapter extensive information powers are given to the Revenue.

The scope of this section is restricted by the meaning of assets as defined in subs. (6) and the requirement of an *overall* 10% increase in higher rate tax liability, from which it follows that the section only deals with extreme cases of avoidance.

2.3.7 Dividend stripping (TA 1970, companies s. 281)

TA 1970, s. 281 reads as follows:—

(1) The provisions of this section apply where one company (in this section referred to as "the first company") has a holding in another company (in this section referred to as "the second company") and the following conditions are fulfilled:—

- (a) that the holding amounts to, or is an ingredient in a holding amounting to, 10% of all holdings of the same class in the second company,
- (b) that the first company is not a dealing company in relation to the holding,
- (c) that a distribution is or has been made after 29 April 1969 to the first company in respect of the holding, and
- (d) that the effect of the distribution is that the value of the holding is or has been materially reduced.

(2) Where this section applies in relation to a holding s. 280 above shall apply in relation to any disposal of any shares or securities comprised in the holding, whether the disposal is by the first company or by any other company to which the holding is transferred by a transfer to which s. 273 above applies, as if the distribution were a depreciatory transaction and, if the companies concerned are not members of a group of companies, as if they were:

Provided that the distribution shall not be treated as a depreciatory transaction to the extent that it consists of a payment which is required to be or has been brought into account, for the purposes of corporation tax on chargeable gains, in computing a chargeable gain or allowable loss accruing to the person making the ultimate disposal.

(3) This section shall be construed as one with s. 280 above.

(4) For the purposes of this section a company is "a dealing company" in relation to a holding if a profit on the sale of the holding would be taken into account in computing the company's trading profits.

(5) References in this section to a holding in a company refer to a holding of shares or securities by virtue of which the holder may receive distributions made by the company, but so that:—

(a) a company's holdings of different classes in another company shall be treated as separate holdings, and

(b) holdings of securities which differ in the entitlements or obligations they confer or impose shall be regarded as holdings of different classes.

(6) For the purposes of subs. (1) above:—

(a) all a company's holdings of the same class in another company are to be treated as ingredients constituting a single holding, and

(b) a company's holding of a particular class shall be treated as an ingredient in a holding amounting to 10% of all holdings of that class if the aggregate of that holding and other holdings of that class held by connected persons amounts to 10% of all holdings of that class,

and s. 533 of this Act (definition of connected persons) shall have effect in relation to para. (b) above as if, in subs. (7) of that section, after the words "or exercise control of" in each place where they occur there were inserted the words "or to acquire a holding in".

TA 1970, s. 281 disallows capital losses created by dividend payments and covers the situation where one company (referred to as 'the first company') has a holding in another company ('the second company') and the following conditions are satisfied:—

(a) the holding amounts to 10% of all holdings of the same class in the second company;

(b) the first company is not a dealing company in relation to the holding;
(c) a distribution is or has been made to the first company by the second company in respect of the holding;
(d) the distribution has materially reduced the value of the holding.

The distribution is not treated as one which materially reduces the value of the holding if it has to be taken into account for the purposes of computing the capital gain/loss of the company making the ultimate disposal. The aim of this section is very similar to TA 1970, s. 476 and so it is not surprising to find that the definitions of the terms used in both sections are identical (see **2.3.8**).

2.3.8 Distribution materially reducing value of holding (TA 1970, companies s. 476)

TA 1970, s. 476 reads as follows:—

> (1) Subsection (2) below applies where a company has, as a dealing company, a holding in another company resident in the UK (being a body corporate), and:—
> (a) the holding amounts to, or is an ingredient in a holding amounting to, 10% of all holdings of the same class in that company, and
> (b) after 29 April 1969 a distribution is, or two or more distributions are, made in respect of the holding, and
> (c) the value (at any accounting date or immediately before realisation or appropriation) of any security comprised in the holding is materially reduced below the value of the security at the time when it was acquired, and the whole or any part of this reduction is attributable to any distribution falling within para. (b) above,
>
> and in relation to any security comprised in the holding, the company having the holding is in subs. (2) below referred to as "the dealing company" and so much of any reduction in the value of the security as is attributable to any distribution falling within para. (b) above is in that subsection referred to as "the relevant reduction".
>
> (2) Where this subsection applies, an amount equal to the relevant reduction in the value of a security comprised in the holding:—
> (a) shall, if and so long as the security is not realised or appropriated as mentioned below, be added to the

value of the security for the purposes of any valuation,

(b) shall be treated, on any realisation of the security in the course of trade, as a trading receipt of the dealing company or, in the event of a partial realisation, shall be so treated to an appropriate extent, and

(c) shall be treated as a trading receipt of the dealing company if the security is appropriated in such circumstances that a profit on the sale of the security would no longer form part of the dealing company's trading profits.

(3) References in this section to a holding in a company refer to a holding of securities by virtue of which the holder may receive distributions made by the company, but so that:—

(a) a company's holdings of different classes in another company shall be treated as separate holdings, and

(b) holdings of securities which differ in the entitlements or obligations they confer or impose shall be regarded as holdings of different classes.

(4) For the purposes of subs. (2) above:—

(a) all a company's holdings of the same class in another company are to be treated as ingredients constituting a single holding, and

(b) a company's holding of a particular class shall be treated as an ingredient in a holding amounting to 10% of all holdings of that class if the aggregate of that holding and other holdings of that class held by connected persons amounts to 10% of all holdings of that class,

and s. 533 of this Act (definition of connected persons) shall have effect in relation to para. (b) above as if, in subs. (7) of that section, after the words "or exercise control of" in each place where they occur there were inserted the words "or to acquire a holding in".

(5) Where this section applies in relation to a distribution which consists of or includes interest to which s. 472 above applies, any reduction under that section in the price paid for the securities in respect of which the distribution is made shall be adjusted in such manner as seems appropriate to the Board to take account of subs. (2) above.

(6) For the purposes of this section "security" includes a share or other right and a company is a "dealing company" in

relation to a holding if a profit on a sale of the holding would be taken into account in computing the company's trading profits.

The aim of this section is to counter transactions in shares held by share-dealing companies. The value of those shares would be materially reduced in value by a substantial dividend payment, the reduction in value giving rise to a trading loss which could then be offset against the company's other trading profits.

Before this section can be applied three conditions must be fulfilled:—

(a) the share-dealing company must own a 10% holding in another company; and
(b) the distribution is, or two or more distributions are made, in the respect of the same holding; and
(c) the value of any security at any accounting date, or immediately before realisation, or appropriation, comprised in the holding is materially reduced below the value of the security at the time when it was acquired and the whole or any part of this reduction is attributable to a distribution falling within (b) above.

There is no definition of what is a material reduction but where the value of a security depreciates as a result of a distribution the decline in value is referred to as 'the relevant reduction'.

The treatment of the relevant reduction depends on whether the security is realised or unrealised or treated as trading stock (subs. 2).

Where a transaction falls within this section it might also be within TA 1970, s. 472. It will be recalled that under this section the purchase price paid for the share is adjusted on a time apportionment basis to reflect the interest paid on the share (see **2.3.4**). Under TA 1970, s. 476 (5) the Revenue can alter the revised purchase price (under TA 1970, s. 472) in such a manner as seems appropriate in the circumstances.

2.3.9 Transactions between a dealing company and an associated non-dealing company (TA 1970, s. 486)

TA 1970, s. 486 reads as follows:—

(1) Subject to the provisions of this section, where:—
(a) a dealing company becomes entitled to a deduction, in computing the profits or gains of the company for tax

purposes for any period, in respect of the depreciation in the value of any right subsisting against an associated company, not being a dealing company, or

(b) a dealing company makes any payment to such an associated company, being a payment in respect of which the dealing company is entitled to a deduction in computing its profits or gains for tax purposes for any period,

and the depreciation or payment is not brought into account in computing the profits or gains of the company not being a dealing company, that company shall be deemed to have received on the last day of the period income of an amount equal to the amount of the deduction and shall be chargeable in respect thereof under Case VI of Sch. D.

(2) Where the company not being a dealing company is carrying on a trade, the said income shall, if the company so elects, not be so chargeable but shall be deemed to have been a receipt of the trade, or, if the company is carrying on more than one trade, to have been a receipt of such one of the trades as the company may choose.

(3) Where the said company is carrying on, or was formed to carry on, a trade, then if the said right subsisting against the company was a right to the repayment of moneys lent for meeting expenditure which has proved (in whole or in part) abortive, or the payment to the company was made for meeting such expenditure, and the expenditure is such that the company is not entitled in respect thereof to any allowance or deduction in computing losses or gains, subs. (1) above shall not apply in so far as the expenditure proved abortive.

(4) For the purposes of this section:—

(a) "company" includes any body corporate,

(b) "dealing company" means a company dealing in securities, land or buildings and includes any company whose profits on the sale of securities, land or buildings are part of its trading profits,

(c) two or more companies shall be treated as associated companies if one has control of the other or others, or any person has control of both or all of them,

(d) references to a company having control of another company shall be construed as references to its having control thereof either by itself or in conjunction with any person having control over the first-mentioned company, and "control" has the meaning given by s. 534 of this Act,

(e) "securities" includes shares and stock.

(5) Where it appears to the Board that by reason of any transaction or transactions a person may by virtue of this section have incurred any liability to tax, the Board may by notice in writing served on him require him, within such time not less than twenty-eight days as may be specified in the notice, to furnish information in his possession with respect to the transaction or any of the transactions, being information as to matters, specified in the notice, which are relevant to the question whether he has incurred such a liability as aforesaid.

TA 1970, s. 486 covers the computation of a dealing company's profits for accounting periods ending after 5 April 1960 where the dealing company:—

(a) becomes entitled to a deduction 'in respect' of the depreciation of any right subsisting against an associated non-dealing company; or
(b) makes a payment to a non-dealing company which entitles the dealing company to a deduction and the receipt is not taxable in the hands of the non-dealing company.

In either case, the non-dealing company is deemed to have received income equivalent to the payment and the income is chargeable to tax under Sch. D, Case VI. There are, however, two exceptions, namely where the non-dealing company carries on a trade and elects to treat the payment as a trading receipt, or where the company was formed to carry on a trade and the right or payment arises in respect of expenditure incurred by the non-dealing company which has proved abortive and disallowable in computing trading profits.

2.4 Conclusions

This chapter has reviewed both the litigation and the two tax-avoidance devices, generally known as 'dividend stripping' or 'bond washing', which gave rise to the legislation that was enacted to counter the various abuses. The comprehensive nature of the legislation reflects the number of different abuses that were perpetrated by individuals, companies and exempt taxpayers. The legislation has not only effectively countered particular schemes it has also been effective in preventing variants of these schemes being used by taxpayers subsequently. This, until recently, was unusual because as each loophole in the legislation was closed a variant, based on the same legislation, would be devised. Whilst the legislation has been successful in terms of effectively countering the various abuses the wide ranging nature of the legislation can affect innocent commercial transactions, such as where a number of companies in a group are being re-organised for bona fide commercial reasons and as part of the re-organisation dividends are paid by some companies in the group to others. It follows that when such transactions are being contemplated advisers should pay very careful attention to these sections in order to see whether they impinge on the transactions. The other point that should be brought to the attention of advisers is that these sections are often ignored in tax planning work generally and the potential scope of the legislation not fully appreciated; it is hoped that this chapter has provided a salutary warning to those who would otherwise ignore the provisions at their peril.

3 Transfer of assets overseas

3.1 Introduction

Amongst professional advisers perhaps the most feared anti-avoidance section of TA 1970 is s. 478, formerly FA 1936, s. 18. Prior to the introduction of this Act a number of wealthy UK residents had transferred their income producing assets overseas and at a later date received the accumulated income (and in many cases the original capital as well) as tax free capital in the UK. It is to this mischief that s. 18 was directed. This chapter will review the scope and coverage of TA 1970, s. 478, as amended by FA 1981, ss. 45 and 46 and the procedural issues these sections give rise to and set out in TA 1970, ss. 480 and 481. The most recent sections have been introduced as a result of the House of Lords' decision in *Vestey v IRC (No. 1 and 2)* [1980] STC 10, HL and the attendant publicity surrounding the case. Before examining these sections in more detail it should be noted that in practice no argument has been too esoteric for the Revenue to pursue in connection with s. 478 and the courts, until recently, have supported this policy by construing the section very widely. This has arisen because most of the early litigation came before the courts during the war when it was thought unpatriotic to avoid UK tax. These decisions have had to be followed in later cases for two reasons: firstly, most of the important cases were decided by the House of Lords prior to 1966, when they first gave themselves the freedom to depart from their earlier decisions; and secondly, the reluctance of the judiciary generally to either distinguish earlier authorities or to depart from them.

The first four sections of the chapter will review the substantive issues; sections 6 and 7 will examine the procedural issues. Each section will be self-contained in terms of any conclusions which follow from the text. Section 7 will discuss briefly the effect of the recent legislative amendments.

3.2 TA 1970, s. 478 and FA 1981, ss. 45 and 46

TA 1970, s. 478 as amended by FA 1981 reads as follows:—

TRANSFER OF ASSETS ABROAD

478 Provisions for preventing avoidance of income tax by transactions resulting in the transfer of income to persons abroad

For the purpose of preventing the avoiding by individuals ordinarily resident in the UK of liability to income tax by means of transfers of assets by virtue or in consequence whereof, either alone or in conjunction with associated operations, income becomes payable to persons resident or domiciled out of the UK, it is hereby enacted as follows:—

(1) Where by virtue or in consequence of any such transfer, either alone or in conjunction with associated operations, such an individual has, within the meaning of this section, power to enjoy, whether forthwith or in the future, any income of a person resident or domiciled out of the UK which, if it were income of that individual received by him in the UK, would be chargeable to income tax by deduction or otherwise, that income shall, whether it would or would not have been chargeable to income tax apart from the provisions of this section, be deemed to be income of that individual for all the purposes of the Income Tax Acts.

(2) Where, whether before or after any such transfer, such an individual receives or is entitled to receive any capital sum the payment whereof is in any way connected with the transfer or any associated operation, any income which, by virtue or in consequence of the transfer, either alone or in conjunction with associated operations, has become the income of a person resident or domiciled out of the UK shall, whether it would or would not have been chargeable to income tax apart from the provisions of this section, be deemed to be the income of that individual for all the purposes of the Income Tax Acts.

In this subsection, "capital sum" means subject to subs. (2A) of this section:—

(2A) For the purposes of subs. (2) of this section there shall be treated as a capital sum which an individual receives or is entitled to receive any sum which a third person receives or is entitled to receive at the individual's direction or by virtue of the assignment by him of his right to receive it.

(2B) Income shall not by virtue of subs. (2) of this section be deemed to be that of an individual for any year of assessment by reason only of his having received a sum by way of loan if that sum has been wholly repaid before the beginning of that year.

(3) Subsections (1) and (2) of this section shall not apply if the individual shows in writing or otherwise to the satisfaction of the Board either:—

(a) that the purpose of avoiding liability to taxation was not the purpose or one of the purposes for which the transfer or associated operations or any of them were effected; or

(b) that the transfer and any associated operations were bona fide commercial transactions and were not designed for the purpose of avoiding liability to taxation.

The jurisdiction of the Special Commissioners on any appeal shall include jurisdiction to review any relevant decision taken by the Board in exercise of their functions under this subsection.

(4) For the purposes of this section, "an associated operation" means, in relation to any transfer, an operation of any kind effected by any person in relation to any of the assets transferred or any assets representing, whether directly or indirectly, any of the assets transferred, or to the income arising from any such assets, or to any assets representing, whether directly or indirectly, the accumulations of income arising from any such assets.

(5) An individual shall, for the purposes of this section, be deemed to have power to enjoy income of a person resident or domiciled out of the UK if:—

(a) the income is in fact so dealt with by any person as to be calculated, at some point of time, and whether in the form of income or not, to enure for the benefit of the individual, or

(b) the receipt or accrual of the income operates to increase the value to the individual of any assets held by him or for his benefit, or

(c) the individual receives or is entitled to receive, at any time, any benefit provided or to be provided out of that income or out of moneys which are or will be available for the purpose by reason of the effect or successive effects of the associated operations on that income and on any assets which directly or indirectly represent that income, or

(d) the individual may, in the event of the exercise or successive exercise of one or more powers, by whomsoever exercisable and whether with or without the consent of any other person, become entitled to the beneficial enjoyment of the income, or

(e) the individual is able in any manner whatsoever, and whether directly or indirectly, to control the application of the income.

(6) In determining whether an individual has power to enjoy income within the meaning of this section, regard shall be had to the substantial result and effect of the transfer and any associated operations, and all benefits which may at any time accrue to the individual (whether or not he has rights at law or in equity in or to those benefits) as a result of the transfer and any associated operations shall be taken into account irrespective of the nature or form of the benefits.

(7) For the purposes of this section, any body corporate incorporated outside the UK shall be treated as if it were resident out of the UK whether it is so resident or not.

(8) For the purposes of this section:—

(a) a reference to an individual shall be deemed to include the wife or husband of the individual,

(b) "assets" includes property or rights of any kind and "transfer", in relation to rights, includes the creation of those rights,

(c) "benefit" includes a payment of any kind,

(d) references to income of a person resident or domiciled out of the UK shall, where the amount of the income of a company for any year or period has been apportioned under para. 1 of Sch. 16 to the Finance Act 1972, include references to so much of the income of the company for that year or period as is equal to the amount so apportioned to that person, and that amount shall be treated as increased by such proportion thereof as corresponds to the rate of advance corporation tax applicable to a distribution made at the end of the accounting period to which the apportionment relates,

(e) references to assets representing any assets, income or accumulations of income include references to shares in or obligations of any company to which, or obligations of any other person to whom, those assets, that income or those accumulations are or have been transferred.

(9) Any amount which by virtue of subs. (8) (d) of this section is treated as the income of any person for the purposes of this section shall also be treated for those purposes as payable to that person.

FA 1981, s. 45 reads as follows:—

45 (1) This section has effect where:—

(a) by virtue or in consequence of a transfer of assets, either alone or in conjunction with associated operations, income becomes payable to a person resident or domiciled outside the UK; and

(b) an individual ordinarily resident in the UK who is not liable to tax under s. 478 of the Taxes Act (prevention of tax avoidance by transfers of assets abroad) by reference to the transfer receives a benefit provided out of assets which are available for the purpose by virtue or in consequence of the transfer or of any associated operations.

(2) Subject to the provisions of this section, the amount or value of any such benefit as is mentioned in subs. (1) above, if not otherwise chargeable to income tax in the hands of the recipient, shall:—

(a) to the extent to which it falls within the amount of relevant income of years of assessment up to and including the year of assessment in which the benefit is received, be treated for all the purposes of the Income Tax Acts as the income of the individual for that year;

(b) to the extent to which it is not by virtue of this subsection treated as his income for that year and falls within the amount of relevant income of the next following year of assessment, be treated for those purposes as his income for the next following year,

and so on for subsequent years, taking the reference in para. (b) to the year mentioned in para. (a) as a reference to that and any other year before the subsequent year in question.

(3) Subject to subs. (9) below and to s. 46 (1) below, the relevant income of a year of assessment, in relation to an individual, is any income which arises in that year to a person resident or domiciled outside the UK and which by virtue of or in consequence of the transfer or associated operations referred to in subs. (1) above can directly or indirectly be used for providing a benefit for the individual or for enabling a benefit to be provided for him.

(4) Income tax chargeable by virtue of this section shall be charged under Case VI of Sch. D.

(5) An individual who is domiciled outside the UK shall not, in respect of any benefit not received in the UK, be chargeable to tax under this section by reference to relevant income which is such that if he had received it he would not, by reason of his being so domiciled, have been chargeable to income tax in respect of it; and subss. (4) to (7) of s. 122 of the Taxes Act (income applied outside the UK treated in certain cases as received in the UK) shall apply for the purposes of this subsection as they would apply for the purposes of subs. (3) of that section if the benefit were income arising from possessions outside the UK.

(6) Where:—

(a) the whole or part of the benefit received by an individual in a year of assessment is a capital payment within the meaning of ss. 80 or 81 (2) below (because not falling within the amount of relevant income referred to in para. (a) of subs. (2) above); and

(b) chargeable gains are by reason of that payment treated under either of those sections as accruing to him in that or a subsequent year,

para. (b) of that subsection shall apply in relation to any year of assessment ("a year of charge") after one in which chargeable gains have been so treated as accruing to him as if a part of the amount or value of the benefit corresponding to the amount of those gains had been treated under that subsection as his income for a year of assessment before the year of charge.

(7) Subsection (3) of s. 478 of the Taxes Act (exemption from charge where transfer of assets is not for tax avoidance) shall apply in relation to this section as it applies in relation to subss. (1) and (2) of that section; and subss. (4), (7), (8) and (9) of that section shall apply for the interpretation of this section.

(8) Section 481 of the Taxes Act (information powers) shall have effect as if this section were included in Chapter III of Part XVII of that Act; in s. 31 (3) (b) of the Taxes Management Act 1970 (assessments against which appeal lies to the Special Commissioners) after "1972" there shall be inserted the words "or under s. 45 of the Finance Act 1981".

(9) This section applies irrespective of when the transfer or associated operations referred to in subs. (1) above took place but applies only to benefits received and relevant income arising on or after 10 March 1981.

FA 1981, s. 46, as amended, reads as follows:—

46 (1) No amount of income shall be taken into account more than once in charging tax under the provisions of s. 478 of the Taxes Act (prevention of tax avoidance by transfer of assets abroad) and s. 45 above; and where there is a choice as to the persons in relation to whom any amount of income can be so taken into account:—

(a) it shall be so taken in account in relation to such of them, and if more than one in such proportions respectively, as appears to the Board to be just and reasonable; and

(b) the jurisdiction of the Special Commissioners on any appeal against an assessment charging tax under those provisions shall include jurisdiction to review any relevant decision taken by the Board under this subsection.

(2) In subs. (1) above references to an amount of income taken into account in charging tax are:—

(a) in the case of tax which under s. 478 is charged on income, to the amount of that income;

(b) in the case of tax charged under that section by virtue of s. 480 (4) of the Taxes Act, to an amount of the income out of which the benefit is provided equal to the amount or value of the benefit charged;

(c) in the case of tax charged under s. 45 above, to the amount of relevant income taken into account under subs. (2) of that section in charging the benefit.

(3) In subs. (2) of the said s. 478 for the words "'capital sum' means" there shall be substituted the words "'capital sum' means, subject to subs. (2A) of this section" and after that subsection there shall be inserted:—

"(2A) For the purposes of subs. (2) of this section there shall be treated as a capital sum which an individual receives or is entitled to receive any sum which a third person receives or is entitled to receive at the individual's direction or by virtue of the assignment by him of his right to receive it.

(2B) Income shall not by virtue of subs. (2) of this section be deemed to be that of an individual for any year of assessment by reason only of his having received a sum by way of loan if that sum has been wholly repaid before the beginning of that year."

(4) Subsection (2A) of the said s. 478 as inserted by subs. (3) above shall not apply to any direction or assignment given or made before 6 April 1981.

(5) In subs. (5) of the said s. 478 (definition of power to enjoy) for para. (d) there shall be substituted:—

"(d) the individual may, in the event of the exercise or successive exercise of one or more powers, by whomsoever exercisable and whether with or without the consent of any other person, become entitled to the beneficial enjoyment of the income, or."

(6) After subs. (8) of the said s. 478 there shall be inserted:—

"(9) Any amount which by virtue of subs. (8) (d) of this section is treated as income of any person for the purposes of this section shall also be treated for those purposes as payable to that person."

(7) After s. 480 (2) of the Taxes Act there shall be inserted:—
"(2A) An individual who is domiciled outside the UK shall not be chargeable to tax in respect of any income deemed to be his by virtue of the preceding provisions of this Chapter if he would not, by reason of his being so domiciled, have been chargeable to tax in respect of it if it had in fact been his income."

(8) So much of s. 27 (5) of the Finance Act 1975 (capital transfer tax liability of beneficiaries) as provides for a reduction to be made for income tax borne in respect of income shall apply also to income tax borne by virtue of s. 478 of the Taxes Act or s. 45 above in respect of property other than income.

3.3 The scope of TA 1970, s. 478 (1) and (2)

3.3.1 Subsection (1). Power to enjoy the income of a person resident or domiciled outside the UK

One of the distinguishing features of this section is the enacted preamble. This sets out the mischief at which the section is directed – the avoidance of income tax by individuals ordinarily resident in the UK transferring assets overseas and as a result of the transfers income becomes payable to persons resident or domiciled outside the UK. However, before subs. (1) can be invoked the individual concerned must also have power to enjoy the income of the person resident or domiciled outside the UK. Where the conditions in the preamble and subs. (1) are satisfied the individual concerned will be charged to income tax on the income of the person resident or domiciled outside the UK, irrespective of whether the income would otherwise be chargeable to income tax.

3.3.2 Transfers of assets

The words 'assets' and 'transfer' are defined in a non-exhaustive manner: the former includes property or rights of any kind and the latter is defined in terms of rights and includes the creation of those rights. The term 'creation of those rights' is capable of a very wide connotation and would include the incorporation of a foreign company and subscribing for shares in such a company.

It was stated earlier that s. 478 has been widely interpreted by the judiciary and rather like the courts' interpretation of s. 460, the normal rules of statutory interpretation have been abrogated in many cases. Examples of this can be seen from the transactions which have been held to be transfers of assets for the purpose of subss. (1) and (2).

(a) Until the recent *Vestey* case [1980] STC 10, HL it was not necessary for the Revenue to establish that the person assessed to tax was the person who had effected the 'transfer of assets' or any of the 'associated operations'. The House of Lords' decision in the *Vestey* case specifically overruled the ratio of the *Congreve* case (1948) 30 TC 163 in which it was held that the person charged to tax need not necessarily be the transferor. FA 1981, s. 45 restores the position to that which existed prior to the *Vestey* decision and charges to income tax benefits received by individuals ordinarily resident in the UK, where the transfers of assets overseas have been effected by persons other than the resident individual.
(b) A transfer of assets by a person who at the date of the transfer was not ordinarily resident in the UK, *IRC v Herdman* (1969) 45 TC 394 and *Phillipi v IRC* (1969) 47 TC 75.
(c) A transfer of assets to a person who at the time was resident in the UK, but who subsequently became non-resident, *Congreve v IRC* (1948) 30 TC 163.
(d) A transfer of assets from one country to another where conditions set out in the preamble are satisfied, *Ramsden v IRC* (1957) 37 TC 619.

3.3.3 Associated operations

This term includes an operation by any person on the assets transferred, or on any assets representing those transferred; or on any income, or accumulations of income which arise from either the assets transferred or those assets which represent the assets transferred. The term assets includes references to shares in or obligations of any company or any person to whom these assets, that income or those accumulations of income are, or have been, transferred.

It is clear from the definition that an associated operation can be effected by any person, irrespective of whether he is the recipient of the income or the original transferee. Whilst this definition is extremely wide it is not without limits. It was held in *Bambridge v IRC* (1955) 36 TC 313 that death was not an associated operation. The question of whether a series of transactions are associated operations is a factual one, as can be seen from *Fynn v IRC* (1958) 37 TC 629 and *IRC v Herdman* (1969) 45 TC 394.

In *Fynn v IRC* (1958) 37 TC 629 a UK resident transferred certain investments to a company incorporated in Eire and in consideration was allotted shares in the company. Some time later these shares were settled on irrevocable trusts in favour of his children. Subsequently the company purchased further investments by borrowing on a secured loan from its bankers, which was later repaid by borrowing from the transferor on an unsecured basis. It was held at first instance that the assets transferred, together with the subsequent charge and the unsecured loan, were not associated operations. The basis of the decision was entirely factual; the company's bankers were not pressing for repayment and there was no restriction on the way the unsecured loan was to be applied. There was, therefore, no connection between the unsecured loan, the assets transferred and the charge.

In a more recent case, *IRC v Herdman* (1969) 45 TC 394, assets were transferred to a company resident in Eire in consideration for shares and debt. The company then accumulated profits and managed the assets transferred in such a manner as to leave sufficient funds to reduce the debt, which was owed to a UK resident. It was held by the Northern Ireland Court of Appeal that the accumulation of profits and the management of the company's assets were associated operations. This point was not discussed specifically by the House of Lords but the speech of Lord Pearce did cast some doubt on this finding by pointing out that creditors' rights were unaffected by the company's accumulation policy. This it is submitted is not the correct view. By accumulating income the company would be more able to satisfy their debt obligations.

The other major points in connection with this term are set out below; the following have been held to be associated operations:—

(a) where a person ceases to be resident in the UK and becomes resident elsewhere, *Congreve v IRC* (1948) 30 TC 163;
(b) where a company transfers its residence overseas, *Latilla v IRC* (1943) 25 TC 107;
(c) lapse of time between two transactions, *Corbett's Executors v IRC* (1943) 25 TC 305;
(d) the transfer of an interest in an overseas partnership to a limited company incorporated overseas, *Latilla v IRC* (1943) 25 TC 107.

3.3.4 The scope of the word 'individual'

The use of the word individual restricts the scope of the section to natural persons but would include the wife or husband of the individual (TA 1970, s. 478 (8) (a)), an important point in *Vestey v IRC* [1980] STC 10, HL. However, a person's widow is excluded, *Vestey's Executors v IRC* (1949) 31 TC 1. An unresolved question is whether an individual who is non-resident for a complete fiscal year, but who is ordinarily resident in that year, can be charged to income tax for that year under s. 478. Some people argue that no tax can be imposed. Two arguments can be advanced in favour of this proposition:

(a) The statement by Lord Herschell in *Colquhoun v Brooks* (1889) 2 TC 490. The Income Tax Acts themselves impose territorial limits; either (1) the source from which the taxable income is derived must be situated in the UK, or (2) the person whose income is to be taxed must be resident there.
(b) TA 1970, s. 108 which covers the charging provisions of Sch. D. This taxes income from trading where either the person is resident in the UK and trades either here or abroad, or where a person is non-resident but trades in the UK. Thus a non-resident individual with income derived from assets abroad would appear to be outside the scope of the section.

It is submitted that this view is incorrect. Section 478 makes no reference to an individual's residential status; the section is clearly directed at individuals ordinarily resident in the UK, whether resident or not, the non-resident who might escape the provisions of s. 108 can, it is submitted, be taxed on the basis of s. 478 despite some judicial dicta to the contrary. The particular remark referred to was made prior to the predecessor of s. 478, FA 1936, s. 18.

The term individual in subss. (1) and (2) does not include the plural. Under normal rules of statutory interpretation the singular usually includes the plural, except where the context admits otherwise. This point was decided in *Vestey's Executors v IRC* (1949) 31 TC 1. It was held by the House of Lords that s. 1 of the Interpretation Act 1889 was not applicable as the context in which the word was used did not include the plural.

3.3.5 Capital sums – subs. (2) as amended

This subsection covers the situation where as a result of a transfer satisfying the conditions set out in the preamble (see **3.3.1** above) the individual, whether before or after the transfer, receives or is entitled to receive a capital sum. This term now includes indirect benefits of the kind illustrated in *Potts' Executors v IRC* (1951) 32 TC 211. The effect of this subsection is to impute to the individual in receipt of a capital sum the income which has become that of the person resident or domiciled outside the UK. The charge to tax is based on the income which 'has become' the income of the non-resident or domiciled UK person. Two views are tenable as regards the scope of this subsection:—

(a) A narrow view: the subsection only applies to income which becomes the income of the non-resident person before the capital sum is received, that is 'has become' refers to income accruing *before* the capital sum was received.
(b) A wider view: once a capital sum has been received the Revenue can look at the situation on a year by year basis and can raise an assessment for the year in which the capital sum is received and each subsequent year, presumably ad infinitum.

The differences between these views can be illustrated by an example. Suppose a UK resident transfers assets to a non-resident on 1 January 1980 and receives a capital sum of £75 on 31 March 1980 and that the income of the non-resident non-domiciled person attributable to the transfer is £50 in 1979–80 and £200 in 1980–81, 1981–82, 1982–83 and 1983–84. If the first interpretation is correct the resident will be taxed on £50. If the alternative view is correct *all* income attributable to the transfer (i.e. £200 from 1979–80 onwards) can be taxed in the hands of the UK resident.

Some people take the view that (a) is correct on the basis that the intention of the legislation was to prevent individuals resident in the UK from accumulating income overseas and thereafter receiving the income as capital. However it should be pointed out that in relation to TA 1970, s. 478 (1) the courts have held that the correct approach is to examine the position on a year by year basis.

It is this author's view that the first view is correct. This is based on three propositions – two strong and one weak.

The stronger arguments:—

(a) The 'mischief' argument referred to above. Although it must be conceded that the courts in interpreting other avoidance sections have not taken such a narrow view, particularly in relation to TA 1970, s. 460, in view of the recent *Vestey* decision [1980] STC 10, HL it is likely that a more restricted view would be taken of the subsection.
(b) FA 1981, s. 45 (2).
This defines the quantum of charge a non-transferor will be liable to under s. 45 where he receives a benefit by virtue of or in consequence of a transfer or of any associated operations.

Where the benefit relates to two or more fiscal years it will be treated as follows:—

(i) in the year of receipt as income of the fiscal year in which the benefit was received to the extent that it represents income of the year of receipt or some prior year;

(ii) to the extent that the benefit is not covered by (i) as income of the following year of assessment.

The weaker argument:—

(c) This is based on the *Vestey* case [1980] STC 10, HL; if the second interpretation is followed it could be argued that the Revenue have no statutory basis on which to assess the taxpayer; the subsection does not prescribe the basis on which the taxpayer would be assessed and in particular which events will give rise to an assessment and when, if ever, the Revenue will be unable to raise further assessments. This type of argument found favour in the recent *Vestey* case but it must be doubted whether it is applicable to this subsection. On a literal application of the section it is clear that once a capital sum has been received the Revenue can assess the UK resident on all the subsequent income to which the transfer gives rise, irrespective of the potential inequity and harshness to which it may give rise and irrespective of whether further capital sums are received. On balance the author feels that at the present time the courts would adopt a narrow view in preference to the wider view.

3.4 Exceptions

TA 1970, s. 478 (3) provides two exceptions: (a) where the avoidance of tax was not the purpose or one of the purposes of the transfer or associated operations and (b) the transfer and any associated operations were bona fide commercial transactions not designed or intended to avoid tax. This exemption will also apply to transfers of assets which would otherwise be chargeable to tax under FA 1981, s. 45.

The first question this subsection gives rise to is the meaning to be attributed to the word taxation and whether it:—

(a) includes not only income tax but also capital transfer tax; and

(b) is limited to UK taxation and so will not preclude the taxpayer from succeeding where the defence is that he intended to avoid overseas tax.

In *Sassoon v IRC* (1943) 25 TC 154 it was held at first instance that taxation included death duties and this decision was affirmed by the

Court of Appeal. Both the court at first instance and the Court of Appeal acted on the assumption that foreign taxation was irrelevant in this context. This question was also raised in *IRC v Herdman* (1969) 45 TC 394 and touched upon in *Phillipi v IRC* (1971) 47 TC 45. In the former case the Special Commissioners held that taxation in the UK included Northern Ireland estate duty and no adverse comment was made on this finding by the higher courts. In the latter case there is certain dicta which supports the view of the Special Commissioners in the former.

It is apparent from reading the subsection that the onus on the taxpayer is greater under (a) than (b) in subs. (3). Under subs. (3) (a) the taxpayer has to show that in respect of each and every transfer and associated operation every single purpose and aim was unconnected with taxation so that this defence would not be available where one of a whole series of transactions related to taxation. Under subs. (3) (b) it is only necessary to show that the transactions were of a bona fide commercial nature and not effected primarily for avoiding tax. This suggests some flexibility and so it has been suggested that bona fide commercial transactions could be effected in a tax efficient manner and still fall within this exception. On a fair reading of the two exceptions this proposition is probably correct. If the matter were litigated it is unlikely that the courts would apply the observations of Lord Upjohn in *IRC v Brebner* (1967) 43 TC 705 and referred to in Chapter 1 in connection with TA 1970, s. 460 (see **1.5** above).

However, as has already been pointed out, the Revenue have found no argument too esoteric in relation to this section and so it could be argued that minimising tax is the same as avoiding tax. This, in the author's view, would be a very strict interpretation and would be out of context in relation to the exhaustive conditions set out in exception (a).

The scope of exemption (b) was considered by the House of Lords in *IRC v Herdman* (1969) 45 TC 394. It was held that the bona fide commercial test only has to be satisfied in relation to transfers and associated operations which actually confer on the taxpayer power to enjoy the income of the non-resident person.

It is thought by many people that trading income, in contrast to investment income, is not within the scope of s. 478. This view is not shared by the Revenue and nothing in the section indicates that it is restricted to investment companies. Two arguments can be put forward in support of this view. Firstly, the words in the preamble 'transfer of assets by virtue or in consequence whereof income becomes payable . . .' cannot include income which only arises as a result of a series of receipts and payments. What the non-resident receives initially is receipts which subsequently become income. Secondly, the income has not become payable as a result of a transfer of assets but as a result of trading. The transfer of assets merely expedited the trading. Support for this view, although only obiter, can be found in the judgment of Megarry J in *Lord Chetwode v IRC* (1974) STC 474 at 482. This point was not discussed in the higher courts. Against this it is argued that at any one point in time it is possible to ascertain what profit has been earned and if this has arisen as a result of a transfer of assets the income has become payable within the meaning of the preamble.

It has also been suggested that most trading activities would be protected by the exemption in subs. (3) (b). However, when foreign partnerships had the privilege of the remittance basis the Revenue invariably asked why the partnership was resident overseas when it could have been, with greater convenience, resident in the UK. In these cases the Revenue relied on the dicta of Lawrence J in *Latilla's* case (1943) 25 TC 107 at 113, who rejected the taxpayer's argument that the section was only intended to cover investment income. Sumption, *Taxation of Overseas Income and Gains* (3rd edn, Butterworths) at 120, has pointed out that his decision may be explicable on the basis that the income of the partnership had already been ascertained before it became payable to the partners. He points out that this view may not be correct in the case of a sole trader, who cannot ascertain his income at any one point in time but only after the end of an accounting period.

The last point in this context concerns the director who is resident and ordinarily resident in the UK but domiciled overseas. Such a person would only be taxed on his overseas earnings to the extent that they are remitted to the UK. If he had formed the company this benefit would be lost and he would be taxed on the amount charged in the accounts. In *Macdonald v IRC* (1940) 23 TC 449, McNaughton J pointed out that the section expressly provided that the income should be deemed to be that of the resident individual, irrespective of whether it would have been chargeable to income tax.

3.5 Power to enjoy

3.5.1 Introduction

The third condition that must be present before TA 1970, s. 478 (1) can be invoked is that the individual ordinarily resident in the UK must have 'power to enjoy' any income of the person not resident or domiciled in the UK. The term 'power to enjoy' is widely defined in subs. (5) under five headings. Furthermore it is provided in subs. (6) that in determining whether an individual has power to enjoy any income within the meaning of subs. (5) that the 'substantial result and effect' of the transactions should be looked at. This section of the chapter will be divided into two parts: the first will examine the five headings, the second, subs. (6).

3.5.2 Subsection (5) (a). Income is calculated for the benefit of the individual

Under this heading it is only necessary that the income is calculated at some point of time, irrespective of whether it is referred to as income, for the benefit of the individual. The first point to notice is that the income does not have to be dealt with either by the UK resident or the person resident or domiciled outside the UK but by any person, providing it enures for the benefit of the resident. Benefit is defined in subs. (8) (c) as payment of any kind and would include benefits in kind such as interest-free loans. The words 'so dealt with' have been held (see *Lord Vestey's Executors v IRC* (1949) 31 TC 1 per Lord Simmonds at 85) to predicate some activity by some person and so there must be a positive act by somebody.

The benefit may arise immediately or at some future date after the transfer or associated operation and may take the form of either capital or income. In *Latilla v IRC* (1943) 25 TC 107 it was held that where a non-resident company redeemed non-interest bearing debentures of a resident individual from profits, the redemption (albeit a capital payment) was within subs. (5) (a).

3.5.3 Subsection (5) (b). Increases in the value of assets held by an individual or for his benefit

This heading is satisfied where the receipt or accrual of the income increases the value of any assets held by the individual or by some other person on his behalf.

In common with other subsections within s. 478 this subsection has also been widely interpreted by the courts. For example, it was held in *Howard de Walden v IRC* (1942) 25 TC 121 that a debt due from a non-resident to a resident is within the subsection. The obligation to repay the debt is an asset which becomes more valuable if income arises to the non-resident as a result of the original transfer, as more funds will be available to repay the debt. It was held that the UK resident should not be assessed on the increase in the value of the debt but on the income attributable to the assets transferred. The implications of this decision can be seen from this example: suppose a person transfers an asset to a non-resident company and in exchange receives shares in the company but the shares are only a small proportion of the company's outstanding share capital. By virtue of this transfer the UK resident can be assessed on the whole of the company's income even though he is only entitled to a very small proportion of that income.

This subsection was also litigated in *Ramsden v IRC* (1957) 37 TC 619. In this case a UK resident sold shares in a UK company to a company resident overseas. The Special Commissioners found that the taxpayer's account with the overseas company was not a loan account and so not within subs. (2), as the sum owing to him represented the unpaid balance of the purchase price. This was despite the fact that in the Directors' Minute Book the sum was referred to as a loan. The importance of this decision is the finding that unpaid purchase money does not constitute a loan.

However, it remains open to the taxpayer to argue that subs. (5) (b) does not apply where at all times the company which acquired the assets had more than sufficient funds to repay the debt. In such a case the face value of the debt (the asset) would remain unchanged, irrespective of the income which might accrue to the company subsequently, as the accumulated reserves prior to the transfer would be greater than the nominal value of the debt.

3.5.4 Subsection (5) (c). Benefits paid or payable to the individual and associated operations

This heading covers the situation where at any time the individual receives or is entitled to receive any benefit out of the income which arises overseas, or out of monies which are or will be available for the purpose by reason of associated operations on that income and on any assets which directly or indirectly represent that income.

This paragraph comes into operation where either of two conditions are satisfied.

(a) If the UK resident is entitled to receive a benefit, irrespective of whether he actually receives a benefit, e.g. where a UK resident holds shares in an overseas company which confers the right to receive dividends.
(b) Although he may not possess a right to receive the benefit he may subsequently receive one by way of payment. An instance

of this would be where a UK resident was a member of a class of discretionary beneficiaries in an overseas controlled trust. It seems that once a UK beneficiary receives any benefit he will be assessed to tax on the income of the non-resident, both before and after receipt of the benefit.

However, whilst the first part of subs. (5) (c) is very wide the second is more restricted. This is because it deals only with monies available by reason of associated operations and these must affect the income and assets (if any) representing the income.

This subsection was litigated in *Earl Beatty's Executors v IRC* (1940) 23 TC 574 where a UK resident transferred assets by means of a series of transactions to a non-resident company in exchange for non-interest bearing redeemable debentures. An argument was advanced to the effect that on redemption the taxpayer received a repayment of capital equal to the value of the assets transferred and so it could not be said that he received any benefit from the income which arose to the non-resident by virtue of the transfer. This was rejected on the basis that the debentures were charged on both the income and capital of the non-resident company. It followed that, given the wide definition of benefit in subs. (8) (b), the taxpayer was entitled to a benefit out of income within subs. (5) (c).

There have been two other cases where this subsection has been in point. In *Howard de Walden v IRC* (1942) 25 TC 121, which has already been referred to, it was also held that the taxpayer had received repayment of his loan notes out of the income of non-resident companies and so he was within subs. (5) (c). This was also held in *Lee v IRC* (1941) 24 TC 207; here the UK resident taxpayer transferred assets to a non-resident company in exchange for shares in that company. As the taxpayer was entitled to receive a dividend out of the company's income he had 'power to enjoy' within para. (5) (c).

3.5.5 Subsection (5) (d). The exercise of a power and beneficial enjoyment of income

Prior to FA 1981 this subs. (5) (d) read as follows:—

> 'The individual has power, by means of the exercise of any power of appointment or power of revocation or otherwise, to obtain for himself, whether with or without the consent of any other person, the beneficial enjoyment of the income, or may, in the event of the exercise of any power vested in any other person, become entitled to the beneficial enjoyment of the income.'

This paragraph appears to cover as a class UK beneficiaries of an overseas discretionary trust. It is also clear from the paragraph that even if the power is never exercised so that an individual never becomes entitled to the beneficial ownership of the income, if it exists and the resident individual can benefit from it, he will be within the paragraph.

It can be argued that this subsection only deals with powers relating to settlements (trust powers) which by their very nature are similar in principle to powers of appointment and revocation. This view it is submitted is correct. Whilst no argument has been too fanciful for the Revenue to pursue it is inconceivable that this view is incorrect and so a power to declare dividends would not be within para. (d). It is also likely that the word 'consent' would be construed restrictively in relation to the exercise of the power. This is based on a first instance judgment in a similar context by Atkinson J in *Wolfson v IRC* (1949) 31 TC 141.

In a more practical context the scope of this section has been considered by many advisers in relation to what has come to be known as 'the two-tier arrangement'. Under this arrangement, the income-producing assets were transferred to an overseas investment company, usually located in a tax haven. The shares in this company were held by an overseas discretionary trust, whose discretionary objects included UK beneficiaries. It was argued that this arrangement did not fall within TA 1970, s. 478 as the trustees did not have any income to which the section applied.

The question then becomes – do the UK beneficiaries have power to enjoy the income of the investment company? At first glance, it seems that this subsection would apply but three arguments are advanced to the contrary:—

(a) The UK beneficiaries can only enjoy the income of the investment company if two powers are exercised. That is if the directors exercise their power to declare a dividend and the trustees exercise their power to distribute the dividends declared by the company.

It was contended that as the singular word power is used the context precludes the operation of the Interpretation Act 1979. Under s. 1 of this Act the singular includes the plural unless the context admits otherwise. The context would seem to admit otherwise; it was also held in *Lord Vestey's Executors v IRC* (1949) 31 TC 1 that the word individual in what is now s. 478 (1) did not include a group of individuals. Whilst it would be incorrect to equate the interpretation of the word individual with the word power it does lend some support for the contention that the word power is to be interpreted as referring to the singular and not the plural. It is this author's view that in this context the singular does not include the plural.

This argument has now been countered by FA 1981, s. 46 (5), which amends and enacts a revised para. (d). The new paragraph provides as follows:—

> 'The individual may, in the event of the exercise or successive exercise of one or more powers, by whomsoever exercisable and whether with or without the consent of any other person, become entitled to the beneficial enjoyment of the income.'

(b) The word power refers to a fiduciary power and does not include the directors' power to declare a dividend. The question of whether the new subs. (5) (d) affects this point will be discussed below after the third argument has been outlined.

(c) This is a form of 'belt and braces' argument. Even if a dividend is declared and passed on to the beneficiaries by the trustees it cannot be said that they have power to enjoy the company's income. What they in fact obtain is beneficial enjoyment of the dividend declared by the company. It seems to this author as if they would obtain beneficial enjoyment of the company's income if all the income of the company were distributed. Something less than a full distribution would be outside the scope of the subsection if this argument were pursued to its logical conclusion.

It is this author's view that the second and third arguments are unaffected by the revised subs. (5) (d). However, it would be unwise to set up new two-tier arrangements which relied exclusively on these two arguments. The question of whether the pre-FA 1981 arrangements will succeed is one that is likely to be taken all the way to the House of Lords. The taxpayer's arguments would be considerably strengthened where the overseas trust was very wide and open ended with many different and unconnected beneficiaries. It must be said that despite the decision in the second *Vestey* case [1980] STC 10, HL it is unlikely that the current House of Lords would interpret subs. (5) (d) narrowly and so the prospects of the taxpayer succeeding are, as with this section in general, not very high.

3.5.6 Subsection (5) (e). Direct or indirect control of the income

This heading will be satisfied where the individual is able, whether directly or indirectly, to control the application of the income.

In *Lord Vestey's Executors v IRC* (1949) 31 TC 1 it was held that a power to direct investments was not within the paragraph, even though this might include a power to direct funds to be loaned to the person having the right, provided the loans were on commercial terms. Viscount Simmonds and Lord Morton in *Lord Vestey's Executors v IRC* (1949) 31 TC 1 at 14 held that a power of appointment which did not include either the holder of the power or his wife was not a power to enjoy the income.

The only other case relating to this subs. (5) (e) is *Lee v IRC* (1941) 24 TC 207. It was held that where a UK resident controls an overseas company, even though he is not a director, he has power to enjoy the company's income. This is because although he has no direct power to control the company he can indirectly, through removing the directors, control the company.

3.5.7 Subsection (5) (f). Substantial result and effect

This subsection provides that in determining the question of whether an individual has power to enjoy income regard should be had to the substantial result and effect of the transfer and any associated operations and all benefits which may at any time accrue to the individual (whether or not he has rights at law or in equity in or to those benefits) as a result of the transfer and any associated operations will be taken into account irrespective of their nature or form.

The scope of this section was discussed by Lord Normand in *Lord Vestey's Executors v IRC* (1949) 31 TC 1 at 88 and 89 where he said:—

> 'The court must first determine the meaning and effect of the documents before this provision is applied and it must then consider whether their effect, though in form not beneficial to the settlor, is so in substance. The contrast is between substance and form, so if it can be shown in the present case that the effect of the transfer and the associated operations is to vest a benefit in (for example) a company over which the settlor has complete control, the court may then say that, though in form the company benefits, in substance the company and the settlor are one and the settlor therefore benefits. But the court cannot take this last step unless it is shown that the settlor has himself the legal control and no reliance must be placed on his influence over others who are not in law bound to follow his directions.'

Whilst it has been argued by some people that the effect of this subsection is to abrogate the rule of law, it is clear from the speech of Lord Normand that there are restrictions on how widely the judiciary can interpret this subsection and following the recent *Vestey* decision [1980] STC 10, HL further support for this view can be found.

3.6 Quantum, assessment and collection

3.6.1 Quantum

In connection with the quantum of charge three problems have been discussed in the courts:—

(a) whether tax can be assessed on the entire income of the non-resident, irrespective of what the UK resident is entitled to receive or receives, or whether the charge is limited to the income attributable to the assets transferred;

(b) how to compute the income chargeable to income tax and in particular, in the case of investment companies, whether management charges are deductible. Similar problems will also arise in connection with trading companies;

(c) where more than one individual is entitled to the income of a non-resident discretionary trust.

This section will examine each problem separately in turn and the implications of FA 1981. In *Howard de Walden v IRC* (1942) 25 TC 121 the question of quantum was discussed by Lord Greene MR in a case where a resident individual only had power to enjoy a proportion of the income of a non-resident. He held that the quantum was not limited to this sum and the taxpayer could be assessed on all the income of the person not resident or domiciled in the UK.

Lord Greene's discussion of quantum was subsequently discussed by the Court of Appeal in *Congreve v IRC* (1948) 30 TC 163. Cohen LJ also rejected the view that tax was only chargeable on the income attributable to the assets transferred. In the House of Lords the question of quantum was left open for further consideration. The harshness of this finding is readily apparent when an extreme example is considered. A UK resident who owns 5% or less of the shares in an overseas company can be assessed on the whole of the income of the company. Sumption, *Taxation of Overseas Income and Gains* (3rd edn, Butterworths) at 127 has commented on this interpretation as follows:—

> 'Stripped of its parentheses and qualifications the section reads:—
>
> "Where any individual has power to enjoy *any income* of a person resident or domiciled outside the UK *that income* shall be deemed to be income of that individual."
>
> It is difficult to see how the words "that income" can describe anything except the income referred to earlier, which is income which the individual has power to enjoy, and not the whole of the income payable "by virtue or in consequence" of the transfer and any associated operations.'

In the second *Vestey* case [1978] STC 567 referred to above Walton J held that the only income to which s. 478 relates is the income which becomes payable to the non-resident as a result of a transfer. Prior to the decision in the second *Vestey* case the Revenue usually mitigated the harshness of this rule. For example, where a UK individual was a shareholder in a non-resident company he was only taxed on the company's income on a pro rata basis to his shareholding. This practice was condemned by Walton J in *Vestey v IRC* (*No. 2*) [1979] STC 567 who doubted the legitimacy of this concession and extra statutory concessions in general. Presumably the Revenue do not feel it necessary to enact this concession as the taxpayer is unlikely to challenge it.

The second problem relates to the deductibility of management charges. This arose in *Chetwode v IRC* [1974] STC 474. The case concerned a Bahamian trust company which received investment income out of which it paid certain management charges for such services as investment advice, bank charges and security handling fees. It was held by the House of Lords that 'income of a person resident or domiciled out of the UK' means the income referred to in the preamble as the income which 'becomes payable to such persons'. On this basis management charges were not deductible and so the gross income and not the net sum fell to be assessed on the UK resident.

The other half of the second question relates to the income of trading companies and whether the Revenue are entitled to go behind the published accounts. On this point Lord Greene MR in *Latilla v IRC* (1943) 25 TC 107 at 116 commented that this would not be legitimate. The income payable to a partner had to be determined in accordance with the partnership agreement. In this case the assessments were based on trading profits after expenses and this point was not taken in the House of Lords. On this basis it seems that income in this context must refer to profit after deducting allowable expenses from taxable receipts. Support for this proposition, albeit obiter, can be found in the speech of Megarry J in the *Chetwode* case (see **3.3** above).

The third question related to the quantum of charges where a beneficiary of an overseas trust received a capital sum from a non-resident discretionary trust. This problem arose in the second *Vestey* case [1980] STC 10, HL in a rather acute form. One of the arguments advanced by the Crown was that they could assess *each* beneficiary who had received a capital sum on the entire income of the trust commencing with the first year he received a capital payment and in each succeeding year until either the trust was dissolved or he ceased to be a beneficiary.

Both Lords Wilberforce and Dilhorne agreed that if the decision in *Congreve v IRC* (1948) 30 TC 163 was correct the Crown was entitled to a multiple of the tax on the income, the relevant multiple depending only on the number of appointments. A unanimous House of Lords reversed this decision and held that UK residents in receipt of capital sums will not be within s. 478 where they were not the original transferors. The position has now been amended by FA 1981, s. 45. This clause charges to tax individuals ordinarily resident in the UK who are in receipt of benefits that arise from transfers of assets (irrespective of any associated operations) overseas and which have not been effected by the individuals in receipt of the benefit. The new section will work as follows:—

(a) Where an individual is in receipt of a benefit in a year of assessment and satisfies the other conditions set out in s. 45 he will now be assessed on that benefit. The quantum of assessment will depend on what the clause refers to as 'the relevant income'.

(b) The relevant income is defined in subs. (3) as:—

'. . . any income which arises in that year to a person resident or domiciled outside the United Kingdom and which by virtue of or in consequence of the transfer or associated operations . . . can directly or indirectly be used for providing a benefit for the individual or for enabling a benefit to be provided for him.'

(c) Where the value of benefit received is less than, or equal to, the amount of relevant income for years of assessment up to and including the year of assessment in which the benefit is received the value of the benefit will be treated as income of the individual for that year.

(d) Where the benefit is in excess of the relevant income the excess will be taxed in the next year of assessment if the excess is less than, or equal to, the relevant income for that year of assessment.

(e) This year by year method of assessment will continue until the relevant income exhausts the benefit.

(f) This mechanism of assessment will only apply to benefits received and relevant income which arises on or after 10 March 1981.

(g) Where a UK beneficiary is in receipt of a capital sum which is subject to income tax under either TA 1970, s. 478 or FA 1981, s. 45 and also to Capital Transfer Tax (CTT) the beneficiary will pay CTT on the capital sum minus the income tax assessed on that sum. In the case of liability under TA 1970, s. 478 (2) it must be doubted whether the legislation actually achieves the purpose. It could be argued that the event which gives rise to a liability under s. 478 (2) is the receipt of a capital sum but that tax is payable in respect of something quite different, the income payable to the non-resident. The two amounts are unrelated and so it is arguable that the liability to tax is not in respect of the capital sum.

Where an individual is not domiciled in the UK and receives a benefit outside the UK he will not be chargeable to tax on the benefit and for this purpose TA 1970, s. 122 (4)–(7) (overseas income applied outside the UK which is treated as income received in the UK) is to be applied in determining whether the benefit is received in the UK.

Where an individual is in receipt of a loan which gives rise to a liability under s. 478 (2B) the liability will cease in the fiscal year following that in which the loan is repaid in full.

The last point relates to the words 'whether it would or would not have been chargeable to income tax apart from the provisions of this section, be deemed to be income of that individual for all purposes of the Act'. In *Macdonald v IRC* (1940) 23 TC 449, a non-resident company held income in trust for a taxpayer who, as the law then stood, was assessed on the remittance basis in the UK – it was held that the above words were applicable and that tax was chargeable under TA 1970, s. 478 in priority to the more favourable remittance basis.

3.6.2 Assessment and collection

These two matters are governed by TA 1970, s. 480, as amended by FA 1981, s. 45. This section provides as follows:—

(a) Income tax at the basic rate will not be charged on any income which has borne tax at the basic rate by deduction or otherwise. Income tax assessed by virtue of TA 1970, s. 478 will be assessed under Case VI of Sch. D. In *IRC v Herdman* (1969) 45

TC 394 dividends which were paid under deduction of tax, which was subsequently refunded under the terms of a double tax treaty, were held by the Court of Appeal in Northern Ireland (this point was not taken in the House of Lords) not to have borne tax.

(b) In computing the income tax liability of an individual chargeable under TA 1970, s. 478 the same deductions and reliefs will be allowed as would have been allowed if the income deemed to be his by virtue of s. 478 had actually been received by him.

(c) Where an individual has been charged income tax on any income deemed to be his and that income is subsequently received by him it will not be taxed twice.

(d) An individual who has power to enjoy the income of a person abroad, by reason of receiving a benefit within the meaning of s. 478 (5) (c) will be chargeable to income tax for the year of assessment in which benefit is received on the amount or value of that benefit, except insofar as it is shown that the benefit derives directly or indirectly from income in respect of which he has already been charged to tax for that or a previous year of assessment.

(e) A non-UK domiciled individual will not be chargeable to income tax on any income deemed to be his under this section (as amended) if the income would not otherwise be taxable in the UK (FA 1981, s. 45 (5)).

(f) Section 46 (1) provides that income shall not be taxed under both TA 1970, s. 478 and FA 1981, s. 45; where there are a number of persons who are in receipt of a benefit, the income can be allocated to such persons as appears to the Board to be just and reasonable.

For this purpose income means the amount or value of the benefit, FA 1981, s. 46 (2) (b). Where income is charged under s. 45, references to income in (f) above relate to the amount of relevant income taken into account under subs. (2) of s. 46 in charging the benefit. An assessment to tax under s. 45 will also be under Sch. D, Case VI and any appeal against an assessment will be heard by the Special Commissioners.

The last two points relate to the treatment of 'benefits' in TA 1970, s. 480 (4).

(a) These are taxable unless the individual can show that it derives directly or indirectly from income which has already been assessed to tax, either for that or an earlier year of assessment.

(b) It was once thought that s. 480 (4) added to the penal nature of these two sections as it refers to s. 478 (5) (c) which treats the receipt of benefits from a non-resident's income as power to enjoy that income. The argument being that s. 480 (4) might impose a charge where one would not have arisen in the absence of a foreign element. For instance, no liability to income tax would arise where a maintenance and accumulation trust constituted under English law distributed capital. It can also be argued that s. 480 (4) restricts the view taken by the Revenue that liability can be extended to the whole of the non-resident's income as subs. (4) restricts the charge to the value of the benefit.

3.7 Powers of the Inland Revenue

3.7.1 Generally

These are set out in TA 1970, s. 481 and also apply to FA 1981, s. 45.

> 'The Board . . . may by notice in writing require any person to furnish them within such time as they may direct (not being less than twenty-eight days) with such particulars as they think necessary,' s. 481 (1).

These particulars are spelt out in more detail in subs. (2) as follows:—

(a) the transactions in which he was acting on his own behalf and those where he was acting on behalf of others;
(b) transactions which in the opinion of the Board it is proper that they should investigate notwithstanding that in the opinion of the person to whom the notice is given no liability to tax will arise;
(c) whether the person to whom the notice is given has taken or is taking and if so, what part, in any of the transactions specified in the notice.

This subsection has been considered in two cases at first instance: *Royal Bank of Canada v IRC* (1971) 47 TC 565 and *Clinch v IRC* [1973] STC 155. In the former the Board had actual transactions in mind whereas in the latter case they went much further and went on what is known in the legal profession as a 'fishing exercise'. In *Royal Bank of Canada v IRC* (1971) 47 TC 565 the Revenue requested information relating to certain sales of gilt-edged stocks carried out by the London branch between 1 June 1964 and 22 June

1965 on behalf of P Ltd, a company incorporated in the Bahamas. In summary, the notice required the Bank to supply:—

(a) full particulars of the manner in which the instructions for each sale were received, and the names and addresses of all persons who gave such instructions or held themselves out as representing P Ltd;
(b) full particulars of any agreement, arrangement or understanding pursuant to which any of the sales were effected and to which the Bank or any officer, employee or agent was a party;
(c) the names and addresses of the persons known or believed by the Bank or any officer, employee or agent to have had control of or a beneficial interest in P Ltd at the time of the sales or thereafter;
(d) the name and address of the representative of P Ltd with whom a certain matter was discussed by a representative of the Bank on 28 January 1966.

The bank took out an originating summons asking whether it was bound to furnish any and if so which of the particulars required by the notice. They also contended that questions (c) and (d) were outside the scope of the section as they did not relate to transactions but only to names and addresses and that if any of the questions were bad the whole notice was ineffective. Megarry J held that the Revenue were entitled to all the information which they thought necessary for their purposes and that if a paragraph in a notice contained an unauthorised question the rest of the notice was not invalidated. However, he did add the rider that where the unauthorised question was so intertwined with the others there might be cases where the whole notice was invalid and added that the Revenue's powers under this subsection were not unlimited.

In *Clinch v IRC* (1973) 49 TC 52 the plaintiff from November 1964 to November 1970 was the London representative and the managing director of a wholly-owned English subsidiary of a bank incorporated in Bermuda which specialised in the formation and management of companies, settlements, etc, in Bermuda. On 31 January 1972, the Revenue served on him a notice requiring him on or before 7 April 1972, to furnish particulars relating to such transactions and operations in which he or his staff had acted since 5 April 1965, for a UK customer. A summary of the transactions and operations specified in the notice are set out below:—

(a) The formation or management of foreign companies, the name of the company, the date and place of incorporation.
(b) The formation or management of foreign partnerships, including the name and address of the partnership, the country in which it was constituted, the name and address of the partners.

(c) The formation of any settlement, together with the name and address of the settlor, the date and nature of any document regulating the settlement.
(d) The transfer of assets to any foreign company, foreign partnership or foreign settlement.
(e) The acquisition of any interest in the share capital or loan capital of any foreign company or in or under any foreign partnership or foreign settlement.

It was estimated that it would take five months working full-time to comply with the notice and an administrative action was brought to invalidate the notice on the grounds that it was vexatious and an abuse of statutory powers and so ultra vires and was unduly burdensome and oppressive.

Ackner J held that the notice was valid as the commissioners were empowered to ask such questions as they thought necessary and in particular questions about unidentified principals. To establish that a notice was invalid the applicant must show that the commissioners have taken matters into account which they ought not to have done, or asked for particulars which no reasonable body of commissioners would include in such a notice.

In the above case, it was held that the managing director of the Bank had been unnecessarily pessimistic about the time it would take him to comply with the notice and even if he were correct he should have kept better records in order to comply with his statutory duty. Ackner J did indicate two limitations on the powers of the Revenue:—

(a) the managing director of the Bank was only to be expected to obtain information which was within his own knowledge and was not expected to make inquiries in Bermuda, or elsewhere; and
(b) the notice would have been unduly burdensome and oppressive if due to its obscurities and ambiguities it would be necessary for the recipient to have an accountant and lawyer constantly advising him how to comply with the notice.

3.7.2 Solicitors

TA 1970, s. 481 (3) relates to the protection conferred on solicitors in connection with transactions falling within s. 478. This subsection provides the following:—

(a) A solicitor shall not be deemed to have taken part in a transaction falling within TA 1970, s. 478 by reason only of giving professional advice in connection with that transaction;

and in relation to anything done by him on behalf of a client he shall not be compelled to do more than state that he is or was acting on behalf of a client and to state the name and address of his client.

(b) In connection with the transfer of any asset by or to an individual ordinarily resident in the UK to or by any company, or any associated operation in relation to any such transfer, a solicitor will only have to supply the names and addresses of the transferor and the transferee or the persons concerned in the associated operations.

(c) Where the matter relates to the formation and management of a company the name and address of the company and where it relates to the formation of a trust and income becomes payable to a person resident or domiciled out of the UK the name and address of the settlor and of that person.

Company for the purposes of (a) to (c) above means a non-trading company resident or incorporated outside the UK which is, or would be, if it was resident in the UK, a close company.

An undecided question is how narrowly or otherwise the term professional advice will be construed. Solicitors frequently give advice to their clients on other than strictly legal matters.

A narrow construction would restrict the scope of the exemption but subs. (3) (a) refers to 'anything done by the solicitor . . .' and makes no reference to his professional activities. If a solicitor had carried out the transactions which were the subject of the notice in the *Royal Bank of Canada* case it would seem on a fair reading of the subsection that he would be protected. The same considerations will also apply to the formation and management of a company or the creation and execution of trusts which might be part of a scheme falling within s. 478. The Revenue have been known to take the view that a solicitor who separately practised as a solicitor and tax consultant could not, in respect of the latter, take advantage of the exemption. They also do not agree that everything a solicitor does on behalf of a client is necessarily effected by him in the exercise of his profession as a solicitor. It is obvious from this brief discussion that the scope of this exemption is far from clear and caution should be exercised by solicitors in connection with transactions which might fall within s. 478.

3.7.3 Banks

Subsection (4) also confers on banks a limited form of protection from disclosing the affairs of their customers. It was noted above in the *Royal Bank* case (1971) 47 TC 565 that this exemption has been construed strictly. It is provided in subs. (4) that s. 480 shall not impose on any bank the obligation to furnish any details of ordinary banking transactions between the bank and a customer carried out in the ordinary course of banking business, unless the bank has acted or is acting on behalf of the customer in connection with the formation or management of a company or in connection with the creation or execution of a settlement.

In the *Royal Bank* case (1971) 47 TC 565 Megarry J set out four limitations on this subsection:—

(a) no protection will be given where the information relates to the name and address of some person, unrelated to anything that could be referred to as a transaction;
(b) 'ordinary banking transactions';
(c) customer and banker transactions;
(d) transactions 'carried out in the ordinary course of banking business'.

On questions of 'ordinary banking transactions or business', these were ones of mixed fact and law, the onus of which was on the appellants to demonstrate.

The penalties for not complying with a notice without a reasonable excuse must not exceed £50 and a further penalty, not exceeding £10 per day, can be imposed for failure to comply with an adjudication notice, by either the Court of Appeal or the commissioners.

3.8 Conclusions

These fall into two categories: those which relate to s. 478 and the scope of FA 1981, ss. 45 and 46.

It would be crass to reiterate that the provisions of s. 478 have been construed widely and in particular the words, 'transfer of assets', 'associated operations' and 'power to enjoy'. What is not clear from the legislation and the case-law is the scope of the bona fide commercial transaction exemption in subs. (3) (b). For instance, suppose an individual who is resident and ordinarily resident in the UK but domiciled abroad wishes to undertake freelance consultancy assignments abroad. If he forms a limited company in this country which hires his consultancy services for the overseas assignments he will only be entitled to a 25% deduction in respect of the emoluments he receives for those duties (this assumes that he satisfies the 30-day rule). However, if he procured the formation of an overseas controlled company any emoluments he received from that company for his services overseas would only be taxed on the remittance basis. Ignoring the other question as to whether trading companies are within s. 478, would the transfer that gave rise to the formation of the overseas company be within subs. (3) (b)? This author feels that such a transaction would be within the criteria laid down in *IRC v Brebner* (1966) 43 TC 705 but in the final analysis it would all depend on the particular facts of the case. As the question in all cases will be factual the professional adviser can never be certain that his view would be accepted by the Special Commissioners. It follows that any advice on this subsection must be subject to this caveat. This author has also seen what can only be described as ingenious schemes to avoid s. 478 in connection with transfer of assets which yield investment income. Most of these inevitably rely on the Inland Revenue not being fully appraised of all the facts and so these are outside the scope of this book. It follows that these schemes are not worth contemplating and both taxpayers and advisers should be very wary of any such schemes.

The new amending clauses contained in FA 1981 extend the scope of the legislation beyond that originally contemplated by FA 1936. It is clear from the above review that the new sections will cover the situation where a UK beneficiary receives a capital sum from an overseas trust formed by an individual other than the beneficiary and the two-tier arrangement described in **3.5.5** above. The new legislation will not cover the situation where a UK settlor forms an overseas trust for UK beneficiaries and the trust accumulates income which is only distributed to beneficiaries after they have emigrated from the UK.

What is not clear is whether the new legislation covers benefits such as:—

(a) rent-free accommodation in the UK;
(b) interest-free loans to UK beneficiaries;
(c) the use of a car.

If the assets of the trust are used to finance one of these items the trust will not have any relevant income out of which to provide these benefits. The benefits will have been financed from capital and not income. This seems to indicate that these benefits are not within the taxing net of the new legislation but given the current attitude of the courts to tax avoidance it is not unlikely that the term 'income' will be construed widely. A wide interpretation would include notional income. This means that the annual value of the house, etc, would be treated as the relevant income of the trust and the amount on which the beneficiary would be assessed to tax. Whilst no argument has been too esoteric for the Revenue to pursue, this author feels that this argument would not succeed before the courts on the grounds that clear words are necessary before the subject can be taxed and these are absent in s. 45, which seems only to contemplate income in the form of a cash receipt and not notional income.

4 Migration of companies

4.1 Introduction

The provisions of FA 1951, s. 36 (now TA 1970, s. 482) were enacted to prevent companies reducing their overall tax liabilities by transferring their residence overseas. The original legislation was preceded by an exodus of companies after the First World War and a number of mining companies after the Second World War. This legislation also prevents close companies from losing their close company status under TA 1970, s. 282 (1) (a). But for s. 482 a UK close company could become non-close by transferring the management and control of the company overseas. This chapter will examine the provisions of s. 482 and discuss how these provisions affect UK companies wanting to set up some form of permanent establishment overseas. The last section of the chapter will review the two Inland Revenue Consultative Papers issued in January 1981 – Tax Havens and The Corporate Sector and Company Residence.

4.2 The statutory provisions

4.2.1 TA 1970, s. 482 provides as follows:—

(1) Subject to the provisions of this section, all transactions of the following classes shall be unlawful unless carried out with the consent of the Treasury, that is to say:—

(a) for a body corporate resident in the UK to cease to be so resident; or

(b) for the trade or business or any part of the trade or business of a body corporate so resident to be transferred from that body corporate to a person not so resident; or

(c) for a body corporate so resident to cause or permit a body corporate not so resident over which it has control to create or issue any shares or debentures; or

(d) except for the purpose of enabling a person to be qualified to act as a director, for a body corporate so resident to transfer to any person, or cause or permit to be transferred to any person, any shares or debentures of a body corporate not so resident over which it has control, being shares or debentures which it owns or in which it has an interest.

(2) Nothing in para. (c) of subs. (1) of this section shall apply to the giving to the bankers of the body corporate not resident in the UK of any security for the payment of any sum due or to become due from it to them by reason of any transaction entered into with it by them in the ordinary course of their business as bankers.

(3) Nothing in the said para. (c) shall apply to the giving by the body corporate not resident in the UK to an insurance company of any security for the payment of any sum due or to become due from that body corporate to that company by reason of any transaction entered into with that body corporate by that company in the ordinary course of that company's business by way of investment of its funds.

(4) Any consent granted by the Treasury under this section:—

(a) may be given either specifically (that is to say, so as to apply only to specified transactions of or relating to a specified body corporate) or generally (that is to say, so as not only to apply as aforesaid); and

(b) may, if given generally, be revoked by the Treasury; and

(c) may in any case be absolute or conditional; and

(d) shall be published in such a way as to give any person entitled to the benefit of it an adequate opportunity of getting to know of it, unless in the opinion of the Treasury publication is not necessary for that purpose.

(5) Any person who, whether within or outside the UK, does or is a party to the doing of any act which to his knowledge amounts to or results in, or forms part of a series of acts which together amount to or result in, or will amount to or result in, something which is unlawful

under subs. (1) of this section shall be guilty of an offence under this section, and in any proceedings in respect of such an offence against a director of the body corporate in question (that is to say, the body corporate which is or was resident in the UK) or against any person who was purporting to act in that capacity:—

(a) it shall be presumed that he was a party to every act of that body corporate unless he proves that it was done without his consent or connivance; and

(b) it shall, unless the contrary is proved, be presumed that any act which in fact amounted to or resulted in, or formed part of a series of acts which together amounted to or resulted in or would amount to or result in, something which is unlawful under subs. (1) of this section was to his knowledge such an act.

(6) Any person who is guilty of an offence under this section shall be liable on conviction on indictment to imprisonment for not more than two years or to a fine not exceeding £10,000 or to both, and proceedings in respect of such an offence alleged to have been committed by a person may be taken before the appropriate court in the UK having jurisdiction in the place where that person is for the time being:

Provided that where the person in question is a body corporate which is or was resident in the UK, the maximum amount of the fine shall be three times the corporation tax, profits tax, capital gains tax and income tax paid or payable which is attributable to the income, profits or gains (including chargeable gains) arising in the thirty-six months immediately preceding the commission of the offence, or £10,000, whichever is the greater.

(7) A body corporate shall be deemed for the purposes of this section to be resident or not to be resident in the UK according as the central management and control of its trade or business is or is not exercised in the UK:

Provided that if it is shown that it has been established as between the Crown and a body corporate for any income tax, corporation tax or profits tax purpose that the body corporate was resident or ordinarily resident in the UK for any year of assessment or other period, it shall be presumed, except so far as the contrary is proved, that that body corporate was resident in the UK for the purposes of this section at the beginning of that year of assessment or other period and that it continued to be so resident at all times thereafter.

(8) Where the functions of a body corporate consist wholly or mainly in the holding of investments or other property, the holding of the investments or property shall be deemed for the purposes of this section to be a business carried on by the body corporate.

(9) Notwithstanding anything in the preceding provisions of this section, in no event shall a mere transfer of assets by a body corporate not resulting in a substantial change in the character or extent of the trade or business of that body corporate be treated for the purpose of this section as a transfer of part of the trade or business thereof.

(10) In this section:—
"share", "debenture" and "director" have, in relation to any body corporate, the meanings respectively assigned to them by s. 455 of the Companies Act 1948 in relation to a company;
"control" (except in the expression "central management and control"), has, in relation to a body corporate, the meaning given by s. 534 of this Act;
"transfer", in relation to shares or debentures, includes a transfer of any beneficial interest therein;
"insurance company" means a body corporate lawfully carrying on business as an insurer, whether in the UK or elsewhere, and "funds" in relation to an insurance company means the funds held by it in connection with that business,
and a body corporate shall not be deemed for the purposes of this section to cease to be resident in the UK by reason only that it ceases to exist.

(11) No proceedings for an offence under this section shall be instituted, in England or Wales, except by or with the consent of the Attorney General, or in Northern Ireland, except by or with the consent of the Attorney General for Northern Ireland.

(12) This section shall come into force for all purposes on 6 April 1970 to the exclusion of the provisions thereby re-enacted:

Provided that any offence committed before 6 April 1970 shall not be punishable under this section, and neither this subsection nor any other provision of this Act shall prevent any such offence from being punishable as if this Act had not been passed.

4.2.2 Definitions

Residence as defined in subs. (7) gives statutory recognition to judicial dicta in *De Beers Consolidated Gold Mines Ltd v Howe* (1906) 5 TC 198; *Egyptian Delta Land and Investment Co Ltd v Todd* (1928) 14 TC 119; *Unit Construction Co Ltd v Bullock* (1960) 38 TC 712.

Control is defined by TA 1970, s. 534 as the power of a person to secure by means of holding shares or the possession of voting power or by any powers conferred by the Articles of Association or analogous document that the affairs of the company are conducted in accordance with that person's wishes.

4.3 The scope of coverage of TA 1970, s. 482

Subsection (1) sets out four classes of transaction which will be unlawful unless prior consent of the Treasury has been obtained. These are:—

(a) where a UK resident company becomes non-resident;
(b) where a UK resident company transfers all or any part of its trade or business to a non-resident person;
(c) where a UK resident company allows a non-resident company over which it has control to issue shares or debentures; and
(d) except for the purpose of enabling a person to be able to act as a director, where a UK resident company transfers any shares or debentures it owns in a non-resident company over which it has control to any person.

The scope of the first class of transaction (i) is self explanatory. In the case of (ii) a 'blur' is put on this category of transaction by subs. (9). A transfer of assets will not be within (ii) where the transfer does not result in a substantial change in the character or extent of the trade or business. The question of what constitutes a substantial change will depend on the facts of the case and a decision of the Special Commissioners on this point will almost certainly be decisive. Companies proposing to take advantage of this proviso should make a thorough painstaking review of the relevant transactions in order to rebut any arguments of the Revenue to the contrary.

It is under this subsection that a number of UK industrial companies have formed investment companies in tax havens. These off-shore companies have been used to invest surplus cash arising in the UK companies. By investing off-shore the interest can be accumulated at a lower tax rate and in some cases, without bearing any tax. If the UK companies are short of cash this can be borrowed from the off-shore company. It is argued that the formation and transfer of assets abroad is outside the scope of the section if the investment in the off-shore company and the resultant income is not substantial in relation to the group's activities and income.

An example of another transaction, which arguably might not be covered by (ii) is where a UK resident company transfers its trade or business to a UK resident partnership, and the resident company is wound up; a transfer by the UK resident partnership's trade overseas would not appear to be within (ii), although it might be within TA 1970, s. 478. If the Revenue can establish a link between the formation of the partnership, the transfer by the company to the partnership, the winding up of the company and the transfer of the trade by the partnership overseas this view is incorrect. To succeed the taxpayer would have to justify commercially each transaction, which might be difficult in the circumstances.

The third class of transaction prevents a UK resident company losing control of a non-resident company as a result of the latter issuing shares or debentures. An exemption is provided in subss. (3) and (4) where the non-resident company gives a security to a bank in the ordinary course of business or to an insurance company on the same basis.

The fourth class of transaction is an extension of (c) and prevents a UK resident company from losing control of a non-resident company by transferring shares or debentures to another person, irrespective of the latter's residential status.

The effect of the wide ranging nature of subs. (1) is that it will cover a number of innocent transactions not designed to avoid tax. However in practice the use of the consents specified in subs. (4) mitigates the potentially harmful effects of subs. (1) (a)–(d). Subsection (4) specifies three consents which may be:—

(a) given specially;
(b) given generally, but these can be revoked by the Treasury; and
(c) absolute or conditional.

As (b) restricts the power of revocation to a general consent it must be assumed that once a special consent is given it cannot be revoked. No application to the Treasury is necessary for a transaction which is within a class that has already been given general consent. The various general consents are discussed in more detail below.

Subsection (5) provides that any person who, irrespective of residential status, does or is a party to any act which to his knowledge amounts to, or results in something unlawful under this section, shall be guilty of an offence. The extent of the enforceability of this section against foreign lawyers or agents seems questionable and in practice action could only be taken against UK residents. Where proceedings are taken against a director, or against any person who has purported to act in that capacity it is presumed that:—

(a) he was a party to every act of the company unless he proves that it was done without his consent or connivance; and
(b) unless the contrary is proved that any act which amounted to, or resulted in, or would amount to or result in, or formed part of a series of acts which together amounted to or resulted in, or would amount to or result in, something which is unlawful within subs. (1) above, was to his knowledge such an act.

This subsection will also cover innocent transactions. One such example has been highlighted by Sumption, *Taxation of Overseas Income and Gains* (3rd edn, Butterworths) at 51. He describes the situation where the directors of a company are resident both in the UK and abroad, and the UK directors retire leaving the foreign directors to meet in their native country. In such a case the retirement by the UK directors might be an act within subs. (5), as might a decision of the foreign directors not to journey to the UK for board meetings. To date there have been no prosecutions under subs. (6) and it is thought that where offences under the section have taken place, the attitude of the Revenue has been both constructive and reasonable. It is provided by subs. (11) that only the Attorney General can institute proceedings under s. 482.

4.4 Tax planning and overseas operations

4.4.1 General considerations

The setting up of a foreign branch by the UK resident company would not be within subs. (1) (b) as it does not involve setting up a separate entity and so is regarded as part of the UK company.

However, if a UK resident company carried on a trade overseas through a branch but wished to transfer the activities of the branch to a locally incorporated and registered company, the transfer would be within (1) (b) as it would involve transferring part of a trade. Other examples of transfers falling within (1) (b) are:—

(a) where a UK resident company forms an overseas subsidiary to manufacture goods previously produced by the UK parent;
(b) where a UK resident company appoints an overseas selling agent to sell goods that were previously sold direct to overseas customers.

An example where the issue could become 'blurred' is where a UK resident company assigns a contract to a non-resident company for execution as a principal. This might occur where a UK resident company obtains an overseas contract but subsequently decides that it should be performed by one of its overseas subsidiaries and so assigns the benefit of the contract to it. In this case the subsidiary would be acting as principal and so the transaction would be within subs. (1). The transaction would be outside the subsection if the UK resident company sub-contracted the work to the overseas subsidiary and continued to act as principal.

4.4.2 Taxation implications

The profits or losses of an overseas branch of a UK resident company are taxed in the same way as UK trading profits or losses, irrespective of where they arise. This means that the profits or losses of a branch are taxed on the same basis as profits or losses in the UK. It follows that where an overseas branch incurs trading losses these can be offset against trading profits in the UK and vice versa. However, in the latter case, where UK trading losses are being offset against overseas profits the branch may still have to pay local taxes on the overseas profits. However, under the double taxation agreement some relief may be available.

The profits of an overseas subsidiary are treated differently as the profits accrue to an entity resident outside the UK. As a result the subsidiary will pay local taxes on its profits and UK tax will only be payable on the dividends paid by the subsidiary to the UK parent. Whilst these will form part of the parent company's taxable income in the UK, most double tax treaties enable the parent company to offset some or all of the tax paid overseas against the UK tax payable on the dividends received from the subsidiary.

In some countries, notably those in the Eastern Bloc and in the Third World, it is only possible for a UK trading company to form some sort of partnership or joint venture. In such cases, irrespective of whether the partnership or joint venture is controlled in the UK or abroad, its share of the profits or losses will be treated in the same way as branch profits or losses.

On the basis of the above discussion what advice can be tendered? Where a company is of the view that in the early years of its trading overseas losses will arise, it should consider trading as a branch initially and transferring the trade to a local resident company (if it can obtain permission) when the trade becomes profitable. In this way the early trading losses can be utilised immediately rather than against future trading profits. It should be pointed out that this tactic may not be appreciated by the Revenue who, if permission is granted, will lose tax by giving relief for losses incurred by the branch and will only be able to tax overseas profits to the extent they are remitted to the UK.

The potential for deferring a parent company's tax liability in respect of the profits of its overseas subsidiaries has been exploited by a number of companies as follows. A separate subsidiary is formed in a tax haven, such as Switzerland or the Channel Islands, to market the product in the overseas territory. It is also necessary to form two trading companies overseas – one in the country which will produce the goods and the other in the country where the goods will be sold. The goods will then be invoiced through the tax haven company and by judicious use of inter-company pricing the profit on the sale of the goods can be diverted to the tax haven company. In this way no tax will be payable in the territory in which the goods are produced, the tax haven, nor in the territory where the goods are sold nor in the UK.

The cash accumulated in the tax haven can then be lent to other members of the group, including the UK parent. As we shall see in the chapter which covers TA 1970, s. 485 most countries have some form of legislation to counter such abuses but it must be admitted that it is difficult to successfully invoke the legislation where the profits of the tax haven company can be justified commercially. Where these relate to marketing or financial services it is far from easy for a government agency to successfully challenge a company's inter-company pricing policy where the tax haven company provides marketing and financial services for a large group of companies. What is clear from this discussion is that there is a 'grey' area which companies can exploit. This 'grey' area is even more pronounced where the tax haven company actually provides value added to an uncompleted product. For instance, suppose the following situation. An American electronics component company decides to produce and sell the components to the European market. It forms a UK operating subsidiary which will produce an uncompleted component for assembly by a Channel Island subsidiary. The Channel Islands company then sells the completed component to a Dutch subsidiary marketing company for sale in Europe. The logic of the English subsidiary is that it is able to recruit sufficient personnel to produce the product and it is also near the Channel Islands. The Channel Islands operation is limited by the number of available personnel. As the product sold by the UK is only partially completed and has no ready market it will be very difficult for the Inland Revenue to challenge the inter-company transfer price. The profits from the sale of the product can be shared by the Dutch and Channel Island companies. Whilst this case illustrates the potential of tax havens it also highlights their limitations. Tax havens are inevitably small and so the range of activities that can be carried on by companies located in such countries are limited by available personnel, both in terms of quantity and skill. The smaller the value added by such companies the smaller the quantum of profit that can be diverted and vice versa.

4.4.3 Other considerations

These can conveniently be divided into two groups – commercial and miscellaneous.

Other things being equal it will be more desirable to operate overseas through a local subsidiary rather than a branch where:—

(a) a permanent local presence is required by law or is felt to be commercially necessary;
(b) where it is necessary to allow local employees to participate in the profits and management of the company;
(c) local limited liability is required although this could be achieved by the formation of a UK subsidiary to trade overseas;
(d) where a UK image would hinder local trading.

4.4.4 Miscellaneous

In addition the following points should be taken into account.

(a) What types of business structure can be formed and what are the reporting requirements of each?
(b) Must the meetings of directors and shareholders be held in the country of incorporation?
(c) Are there any minimum capital requirements? In most European countries these are not insubstantial.

(d) In some countries the parent of a branch must inform the local authorities that it is trading in the country. Whilst a locally incorporated subsidiary may not have to file details of its parent in practice it is relatively simple for a local government agency to obtain details of the parent.
(e) Are there any local trading restrictions or regulations that might affect the trade to be carried on?
(f) In the case of products which either incorporate a distinctive trade mark or a patented design what is the local law as regards trade marks and patents?
(g) Are there any unusual local provisions relating to such things as goodwill, financing by means of foreign loans and the formation of local partnerships?
(h) In general tax on company profits is paid at an earlier date overseas than in the UK. This is done by means of estimated assessments, which are subsequently revised when the actual profits are known. In effect company tax is paid concurrently with the earning of the profits on which the tax is paid. As most new investment projects will take some time before profits arise this consideration may not be important for a number of years. It may be a more important consideration in service industries, such as marketing and banking, where profits arise very shortly after trading commences.

4.5 General consents

No application to the Treasury for consent is necessary if the transaction(s) falls into one of the categories where consent has already been given. The various privileged categories of transaction are set out below.

4.5.1 Post 1970 companies

Transactions falling within subs. (1) (a) and (b) where the company was incorporated after the passing of TA 1970 for the purpose of carrying on a new trade or business which has not previously been carried on by any person.

The references to a 'new trade' mean that it is new in a commercial rather than technical sense. This exemption will also only apply where 50% of the company's issued share capital both at the date of issue and at the time of the transaction is beneficially owned by persons not ordinarily resident in the UK. The effect of this restricted exemption is that it will only cover some forms of joint enterprise.

4.5.2 Issue of shares in a foreign resident company

The second category of transactions relates to the issue of shares or debentures in a foreign resident company over which a UK company has control and so covers transactions falling with subs. (1) (c). This is permitted where either:—

(a) the issue is for full consideration paid in cash to the company issuing the shares; or
(b) the issue is in payment for any business or property acquired for full consideration.

It is further provided that the shares should not:—

(a) be redeemable preference shares;
(b) be issued to trustees for a non-resident company over which the UK resident company has control, or to trustees for any individual or individuals having control over that UK resident company;
(c) result in the UK resident company losing control of the non-resident company.

4.5.3 Transfer of shares

A transaction within subs. (1) (d) (the transfer of shares or debentures in a non-resident company by a UK resident company) is permitted provided the UK company retains control of the non-resident company. An example of how this privileged category works is shown below.

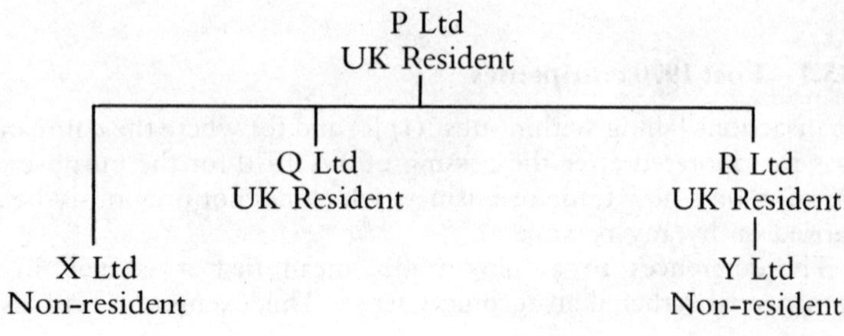

A transfer of shares in X Ltd from P Ltd to Q Ltd or from P Ltd to R Ltd is within this exemption as at all times P Ltd continues to control X Ltd. However, a transfer of shares in Y Ltd from R Ltd to Q Ltd or from R Ltd to P Ltd would not be within this paragraph as it would involve the transferor company, R Ltd, losing control.

4.5.4 Companies resident in Commonwealth territories

A company which is not resident in the UK and incorporated after 31 December 1951 may issue shares or debentures for the purposes of commencing and carrying on a new industrial activity in any Commonwealth territory, provided that it is resident in that territory. Industrial activity for this purpose includes any productive, extractive or manufacturing industry and any public utility, fisheries or any form of husbandry.

4.5.5 Outright sale of shares

The outright transfer by sale of shares or debentures in any overseas company providing:—
(a) the sale must be for full consideration and in cash;
(b) the consideration must not exceed £50,000;
(c) the buyer is not a company over which persons ordinarily resident in the UK have control;
(d) the buyer has no interest in the business of the seller and the seller no interest in that of the buyer;
(e) the sale is not associated with any other operation, transaction or arrangement whereby the business is sold and an interest in that business or part of a business may revert to the seller or to anyone who has an interest in the business of the seller.

4.6 Specific consents

Where a transaction is not within the general consent category an application must be made for a specific consent before the transaction in contemplation can be effected. The application must be addressed to the Treasury, together with a copy of the applicant's latest Balance Sheet and Profit and Loss Account, and where appropriate, a copy of the accounts of the overseas subsidiary where the transaction involves shares or debentures of the subsidiary. The letter must answer the Treasury's official questionnaire, a copy of which is reproduced in Appendix 1.

Whether consent is granted will obviously depend on a number of factors. For instance, the effect of the transaction on the balance of payments will be taken into account and the Revenue will need to be convinced that the transactions will not reduce the amount of UK tax paid by the applicant. It is quite common for consent to be given subject to an undertaking by the applicant. A common requirement is that a certain proportion of the overseas subsidiary's profits should be remitted to the UK.

4.7 Inland Revenue consultative documents: (Tax Havens and Company Residence and The Corporate Sector)

4.7.1 Introduction

These two documents were issued on 26 January 1978. These papers invite views on the case for a statutory redefinition of company residence and the form new legislation might take to counter avoidance of UK tax through the use of tax haven companies.

4.7.2 Company residence

It was stated above that the courts (and s. 482) have equated the term residence with the place of central management and control. In deciding this question considerable weight has been given to the place where formal meetings of the directors are held. The document suggests that this test may not be appropriate as a result of instant communication, improved transport facilities and changes in the mechanisms by which companies decide on and implement policy.

As a result of the current test companies have been able to arrange their residence for tax purposes which have little or no connection with the company's effective place of control. This has given rise to a certain amount of uncertainty in the law, which has been exacerbated by the abolition of exchange control.

A summary of the current proposals is set out below.

(1) Without any change in the general law relating to company residence, companies should be taxed in the UK on the basis of new statutory rules which would bring the tax law of the UK into line with that of a number of other countries, including some of our European Community partners.

(2) Article 4 of the OECD Model Double Taxation Convention of 1977 refers to 'the place of effective management' and there is currently some confusion about the relationship of this concept with the UK test of 'central management and control'. In addition, Article 58 of the EEC Treaty refers to 'central administration' and 'principal place of business' and it is towards these concepts rather than the place where the highest policy decisions are taken that the new tests will be directed.

(3) A trading company would be treated as resident in the UK under the new rules if, for example, its principal day to day management were carried on here, or if its principal administrative functions or its principal place of business were located here. The place where formal meetings of directors are held would no longer have the significance it now has; the place where the working directors actually carried out their administrative functions would be of greater importance. Some modification of these rules might be required to cover companies operating in service industries and non-trading companies, e.g. property investment companies. In these cases existing law might continue to apply.

(4) In many countries such tests are supplemented by a rule that all companies incorporated under the laws of that country are taxed in the same way as resident companies. The introduction of a similar rule in the UK is also being considered.

In practice the proposed changes will only affect a very small proportion of companies. It is directed at two categories of companies. Firstly, those registered overseas and currently treated as resident overseas, often by virtue of directors who play little or no part in the company's management. Secondly, para. 4 is directed at a more recent trend – owing to the high cost of forming companies overseas relative to the cost in the UK, overseas residents have been forming companies in the UK to trade overseas, whether in their own jurisdiction or elsewhere. What is not clear from this document is how the new rules will affect:—

(a) overseas companies who trade in the UK through a branch or agency, sometimes with or without the presence of a director;

(b) the converse of (a): a foreign subsidiary of a UK holding company with common directors.

It is very difficult to comment on this document as the whole document is inevitably cast in very general terms. A more comprehensive review of the effect of the new concepts will only be possible when the Government's proposals are set out in more detail.

4.7.3 Tax Havens and The Corporate Sector

The introductory paragraph of the document notes that TA 1970, s. 482 has been the main provision for countering international tax avoidance and until recently was reinforced by exchange control, which imposed certain constraints on international transfers. The abolition of exchange control has increased the possibilities of tax evasion and avoidance and so the Government have instructed the Revenue to devise a more comprehensive TA 1970, s. 482. One abuse the new section would cover is the recent growth in tax haven companies under the control of a UK parent. This trend has already been noted above in s. **4.4.2**.

A number of other countries have introduced legislation to counter this type of avoidance, the effect of which will be to tax certain types of unremitted income of overseas companies which are controlled by UK resident companies. In summary, where a UK resident company controls such a company it will be taxed in the UK on the unremitted income of that company. The detailed proposals are set out below.

(a) UK resident companies will be treated as liable for a pro rata share of the UK tax charge on the unremitted income and gains of overseas companies which are controlled by UK residents. 'Control' would be defined by reference to existing law and the charge would apply only to corporate shareholders with an interest in excess of 10% in the overseas company. The charge would be computed as if the overseas company were a UK resident company within the charge to corporation tax.

(b) The charge would arise only if the controlled company were resident in a country with a 'privileged tax system' and if it did not distribute a substantial proportion of its profits. A 'privileged tax system' would be one in which a company was not subject to tax in its country of residence or was subject to taxes on profits and gains in that country which were significantly lower than those to which it would have been charged in the UK.

(c) In order to minimise the cost of operation for both companies and the Inland Revenue the new charge will only be imposed at the direction of the Board of Inland Revenue, as with TA 1970, s. 485 (transfer pricing). There will also be tests designed to exclude from tax profits derived by overseas companies from genuine trading activities in the country of residence. Where these tests are satisfied no direction will be made by the Board. The legislation in other countries sets out tests which distinguish income from genuine economic activity in a particular territory from income artificially diverted there for tax avoidance purposes. The tests applied by the Japanese are set out in an appendix to the paper and are reproduced below.

(d) It would be difficult to devise comprehensive tests to ensure that all UK controlled overseas subsidiaries with profits from genuine overseas trading activities are excluded from the charge. An additional exclusion is therefore proposed – where the transactions in a particular accounting period were carried out for bona fide commercial reasons and that tax avoidance was not one of the main objects.

(e) In computing the UK tax charge on an overseas company's income or gains, double taxation relief would be allowed on the same basis as is currently available to UK resident companies. Similar relief would be available against tax charged on any dividend received by a UK shareholder in respect of any tax which the shareholder bears on the income out of which the dividend was paid.

(f) To avoid any overlap, the new provisions would apply to a capital gain only where a charge did not arise on that gain under CGTA 1979, s. 15. That section provides for a charge to capital gains tax on the resident shareholders of a non-resident company which would be a close company if it were resident in the UK. Every person who is resident or ordinarily resident at the time the gain arises to the overseas company (and who, if an individual, is also domiciled in the UK) and who holds shares in it, is treated as if he realised part of the gain. The gain is attributed on the basis of the shareholder's entitlement on liquidation, but not where his interest is less than 5%.

(g) Specific provision might be required to deal with particular problems, such as loans out of income by overseas subsidiaries to the United Kingdom parent.

The above proposals are likely to give rise to the following difficulties:—

(i) the scope of the term 'indirect interest' and the extent to which tax will be exigible where the conditions set out in (a) are otherwise satisfied;

(ii) the meaning of 'significantly lower' in (b) and the extent to which allowances which a company can claim will be taken into account;

(iii) the scope of the words '. . . bona fide commercial reasons and that the avoidance of tax was not one of the main objects of the transactions'. Will it be bona fide commercial to minimise tax in an overseas jurisdiction by setting up an intermediary tax haven company? Or would the latter be included in the term 'profit derived from genuine overseas trading activities'?

4.7.4 Appendix to the Consultative Document

Genuine trade or business activity. Japanese criteria

The Japanese rules apply to the total income of a 'specified foreign subsidiary'. A specified foreign subsidiary is defined as a foreign corporation with a head office or main place of business in a country where the tax burden is significantly lower than in Japan and more than 50% of its stock is owned by Japanese residents. Income derived from genuine trading or business activities is excluded from the scope of the charge. A foreign corporation is not a specified foreign subsidiary if it satisfies all of the following conditions:—

(a) its main business is not to hold securities, patents or copyrights or to lease ships or aircraft;

(b) it has the necessary office, shop, factory or other fixed business premises to conduct its business in the country of incorporation;

(c) it independently administers, controls and manages its business carried on in that country;

(d) where its main business is wholesaling, banking, administration of trusts, dealing in securities, insurance, shipping or air transport, more than 50% of its total gross receipts are derived from unrelated persons; and

(e) dividends received from other specified foreign subsidiaries do not exceed 5% of gross receipts.

4.8 Conclusions

It is clear from the above discussion that in common with other anti-avoidance provisions the scope of the section is very wide and that most overseas transactions other than exports from the UK will require Treasury consent. However, as the section deals exclusively with transactions by companies it can have no application to individuals who control a non-resident company.

Private companies who want to establish a trading entity overseas might wish to consider if it is possible to set up a foreign company with the same shareholders as the UK company. This would avoid s. 482 but may (though not necessarily) contravene another anti-avoidance provision, TA 1970, s. 478. This section covers transactions resulting in the transfer of income to persons abroad. It must follow that before embarking on such a course expert opinion should be obtained. In view of the difficulties such transactions could give rise to, it is perhaps easier and undoubtedly safer, to obtain Treasury permission.

In practice genuine commercial transactions are given a very fair and sympathetic hearing. Permission is usually conditional on remitting a certain proportion of the company's profits in the form of dividends. The proportion will depend on the circumstances, but the level is negotiable and in practice very reasonable.

The chapter also considered the factors to be taken into account in deciding whether overseas operations should be undertaken by a branch or a locally incorporated subsidiary. It was clear from this discussion that the choice will be dictated by the time profile of expected future profits or losses. Where losses are expected in the early years a branch operation will be more advantageous but where profits are expected a subsidiary will be the most tax-efficient entity. The use of tax haven companies was also described and how they can be exploited by means of inter-company pricing policies.

The consultative papers discussed above show that s. 482 and the concept of residence are now under review by the Government. Whilst legislation can be expected in the near future it should be clear from my comments that legislation will be difficult to frame given the 'blurred' distinction in practice between bona fide commercial transactions and tax avoidance. However, practitioners should take heart from the lapse of time between the date these documents are issued and their appearance on the statute book. It is this author's view that we will be very lucky if this proposed legislation reaches the statute book in the Finance Act 1983 and support for this can be found from the recent statement by the Revenue that they are extending the time for comments on these documents from 31 March to 30 June.

4.9 Appendix 1

Migration of companies – applications for consent

HM Treasury questionnaire

Information required

A *For all transactions*

(1) The name of the applicant company.
(2) The nature of the business of the company and the place where its main activities are carried on.
(3) Whether the applicant is a public or private company.
(4) The extent of the overseas holding where residents of the UK hold less than 80% of the capital of any class.
(5) The names of the present and any proposed directors of the company and the addresses of any directors not resident in the UK.
(6) The Tax District to which the company makes its corporation tax returns.
(7) Brief details of any previous application which has been made under the section by or on behalf of the applicant company.
(8) The nature of the proposed transaction.

B *For transactions under subs. (1) (a)* (transfer of residence)

(9) The proposed residence of the company.
(10) Full details of the means by which it is proposed (a) to transfer the residence of the company from the UK and (b) to exercise control and management abroad.

C *For transactions under subs. (1) (b)* (transfer of a trade or business or part of a trade or business)

(11) The name and address of the transferee. If he is an agent the name and address of his principal.
(12) Whether there is any direct or indirect connection by means of shareholding or otherwise, between the applicant company and the transferee or his principal.
(13) The amount of the consideration for the transfer, how it is to be satisfied, and whether it is regarded as full consideration.
(14) If the transfer is to a new company, the reasons why it is necessary for that company to be controlled abroad and full

details of the means by which control and management are to be exercised.

(15) If part only of the company's trade or business is to be transferred, full particulars of that part. (If separate accounts for that part have been prepared copies for each of the last five years should be attached; where accounts have not been prepared an estimate of the turnover and profit in respect of that part for each of these years should be submitted.)

D *For transactions under subs. (1) (c)* (issue of shares or debentures by a non-resident company)

(16) The name of the non-resident company and the nature and extent of the applicant company's control over it (see TA 1970, s. 534, as applied by s. 482 (10)).

(17) The nature of the business of the non-resident company and the place where its main activities are carried on.

(18) The amount and description of the shares or debentures to be issued.

(19) The name(s) and address(es) of the person(s) to whom the shares or debentures are to be issued and full details of any direct or indirect connection, by means of shareholding or otherwise, between such person(s) and either company.

(20) Full details of the consideration where the issue is not for cash.

(21) If the issue represents capitalisation of profits or reserves,
  (a) how the reserves have been created;
  (b) whether any repayment of capital, whether directly or by means of associated transactions, is in contemplation or, on presently known facts, is possible at a future date.

(22) If the issue is other than to the applicant company, the proportion of shares of each class which would be held by the applicant company after the transaction.

E *For transactions under subs. (1) (d)* (transfer of shares or debentures in a non-resident company)

(23) The name of the non-resident company and the nature and extent of the applicant company's control over it (see TA 1970, s. 534, as applied by s. 482 (10)).

(24) The nature of the business of the non-resident company and the place where its main activities are carried on.

(25) The nature and amount of the consideration for the transfer and, where this differs from the current market value, the reasons for the difference.

(26) The name(s) and address(es) of the person(s) to whom the shares or debentures are to be transferred and full details of

any direct or indirect connection by means of shareholding or otherwise, between such person(s) and either company.

(27) The proportion of the shares of each class in the non-resident company which would be held by the applicant company, after the transaction.

F *For all transactions*

(28) An estimate of the difference between the amounts of UK corporation tax (including advance corporation tax (ACT) and corporation tax on chargeable gains) and income tax taking into account the close company provisions if applicable, which would be payable as a result of the proposed transaction and those payable under existing arrangements.

(29) An estimate of the effect of the transaction on the UK Balance of Payments. This estimate should include the provision of the following information:—

(a) details of both the current annual value and the expected value after the proposed transaction has taken place of:—

(i) the company's export earnings

(ii) all funds remitted to the United Kingdom to meet tax, Head Office and other expenses, or out of profits (whether by way of dividends or otherwise);

(b) where application is made under subs. (1) (a) or (b), an estimate of the assets and liabilities to be transferred, indicating the extent to which they represent (i) sterling, (ii) other currencies;

(c) where application is made under subs. (1) (c) or (d) the amount of any payments or receipts which will be remitted from or to the UK as part of the transaction.

(30) The reasons in full for the proposed transaction. (Attention is drawn to the terms of reference of the Advisory Committee which are as follows:—

'They will take into account the significance of any new factors or circumstances which are represented to require the proposed change and any compelling reasons for such applications based on the efficiency and development of the applicant's operations. The Committee will weigh against consideration of this kind the prospective loss of revenue or of foreign exchange to this country which the transaction, if permitted, would entail, and they will inform the Chancellor whether, on a balance of consideration, it would, in their opinion, be in the national interest that permission should be granted.')

5 Tax losses

5.1 Introduction

Prior to the Finance Act 1969 there was a buoyant market in what might be called 'tax-loss' companies. The legislation introduced by that Act halted the market in these companies for a time but after the property collapse in 1974 the same type of newspaper advertisement began to reappear. This chapter will examine in three parts the questions which arise in relation to such companies: the first section will set out the legislation; section two will review the scope of legislation; section three will examine two arrangements which have been put to this author as outside the scope of TA 1970, s. 483.

Before reviewing these three aspects it is necessary to put the legislation into context. This chapter will only focus on trading losses; to date no legislation has been introduced to counter the market in capital loss companies. Under TA 1970, s. 177 trading losses can be off-set as follows:—

(a) against other profits (including capital gains) of the same or preceding accounting period;
(b) against future profits from the same trade indefinitely.

It should be pointed out that in relation to (b) the question of whether the profits arise from the same trade is a question of fact and one which if challenged by the Revenue will be for the Special Commissioners to decide. As their findings will not be lightly overturned companies should ensure that if such companies are purchased the same trade is actually carried on; in practice this may present difficulties. A corollary of this is that it is vital to ensure that when the purchaser acquires the company it has not ceased to trade; this is to counter the Revenue from arguing that a new trade has been set up when the purchaser directs profitable work to the company. The importance of the findings of the Special Commissioners in this matter was highlighted in *J G Ingram & Son Ltd v Callaghan* (1968) 45 TC 151, CA. In this case the company's trade was the manufacture and selling of rubber goods. After a nine-month break, during which the company was taken over by new shareholders, the company resumed the manufacture and sale of similar articles, but in plastic, rather than rubber. The Court of Appeal reaffirmed the findings of the Special Commissioners that a new trade had been set up.

5.2 The legislation (2)

TA 1970, ss. 483 and 484 read as follows:—

483 Change in ownership of company: disallowance of trading losses

(1) If:—

(a) within any period of three years there is both a change in the ownership of a company and (either earlier or later in that period, or at the same time) a major change in the nature or conduct of a trade carried on by the company, or

(b) at any time after the scale of the activities in a trade carried on by a company has become small or negligible, and before any considerable revival of the trade, there is a change in the ownership of the company,

no relief shall be given under s. 177 of this Act (relief for trading losses against future trading profits or total profits) by setting a loss incurred by the company in an accounting period beginning before the change of ownership against any income or other profits of an accounting period ending after the change of ownership.

(2) In applying this section to the accounting period in which the change of ownership occurs, the part ending with the change of ownership, and the part after, shall be treated as two separate accounting periods, and the profits or losses of the accounting period shall be apportioned to the two parts.

The apportionment shall be on a time basis according to the respective lengths of those parts except that if it appears that that method would work unreasonably or unjustly such other method shall be used as appears just and reasonable.

(3) In subs. (1) above "major change in the nature or conduct of a trade" includes:—

(a) a major change in the type of property dealt in, or services or facilities provided, in the trade, or
(b) a major change in customers, outlets or markets of the trade,

and this section applies even if the change is the result of a gradual process which began outside the period of three years mentioned in subs. (1) (a) above.

(4) In relation to any relief available under s. 252 of this Act (company reconstructions) to a successor company, subs. (1) above shall apply as if any loss sustained by a predecessor company had been sustained by a successor company and as if the references to a trade included references to the trade as carried on by a predecessor company.

(5) Where relief in respect of a company's losses has been restricted under this section then, notwithstanding s. 87 (3) of the Capital Allowances Act 1968, in applying the provisions of that Act about balancing charges to the company by reference to any event after the change of ownership of the company, any allowance or deduction falling to be made in taxing the company's trade for any chargeable period before the change of ownership shall be disregarded unless the profits or gains of that chargeable period or of any subsequent chargeable period before the change of ownership were sufficient to give effect to the allowance or deduction.

In applying this subsection it shall be assumed that any profits or gains are applied in giving effect to any such allowance or deduction in preference to being set off against any loss which is not attributable to such an allowance or deduction.

(6) Where the operation of this section depends on circumstances or events at a time after the change of ownership (but not more than three years after), an assessment to give effect to the provisions of this section shall not be out of time if made within six years from that time, or the latest of those times.

(7) Any person in whose name any shares, stock or securities of a company are registered shall, if required by notice in writing by an inspector given for the purposes of this section, state whether or not he is the beneficial owner of those shares or securities and, if not the beneficial owner of those shares or securities or any of them, shall furnish the

name and address of the person or persons on whose behalf those shares, stock or securities are registered in his name.

(8) This section shall not apply if the change of ownership took place before 15 April 1969, and subs. (1) (a) above shall not apply if the major change in the nature or conduct of the trade was completed before that date.

In other respects this section has effect by reference to circumstances and events before that date, as well as by reference to later circumstances and events.

484 Rules for ascertaining change in ownership of company

(1) For the purposes of s. 483 above (in this section called "the principal section") there is a change in the ownership of a company:—

(a) if a single person acquires more than half the ordinary share capital of the company, or

(b) if two or more persons each acquire a holding of 5% or more of the ordinary share capital of the company, and those holdings together amount to more than half the ordinary share capital of the company, or

(c) if two or more persons each acquire a holding of the ordinary share capital of the company, and the holdings together amount to more than half the ordinary share capital of the company, but disregarding a holding of less than 5% unless it is an addition to an existing holding and the two holdings together amount to 5% or more of the ordinary share capital of the company.

(2) In applying subs. (1) above:—

(a) the circumstances at any two points of time with not more than three years between may be compared, and a holder at the later time may be regarded as having acquired whatever he did not hold at the earlier time, irrespective of what he has acquired or disposed of in between,

(b) to allow for any issue of shares or other reorganisation of capital, the comparison may be made in terms of percentage holdings of the total ordinary share capital at the respective times, so that a person whose percentage holding is greater at the later time may be regarded as having acquired a percentage holding equal to the increase,

(c) to decide for the purposes of subs. (1) (b) or (c) above if any person has acquired a holding of at least 5%, or a holding which makes at least 5% when added to an existing holding, acquisitions by, and holdings of, two or more persons who are connected persons within the meaning of s. 533 of this Act shall be aggregated as if they were acquisitions by, and holdings of, one and the same person,

(d) any acquisition of shares under the will or on the intestacy of a deceased person and, if it is shown that the gift is unsolicited and made without regard to the provisions of the principal section, any gift of shares, shall be left out of account.

(3) Where, because persons, whether company members or not, possess extraordinary rights or powers under the articles of association or under any other document regulating the company, ownership of ordinary share capital may not be an appropriate test of whether there has been a major change in the persons for whose benefit the losses may ultimately enure, then in considering whether there has been a change of ownership of the company for the purposes of the principal section, holdings of all kinds of share capital, including preference shares, or of any particular category of share capital, or voting power or any other special kind of power, may be taken into account instead of ordinary share capital.

(4) Where the principal section has operated to restrict relief by reference to a change of ownership taking place at any time, no transaction or circumstances before that time shall be taken into account in determining whether there is any subsequent change of ownership.

(5) A change in the ownership of a company shall be disregarded for the purposes of the principal section if:—

(a) immediately before the change the company is the 75% subsidiary of another company, and

(b) (although there is a change in the direct ownership of the company) that other company continues after the change to own the first-mentioned company as a 75% subsidiary.

(6) If there is a change in the ownership of a company which has a 75% subsidiary (whether owned directly or indirectly), then, unless under subs. (5) above that change in

ownership is to be disregarded, the principal section shall apply as if there had also been a change in the ownership of that 75% subsidiary.

(7) For the purposes of this section:—

(a) references to ownership shall be construed as references to beneficial ownership, and references to acquisition shall be construed accordingly,

(b) a company shall be deemed to be 75% subsidiary of another company if and so long as not less than three quarters of its ordinary share capital is owned by that other company, whether directly or through another company or other companies, or partly directly and partly through another company or other companies,

(c) the amount of ordinary share capital of one company owned by a second company through another company or other companies, or partly directly and partly through another company or other companies, shall be determined in accordance with subss. (5) to (10) of s. 532 of this Act,

(d) "share" includes stock.

(8) If any acquisition of ordinary share capital or other property or rights taken into account in determining that there has been change of ownership of a company was made in pursuance of a contract of sale or option or other contract, or the acquisition was made by a person holding such a contract, and the contract was made on or after 15 April 1969, the time when the change in the ownership of the company took place shall be determined as if the acquisition had been made when the contract was made with the holder or when the benefit of it was assigned to him so that, in the case of a person exercising an option to purchase shares, he shall be regarded as having purchased the shares when he acquired the option.

5.3 The scope of the legislation

This section should be read in conjunction with the legislation.

5.3.1 TA 1970, s. 483 (1) (a) – The two conditions

This subsection prescribes two conditions that must be satisfied before the Revenue can disallow the carry forward of trading losses:—

(a) a change in ownership; and
(b) a major change in the nature or conduct of the trade.

Despite the detailed rules in s. 484 relating to what constitutes a change in ownership, the arrangements which have been designed to be outside the scope of the section have centred on this aspect. The second condition is set out more tersely in s. 483 (3); having said this the terms used in that subsection are capable of a very wide meaning. It follows that where the arrangements rely on (a) the question for the courts would largely be one of law, whereas in the case of (b) it would be one of fact.

5.3.2 Change in ownership

The basic rules are set out in TA 1970, s. 484 (1)–(6). As with most anti-avoidance legislation it is not only comprehensive but very wide ranging.

Subsection (1) sets out the three circumstances which will constitute a change in ownership of the company. These are:—

(a) where a single person acquires more than 50% of the ordinary share capital of the company;
(b) if two or more persons each acquire a holding of at least 5% of the ordinary share capital of the company and the two holdings together amount to more than 50% of the ordinary share capital of the company;
(c) if two or more persons each acquire a holding in a company and the holdings together amount to more than 50% of the ordinary share capital of the company, but disregarding holdings of less than 5% unless it is an addition to an existing holding and the two holdings together are in excess of 5% of the ordinary share capital of the company.

For the purposes of subs. (2) (a) the Revenue can quite arbitrarily decide the relevant two points and it could be that quite innocent transactions might be caught as a result. Such an interpretation would be penal and not merely restorative, the normal canon of anti-avoidance legislation.

From subs. (d) it appears that the acquisition of shares from an intestate can somehow be solicited. If this proposition were litigated the mind boggles at what esoteric arguments the Revenue would advance. The other question to which this clause gives rise is on whom does the burden of proof lie? Presumably, under normal canons it is the taxpayer and it seems that unless the deceased is blessed with life after death the taxpayer will have no alternative but to hope these protestations are met with the same sympathy as the deceased showed by either:—

(a) not making a will and so not divesting the taxpayer of his rights on intestacy; or
(b) making a will and including the taxpayer.

As the Revenue's sense of charity is, to put it no higher, not all it could be in such situations the taxpayer will be left anxiously awaiting the immortality of the deceased.

In the past taxpayers' advisers have circumvented similar legislation by such devices as varying the share rights. Subsection (3) recognises this; what is not clear from the subsection is the meaning of the terms:—

(a) extraordinary;
(b) all kinds of share capital; and
(c) any other special kinds of power.

The difficulty with (a) is identifying what will constitute an ordinary power, as anything else will be regarded as extraordinary. Does it mean extraordinary in relation to shares in general or in relation to particular categories of share capital in a company's share structure? The scope of (b) seems to extend to any instrument of capital issued by a company other than a debt. The third, (c), seems to be of an unknown quantity in that one would normally assume that the term 'extraordinary powers' included 'any other special kind of power'. Presumably the connotation to be given to the term in practice will mean some form of Houdini power hitherto not known to the Revenue but legislated for in advance.

Subsections (4) and (5) of s. 484 provide a measure of relief from the onerous conditions discussed above. Subsection (4) provides that where s. 483 has already restricted relief as a result of a change in ownership no transaction or circumstances occurring prior to that change will be taken into account in determining whether there is any subsequent change of ownership. Subsection (5) provides that there is not a change in ownership where:—

(a) immediately before the change the company is a 75% subsidiary of another company, and
(b) although there is a change in direct ownership of the company, that other company continues after the change to own the first company as a 75% subsidiary.

This relieving subsection is restricted by subs. (6) which provides that relief will be restricted in the case of a subsidiary (75% or more of the equity being owned by the holding company) where there has been a change in the ownership of the holding company, unless subs. (5) applies. Subsection (7) defines the various terms used in the section. These are cast in very wide terms and the only surprise is the brevity of the definition of a 'share'. Whilst it is clear that the definition is illustrative and not exhaustive, from the discussion above one would have expected a more all embracing definition. As the definition currently stands it is somewhat crass and unhelpful.

5.3.3 Company reconstructions

If the trade of a company has been transferred to another company as part of a reconstruction and the predecessor company has incurred trading losses it is possible if the conditions prescribed in TA 1970, s. 252 are satisfied to transfer the losses to the successor company. The most important condition is that on or at any time within two years after the transfer three quarters of the trade, or an interest amounting to that, belongs to the same persons as the trade or interest belonged to at some time within a year before the transfer.

Where these conditions are satisfied TA 1970, s. 483 (4) provides that s. 252 must be read as subject to ss. 483 and 484. It follows that where a company effects a reconstruction two hurdles will have to be overcome if the successor is to benefit from the losses transferred – s. 252 and ss. 483 and 484. In practice the latter sections are often overlooked in schemes of reconstruction; such oversights could prove very expensive and professional advisers in evaluating such schemes should consider very closely whether the exhaustive provisions of ss. 483 and 484 are applicable.

5.3.4 Capital allowances

TA 1970, s. 483 (5) provides a relief from balancing charges where the losses have been restricted as a result of a change of ownership. It is provided that any allowances given prior to the change are to be disregarded to the extent that they have not been offset against profits or gains brought into charge to tax. In effect, in computing any balancing charge the successor is allowed to take into account the written down value of the asset at the date the ownership of the business changed and the allowances claimed by the predecessor but not relieved against his profits or gains.

5.4 The practical implementation of the legislation

A variety of arrangements have been put to the author in an attempt to circumvent the very tightly prescribed conditions set out in TA 1970, ss. 483 and 484. Two such arrangements will now be reviewed.

5.4.1 Case 1

This related to a property development company ('X Ltd') with trading losses in excess of £2 million and a share capital of £200,000, divided into 200,000 £1 shares. The company wishing to purchase the share capital of X Ltd will be referred to as 'Y Ltd'. The transactions suggested were:—

(1) The share capital of X Ltd would be divided into 102,000 preferred ordinary shares of £1 each ('the A shares') plus 98,000 ordinary shares of £1 each ('the B shares').
(2) The Articles of Association of X Ltd would be altered to provide that, save as otherwise expressly provided, all shares in the company would rank *pari passu* in all respects.
(3) The Articles of Association of the company would then provide that the A shares would not carry any voting rights and that their entitlement to dividends and capital would be limited as follows:—
    (a) to a cumulative annual preferred dividend of, say, 5% of the nominal value of the shares;
    (b) to participate *pari passu* with all other shares in dividends declared for any accounting period where the profits exceed, say, £5 million;
    (c) in a winding-up to the repayment of the nominal capital in priority to any repayment being made on any other shares in the company.
(4) The existing shareholders in X Ltd would sell their B shares to Y Ltd, but would retain beneficial ownership of the A shares.

The main question to which these transactions give rise is whether the acquisition of Y Ltd would amount to a change in ownership of X Ltd, within the meaning of s. 484 (3). The crucial question is whether the shares owned by Y Ltd 'possess extraordinary rights or powers under the articles of association'. This raises the question as to whether 'extraordinary' refers to either the rights and powers:—

(a) generally attaching to shares in companies; or
(b) attaching to one class of shares in a company as compared to another class of shares in the company.

In this author's view both views are tenable. In any litigation much would depend on the respective skills of the advocates involved and the outcome would depend on whether the court took a narrow or wide view of the section. This author feels that the former would prevail because:—

(a) the legislation is anti-avoidance in nature;
(b) a finding against the taxpayer would be in accordance with the restorative nature of the legislation;
(c) of recent judicial hostility towards tax avoidance arrangements.

In this context it should be pointed out that even if the taxpayer succeeded on this point the Revenue almost certainly would challenge other aspects of the transaction such as:—

(i) whether a new trade had been set up following the *J G Ingram* case (1968) 45 TC 151, CA referred to in **5.1** above;
(ii) if certain debts were taken over by other members of the taxpayer's group of companies and these were repaid from profits which arose after the change in ownership, whether s. 460 ICTA 1970 could be invoked.

To conclude, from a commercial viewpoint the company may well be worth acquiring but the possible tax benefits of the trading losses should be heavily discounted in evaluating a possible purchase price.

5.4.2 Case II

This concerned a trading company ('X Ltd') with tax losses, whose shares were owned as to 75% by an entrenched majority shareholder ('Z Ltd') and the balance by a minority shareholder, A. The arrangements contemplated were to enable another company, Q Ltd, to purchase X Ltd with the benefits of the tax losses. The share capital of X Ltd consisted of 100 ordinary £1 shares, each fully paid.

The following steps were proposed:—

(1) Z Ltd would incorporate a new wholly owned subsidiary, Y Ltd.
(2) A would sell to Y Ltd 2 of his shares in X Ltd.
(3) Z Ltd would then sell its holding in X Ltd to Y Ltd.
(4) Y Ltd would sell to Q Ltd 3 shares in X Ltd.
(5) A would then sell his remaining 23 shares in X Ltd to Q Ltd.
(6) Z Ltd would sell to Q Ltd its shareholding in Y Ltd.

Diagrammatically this can be represented as follows:—

Before Step 1

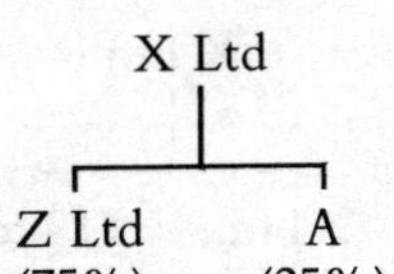

Step 1 Incorporation of a new subsidiary, Y Ltd

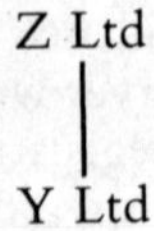

Step 2

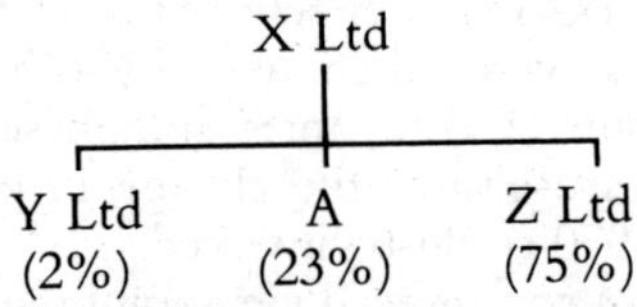

Step 3

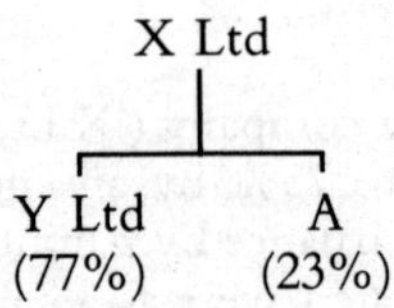

Step 4

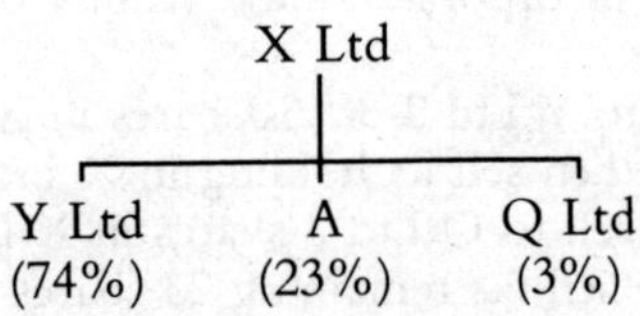

Step 5

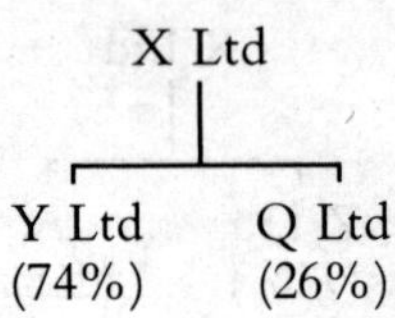

Step 6 X Ltd becomes a wholly owned subsidiary of Q Ltd

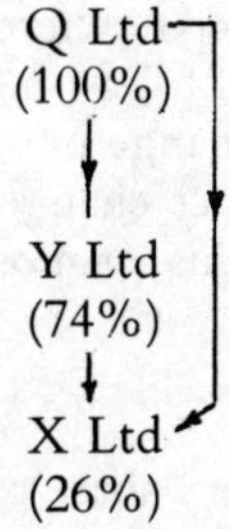

In summary, X Ltd becomes a wholly owned subsidiary of Q Ltd as Q Ltd owns 26% of X Ltd directly and 74% indirectly through Y Ltd which is a wholly owned subsidiary of Q Ltd.

It is crucial to the success of those arrangements that:—

(a) each transaction should be independent of any subsequent transaction;

(b) none of the parties would be under any obligation to enter into any of the transactions.

As an evidential matter this would undoubtedly be difficult to show and probably more to the point, to convince a court. However, on the basis that this difficulty could be overcome it is argued that the transactions would not constitute a 'change of ownership' within s. 484 for the following reasons:—

(a) *Step 1.* Incorporation of Y Ltd. This does not affect the ownership of X Ltd.

(b) *Step 2.* Acquisition of 2 shares by Y Ltd in X Ltd from A. This would not involve a change in the ownership of X Ltd, within either subs. (1) or (3).

(c) *Step 3.* X Ltd would sell to Y Ltd the shares it owns in X Ltd. But for subs. (5) there would be a change of ownership within subs. (1) (a). Indirect holdings in companies can be taken into account by virtue of paras. (b) and (c) of subs. (7).

(d) *Step 4.* Y Ltd sells to Q Ltd 3 shares in X Ltd. This would not be within either subs. (1) or (3).

(e) *Step 5.* A sells his 23 shares in X Ltd to Q Ltd. As with Step 4 this would not be within either subs. (1) or (3).

(f) *Step 6.* Q Ltd would acquire from Z Ltd their shareholding in Y Ltd. This would involve a change in ownership of Y Ltd. However, the ownership of X Ltd would remain unchanged; it is then argued that subs. (6) would not apply as X Ltd at the time of the sale was not, either directly or indirectly, a 75% subsidiary of Y Ltd.

Two points give this author concern about the above arrangements. The first is an evidential one and has already been alluded to. The second concerns Step 6 where it is argued that there is not a change in ownership of X Ltd, as the shares continue to be owned by Y Ltd, there is only a change in ownership in Y Ltd. It follows that there is only an indirect change in the ownership of X Ltd. What worries me about this proposition is subs. (7) (c), which provides:—

> 'The amount of ordinary share capital of one company owned by a second company through another company or other companies, or partly directly and partly through another company or other companies, shall be determined in accordance with subss. (5) to (10) of s. 532 of this Act.'

The latter subsections in effect provide that in determining questions of ownership fractions of a company owned by subsidiaries are to be aggregated. It is my view that at Step 6, if the provisions of subs. (7) (c) and subss. (5) to (10) of s. 532 are applied, Q Ltd in effect purchases 74% of X Ltd and so the transactions are clearly within TA 1970, s. 484 (1) (a). It seems to this author that this argument can only be wrong if:—

(a) the application of subs. (7) (c) is restricted to the question of whether one company is a 75% subsidiary of another; and
(b) by corollary, it has no application in determining whether a single person has acquired more than half the ordinary share capital of a company.

Such a favourable interpretation seems out of context with the general tenor of the legislation. As with the previous case, even if the taxpayer succeeded the Revenue would look very closely at the factual situation to see whether either:—

(a) there had been a major change in the nature or conduct of the trade; and
(b) the activities of the trade prior to any revival had become small or negligible.

As stated above in any marginal situation a finding of the Commissioners could go either way and would be very difficult to overturn on appeal. However, in both cases the taxpayer would be well advised to decide whether to acquire such companies on purely commercial grounds and heavily discount any tax benefits that might arise as a result of effecting arrangements similar to those discussed above.

5.5 Conclusions

As with all the other anti-avoidance sections that have so far been considered this piece of legislation is very widely drawn and is a veritable 'minefield' for the tax planner. In this chapter two cases were considered in relation to how the section might be circumvented and it was shown that the prospects of success were, to put it no higher, of a low order. This may seem a negative view to those whom I would call the commercial tax planners in industry and commerce but is one which I think follows from the mischief aimed at by the legislation. It is to be regretted that it is no longer possible to utilise the tax losses incurred by previous owners. If such losses could be used this would increase the expected return prospective owners would receive on their investment and hopefully this would stimulate economic activity. Unfortunately, what might be called the 'artificial tax planner' abused this relief prior to the introduction of this legislation and thereby jeopardised many potentially bona fide commercial transactions.

6 Transfer pricing. TA 1970, s. 485

6.1 Introduction

In recent years there has been a growing awareness by politicians and government agencies that multi-national corporations might exploit host jurisdictions by pursuing transfer pricing policies aimed at minimising both local and world-wide tax burdens. To counter this possibility most countries now have detailed rules which govern inter-company transactions. Most of these rules contain an element of arbitrariness. This, together with the increasing hostility of government agencies, has created considerable problems for the multi-national corporation. These have also been exacerbated by two further problems:—

(a) where transfer prices are adjusted by one jurisdiction this inevitably increases the profit in that jurisdiction and reduces the profit in another. However, the other country often does not adjust the tax burden to reflect these adjustments;
(b) transfer prices which are acceptable for corporate tax purposes are not necessarily acceptable for customs purposes.

A further problem in some countries, for instance, France, is that the import price of some products (e.g. pharmaceutical goods) determines what price can be charged in the final goods market. This price might be at variance with the pricing policy the multi-national would normally follow. It should be pointed out that transfer pricing covers not only inter-company transfers of goods but also payments for services, intangibles such as royalties and know-how and inter-company debt.

Different considerations apply to each. It was stated earlier that nearly all countries have legislation to counter the possibilities of abusing inter-company pricing. The legislation varies from the very detailed (such as the United States and West Germany) to the very general (the Netherlands). This is not the place to discuss the legislation in these countries but to give an insight into the various approaches. In terms of the spectrum the UK is about in the middle. Whilst we have some legislation (principally TA 1970, s. 485 and FA 1975, s. 17), this has largely supplemented rather than displaced two powerful weapons in the Inland Revenue's armoury:—

(a) TA 1970, s. 130 (a) – that for expenditure to be deductible it must have been incurred wholly and exclusively for the purposes of the trade;

(b) the market value rule established so vividly in *Sharkey v Wernher* (1955) 36 TC 275.

This chapter will examine in three parts the issues to which transfer pricing gives rise. The first will set out the relevant legislation, the second will discuss the scope of the legislation and the third will review the practical issues that have arisen from the legislation and press publicity.

6.2 The legislation

TA 1970, s. 485 reads as follows:—

Transactions between associated persons

485 Sales etc, at undervalue or overvalue

(1) Subject to the provisions of this section, where any property is sold and:—

(a) the buyer is a body of persons over whom the seller has control or the seller is a body of persons over whom the buyer has control or both the seller and the buyer are bodies of persons and some other person has control over both of them; and

(b) the property is sold at a price less than the price which it might have been expected to fetch if the parties to the transaction had been independent persons dealing at arm's length,

then, in computing the income, profits or losses of the seller for tax purposes, the like consequences shall ensue as would have ensued if the property had been sold for the price which it would have fetched if the transaction had been a transaction between independent persons dealing as aforesaid:

Provided that this subsection shall not apply where the buyer is resident in the UK and is carrying on a trade therein, and the price of the property falls to be taken into account as a deduction in computing the profits or gains or losses of that trade for tax purposes.

(2) Subject to the provisions of this section, where any property is sold and:—

(a) the buyer is a body of persons over whom the seller has control or the seller is a body of persons over whom the buyer has control or both the seller and the buyer are bodies of persons and some other person has control over both of them; and

(b) the property is sold at a price greater than the price which it might have been expected to fetch if the parties to the transaction had been independent persons dealing at arm's length,

then, in computing the income, profits or losses of the buyer for tax purposes, the like consequences shall ensue as would have ensued if the property had been sold for the price which it would have fetched if the transaction had been a transaction between independent persons dealing as aforesaid:

Provided that this subsection shall not apply where the seller is resident in the UK and is carrying on a trade therein, and the price of the property falls to be taken into account as a trading receipt in computing the profits or gains or losses of that trade for tax purposes.

(3) The preceding provisions of this section shall not apply in relation to any sale unless the Board so direct, and where such a direction is given all such adjustments shall be made, whether by assessment, repayment of tax or otherwise, as are necessary to give effect to the direction.

(4) Nothing in this section shall be construed as affecting the operation of any of the provisions of the Capital Allowances Act 1968.

(5) In this section, "body of persons" includes a partnership and "control" has the meaning ascribed to it by s. 534 of this Act, and, for the purposes of this section, a sale shall be deemed to take place at the time of completion or at the time when possession is given, whichever is the earlier.

(5A) In determining for the purposes of this section whether any person (alone or with others) has control over a body of persons:—

(a) there shall be attributed to him any rights or powers of a nominee for him, that is to say, any rights or powers which another possesses on his behalf or may be required to exercise on his direction or behalf;

(b) there may also be attributed to him any rights or powers of a person with whom he is connected (within the meaning of s. 533 of this Act, but omitting subss. (5) to (7) and the exception in subs. (4)), including any rights or powers of a nominee for such a person, that is to say any rights or powers which another possesses on behalf of such a person or may be required to exercise on his direction or behalf.

(6) The preceding provisions of this section shall, with the necessary adaptations, have effect in relation to lettings and hirings of property, grants and transfers of rights, interests or licences and the giving of business facilities of whatever kind as they have effect in relation to sales, and the references in the said preceding provisions to sales, sellers, buyers and prices shall be deemed to be extended accordingly.

6.3 The scope of TA 1970, s. 485

6.3.1 The substantive issues

Subsections (1) and (2) are enabling ones. This means that they can only be applied when there is a direction by the Board. To date only a few directions have been made, but as we shall see, the Revenue are now paying increasing attention to this section and pursuant to this a special unit has been set up to review companies' policies.

TA 1970, s. 485 (1) covers the situation where property is sold at below market value and the buyer is a company over whom the seller has control, or the seller is a company over whom the buyer has control, or both the buyer and seller are companies controlled by a third company. Subsection (2) covers a sale under the same conditions but the property is sold at above market value. In both cases the sale will be treated as between independent companies at market value. However, it is provided that subs. (1) will not apply where the buyer is resident and carries on a trade in the UK and the price of the property is taken into account in computing his taxable profits or losses. The converse is true where the seller is both resident and carries on a trade in the UK and the price is taken into account in computing his taxable profits or losses.

What is not clear from the legislation is the extent to which the section could be invoked to cover a purely domestic transaction within a domestic group of companies. TA 1970, s. 485 would be applicable where the transaction, in the case of:—

(a) the buyer, for the purposes of subs. (1); and
(b) the seller, for the purposes of subs. (2),

was not a trading transaction. TA 1970, s. 485 would, therefore, apply where one company in a group either sells or buys an asset that will be held by the other company in the group as an investment and not as trading stock. Whilst TA 1970, s. 485 might at first appear applicable to such cases the scope of the section is restricted where either:—

(a) both parties to the transaction are 75% subsidiaries (directly or otherwise) of a holding company; or
(b) one party is a 75% subsidiary of the other party to the transaction.

In such cases a combination of TA 1970, s. 274 and CGTA 1979, s. 122 and related case law dictate that transactions falling within (a) and (b) are to be recorded at market value. TA 1970, s. 485 is, therefore, rendered otiose. However, in situations other than 75% companies it may well be either directly applicable or supplement existing case law. As both subsections refer to trading in the UK the provisions appear not to cover a UK company whose trading activities are carried on exclusively overseas. Another unusual situation where TA 1970, s. 485 could be invoked is where goods are traded between a UK trading branch of a non-resident UK company and a UK resident company of the non-resident UK company. In such a case TA 1970, s. 485 will not apply to:—

(a) a sale by the branch at an undervalue to the subsidiary; or
(b) a sale to the branch at an undervalue from the subsidiary.

In the converse case the protection of the provision will not be available as although the branch is taxable in the UK it is not resident here. In this unusual case recourse would have to be made to the double tax treaty for a non-discrimination clause. If there was no such clause the provisions would apply and so the transactions would be within TA 1970, s. 485. As stated above, these two cases are very unusual and their importance is largely academic.

6.3.2 TA 1970, s. 485 and s. 233

In terms of practical reality, problems could arise in connection with the overlap between TA 1970, s. 485 and TA 1970, s. 233 (which deals with distributions) where:—

(a) a UK subsidiary buys at an overvalue from an overseas parent company; and
(b) a UK subsidiary sells at an undervalue from an overseas parent company.

The difference between the overvalue and market value in the first case might be treated as a distribution under TA 1970, s. 233 (3) and in the second case, the difference between the invoice price and market value might be treated as both a notional trading receipt and a distribution. To date the Revenue have not taken the distribution point but any settlement with the Revenue should specifically cover this aspect.

6.3.3 TA 1970, s. 130

This section was referred to in **6.1** above where it was stated that a payment between connected companies might be challenged on the grounds that either:—

(a) it was not incurred wholly and exclusively for the purposes of the trade; or
(b) the loss was either not connected with or attributable to the trade.

Whilst it might appear that TA 1970, ss. 485 and 130 overlap, the latter section has been confined to overall categories of expense and not with the appropriateness of the charge. Although recent cases, such as *Ransom v Higgs* (1974) 50 TC 1, have discussed whether a particular trading expense was incurred for bona fide commercial purposes where there is a duality of purpose, TA 1970, s. 485 is a more precise weapon. This being the case the Revenue will prefer to use TA 1970, s. 485 and s. 130 will only be invoked as an alternative.

6.3.4 TA 1970, s. 485 (6)

This subsection states that the provisions of this section and more particularly in practice, the provisions of subss. (1) and (2), will apply to lettings and hirings of property, grants and transfers of rights, interests or licences and the giving of business facilities of any kind. Two points arise in connection with the interpretation of this subsection. Firstly the meaning to be attributed to the words 'necessary adaptations' and secondly the scope of subs. (6) appears very open ended. An example of the latter is the provision of interest-free finance by a UK parent to a foreign subsidiary. The Revenue take the view that this falls within the words 'the giving of business facilities'. For the company to escape from a direction under subs. (1) it would have to successfully argue that one or more of the following defences were applicable:—

(a) the loan should be treated as equity where it is not permissible under the laws of the local territory to pay interest;
(b) the subsidiary is financially not in a position to pay interest on the loan;
(c) the phrase 'a price less than' does not cover a transaction where there is no price.

Where the borrower is a UK resident subsidiary company of an overseas parent a direction under subs. (2) would dictate the substitution of an arm's length interest charge against trading profit. Difficulties with the Revenue have arisen where the outstanding debt of the company is a multiple of the issued equity (otherwise referred to as 'thin capitalisation'). Interest payments on such a debt might be a distribution within TA 1970, s. 233 (2) (d) (iv), although this may be overriden by the terms of the double tax treaty. However, for the Revenue to succeed with the 'thin capitalisation' argument the borrowing of a subsidiary would have to be ignored, and the transaction completely restructured. Such an argument is an abrogation of the rule of law, so fundamental to our constitution. It would surely stretch the adaptations too far to substitute a broad concept of terms on which finance is provided (as opposed to the specific interest rate charged on the loan) for a narrower concept of a price for property contemplated by TA 1970, s. 485 (2) before adaptation.

The legislation is even less clear where the interest-free loan is made by one UK resident company to another related UK resident company. Difficulties with the legislation arise as follows:—

(a) whether or not the borrower or lender is a trader;
(b) adapting the appropriate words, such as 'lender', 'borrower' and 'loan' to subss. (1) and (2);
(c) how the provisions are to operate.

To overcome these difficulties the companies involved should argue that in the case of the borrower the interest on the loan, if charged, would be treated as a charge on income and in the case of the lender, the notional receipt would be taxed under Sch. D, Case III. It is submitted that if this approach is taken the interest-free loan would be outside the scope of TA 1970, s. 485.

6.3.5 The administration of TA 1970, s. 485

TA 1970, s. 485, as originally enacted gave the Revenue no special powers of investigation and the Revenue had to rely on the general powers of the TMA 1970. These were subsequently supplemented by the provisions of FA 1975, s. 17. The additional powers are similar to those given to the Customs and Excise in connection with the administration of value added tax (FA 1972, ss. 35–37).

Under these revised provisions the Board may, by notice in writing, require any company within such time as it may allow (but not less than 30 days) to provide such particulars including details of relevant documents, as may be specified in the notice of any related transaction which appears to the Board to be:—

(a) or to be connected with, a transaction with respect to which the Revenue might give a direction under TA 1970, s. 485; or
(b) relevant for determining whether such a direction could or should be given in any case; or
(c) relevant for determining for the purposes of TA 1970, s. 485 what price any property sold could have fetched had the sale been one between independent persons dealing at arm's length (FA 1972, ss. 35–37).

'Related transaction' is defined in FA 1975, s. 17 (4) as one to which the company concerned or an associated company was a party and in this context two bodies are associated if one is under the control of the other or both are under the control of the same person or persons. Obviously the Revenue would have great difficulties in obtaining information about the activities of companies resident outside the UK and subs. (5) attempts to improve the Revenue's position. This subsection provides that in the case of a transaction where it appears to the Board that a direction under TA 1970, s. 485 might be given and:—

(a) one of the parties is a company resident outside the UK and is a 51% subsidiary of a UK resident company (the parent); and
(b) the other party is, or is a 51% subsidiary body of, the parent,

the Board may require the parent company to make available for inspection any books, accounts or other documents or records whatsoever of the parent body or of any body of persons (including a partnership) over whom it has control and which relates to that transaction or any other transaction (of whatsoever nature) in the same assets, or to transactions (of whatsoever nature) in assets which are similar to the first mentioned transaction (FA 1975, s. 17 (5)). The parent company can apply to the Board to be excused from complying with these requirements in relation to a non-resident company and an appeal lies to the Special Commissioners if the Board refuse to exercise their discretion (FA 1975, s. 17 (6)). Such an application or appeal is only likely to succeed if the parent company can persuade either body that:—

(a) TA 1970, s. 485 has no application to the transactions; or

(b) the information required by the notice is unreasonable.

Perhaps the most ranging power in the Revenue's armoury is contained in subs. (7). This subsection provides that where it appears to the Board that a body of persons (which includes a partnership) may be a party to a transaction with respect to which a direction under TA 1970, s. 485 might be given, they may, for the purpose of determining whether a direction should be made, authorise an inspector on their behalf to enter any premises used in connection with the relevant trade carried on by that body of persons and inspect any books, accounts or other documents and records relating to that trade which he considers necessary for his purposes and may require any such books, accounts, documents, or records to be produced for his inspection. No provision is made in the subsection which enables the inspector to take anything from the premises.

It is to be hoped that this power will be used sparingly and that the courts will be vigilant in order to protect the citizen against possible abuse by the Revenue.

6.4 The practical implementation of the legislation

This section will examine the practical implementation of TA 1970, s. 485. Shortly after FA 1975 the Revenue announced they were setting up a special unit to examine the pricing policies of multinational corporations trading in the UK. To facilitate the smooth working of the legislation the unit sent some of their number to the United States to study how the Internal Revenue Service administers the more detailed United States' legislation.

An investigation by this unit may arise as a result of one or more of the following:—

(a) a reference from the tax district which deals with the company's tax affairs;
(b) a reference as a result of another department, e.g. a request under TA 1970, s. 482 has been known to initiate an enquiry;
(c) a reference from a foreign tax authority;
(d) published information in the press.

The enquiry is usually conducted in some depth and normally involves meetings and correspondence. It is usual for more than one year's assessment to be re-opened and it is obviously desirable, given the interest penalty, that both sides identify problem areas quickly.

Recently the Revenue issued some practice notes ([1981] STI 42–44) which were designed to guide overseas companies which have, or may be thinking of trading in the UK. In these notes a section deals with methods of and considerations taken into account in arriving at arm's length prices. The relevant section of the notes is reproduced below:—

> 'In ascertaining an arm's length price the Inland Revenue will often look for evidence of prices in similar transactions between parties who are in fact operating at arm's length. They may however find it more useful in some circumstances to start with the re-sale price of the goods or services etc, and arrive at the relevant arm's length purchase price by deducting an appropriate mark up. They may find it more convenient on the other hand to start with the cost of the goods or services and arrive at the arm's length price by adding an appropriate mark up. But they will in practice use any method which seems likely to produce a satisfactory result. They will be guided in their search for an arm's length price by the considerations set out in the OECD report on multinationals and transfer pricing. (This report examines the considerations which need to be taken into account in arriving at arm's length prices in general and also in the context of sales of goods, the provision of intra group services, the transfer of technology and rights to use trade marks within a group and the provision of intra group loans).

In practice these methods have been supplemented by:—

(a) comparisons with other taxpayers;
(b) other published economic information and statistics;
(c) representations of the company.

To date one of the problems which has arisen is that the Revenue have been unwilling to disclose in detail the origin and basis of their calculations. In particular, problems have arisen in two areas:—

(a) integrated groups with complicated production schedules. In these cases it has been difficult to identify a market value for each separate part of the production process;
(b) firms who add fixed profit margins to the cost of goods sold abroad by distributors, despite selling at a lower price in the UK. The Revenue have argued that the overseas pricing policy should take into account the losses in the UK whilst the companies have argued that this makes no sense when other foreign distributors are operating on fixed margins.

In the case of inter-company services the Revenue have not been hostile to contributions to head office costs but the taxpayer has obviously been asked to justify these and this has necessitated fairly detailed documentation. This attitude is obviously far more relaxed where the UK company charges an overseas affiliate for services.

The same considerations as those discussed above in connection with goods and services have been applied to charges for tangibles and intangibles. In the former case, legislation has been enacted to counter abuses that arose from cross boundary leasing. The other main charge relates to the cost of finance. The Revenue have argued, particularly in relation to oil companies, that interest should be restricted to a maximum of debt to capital employed of 80%. It is arguable that TA 1970, s. 485 only affects the **rate of interest** and not that debt would have been substituted for equity if the transaction had been at arm's length. Based on the arguments in **6.3** above this view is correct and the Revenue's approach should be firmly and decisively rejected.

In the practice document referred to above two sections are particularly relevant and these cover:—

(a) Exchange of information with other countries

Disclosure is permitted (under strict safeguards) to other countries' tax authorities under agreements for double tax relief and under the directive concerning mutual assistance between tax authorities of the member states of the European Community. (The Inland Revenue may also receive information from other countries under these instruments).

(b) Consultation with other countries

The Inland Revenue recognise that transfer pricing adjustments may have a consequence not only for UK tax but also for foreign tax. They are able, under the terms of some seventy agreements for the relief of double taxation and the prevention of fiscal evasion, to exchange information with the tax authorities of their partner countries on transfer pricing matters and they often do this for the purpose of ensuring that tax is adequately charged in the UK. On the other hand, they are also able to consult and do consult with partner countries with a view to preventing unrelievable double taxation arising from (among other causes) the adjustment of transfer prices. A taxpayer who fears that unrelievable double taxation may result in his own case from some action of the tax authorities of a treaty partner may ask the UK Inland Revenue to enter into such consultation and they will do so whenever the need arises. All that such a taxpayer need do is to write a letter putting his request, and giving the relevant details, to the International Tax Policy Division of the Inland Revenue in Somerset House, London. For such consultation to be effective, however, it will usually be necessary for the request to be made in good time so as not to be frustrated by the expiry of legal limits for tax adjustments either in the UK or in the other country.

6.5 Conclusions

These can be divided into two distinct groups, namely those which relate to the current legislation and those which relate to the form future legislation might take. In practical terms the question of whether a transaction is within TA 1970, s. 485 is a question of law; having established that a transaction is within TA 1970, s. 485 the question of whether the transaction is at an over or under value is one of fact. To date TA 1970, s. 485 has not been litigated but if the transaction falls within the first limb – a question of law – such a case would almost certainly go to the highest appellate courts. However, if the case is within the second limb – a question of fact – a finding by the Special Commissioners will not be lightly overturned by the higher courts. It follows that in the latter cases the importance of assembling the underlying facts skilfully and painstakingly cannot be overstated.

Having said this the next question is what future legislation can we expect and what form will it take? It would not be surprising, given the practice notes issued by the Revenue and referred to above, if detailed legislation similar to that in the United States and Western Germany is introduced here. It must be said that the experience of the United States and Western Germany with its legislation is that legislation does not necessarily lead to greater certainty in the operation of the law, but in many cases to greater uncertainty. In a number of instances this uncertainty has amounted to harassment and it is hoped that if such legislation is introduced in the UK it will be administered in a manner acceptable to both companies and the Revenue.

7 Artificial transactions in land

7.1 Introduction

In practice perhaps the most frequently encountered anti-avoidance section advisers are called upon to interpret is TA 1970, s. 488. This arises because the section covers both direct and indirect gains attributable to land. As a result of the wide nature of the latter advisers often overlook, at their peril, this section when advising on transactions where the land element is not immediately apparent, e.g. the sale of a majority shareholding, the value of which is derived from land. This chapter will review the scope and possible coverage of this section and discuss the two fully reported cases to date this section has given rise to: *Yuill v Wilson* [1980] STC 460 and *Winterton v Edwards Byfield v Edwards* [1980] STC 206. A third case, *Chilcott v IRC* [1981] STI 403, has now been heard but a full report was not available to the author at the date of writing this chapter. As a result it will only be possible to briefly review this case.

TA 1970, s. 488 is not a self-contained provision. TA 1970, s. 489 supplements both TA 1970, ss. 488 and 487 (the sale by an individual of income derived from personal activities) and in the main, defines in more detail the terms used in these sections. The power to obtain information for the purposes of these two sections is set out in TA 1970, s. 490.

This chapter will be of importance not only to property developers but also to any company contemplating a transaction where land is acquired and subsequently resold. It could, therefore, apply where a family controlled company purchased a development site and erected a building on the land, which it subsequently sold and leased back to an institution.

7.2 The statutory provisions

TA 1970, s. 488 reads as follows:—

> **488 Artificial transactions in land**
>
> (1) This section is enacted to prevent the avoidance of tax by persons concerned with land or the development of land.

(2) This section applies wherever:—

(a) land, or any property deriving its value from land, is acquired with the sole or main object of realising a gain from disposing of the land, or

(b) land is held as trading stock, or

(c) land is developed with the sole or main object of realising a gain from disposing of the land when developed,

and any gain of a capital nature is obtained from the disposal of the land:—

(i) by the person acquiring, holding or developing the land, or by any connected person, or

(ii) where any arrangement or scheme is effected as respects the land which enables a gain to be realised by any indirect method, or by any series of transactions, by any person who is a party to, or concerned in, the arrangement or scheme;

and this subsection applies whether any such person obtains the gain for himself or for any other person.

(3) Where this section applies, the whole of any such gain shall for all the purposes of the Tax Acts be treated:—

(a) as being income which arises when the gain is realised, and which constitutes profits or gains chargeable to tax under Case VI of Sch. D for the chargeable period in which the gain is realised, and

(b) subject to the following provisions of this section, as being income of the person by whom the gain is realised.

(4) For the purposes of this section land is disposed of if, by any one or more transactions, or by any arrangement or scheme, whether concerning the land or property deriving its value from the land, the property in the land, or control over the land, is effectually disposed of, and references in subs. (2) above to the acquisition or development of property with the sole or main object of realising the gain from disposing of the land shall be construed accordingly.

(5) For the said purposes:—

(a) where, whether by a premature sale or otherwise, a person directly or indirectly transmits the opportunity of making a gain to another person, that other person's gain is obtained for him by the first-mentioned person, and

(b) any number of transactions may be regarded as constituting a single arrangement or scheme if a common purpose can be discerned in them, or if there is other sufficient evidence of a common purpose.

(6) For the purposes of this section such method of computing a gain shall be adopted as is just and reasonable in the circumstances, taking into account the value of what is obtained for disposing of the land, and allowing only such expenses as are attributable to the land disposed of, and in applying this subsection:—

(a) where a freehold is acquired and the reversion is retained on disposal, account may be taken of the way in which the profits or gains under Case I of Sch. D of a person dealing in land are computed in such a case, and

(b) account may be taken of the adjustments to be made in computing such profits or gains under subss. (2), (3) and (4) of s. 142 of this Act (allowance for tax on premiums on leases).

In the application of this subsection to Scotland, "freehold" means the estate or interest of the proprietor of the *dominium utile* or, in the case of property other than feudal property, of the owner, and "reversion" means the interest of the landlord in property subject to a lease.

(7) Subsection (2) (c) of this section shall not apply to so much of any gain as is fairly attributable to the period, if any, before the intention to develop the land was formed, and which would not fall under para. (a) or para. (b) of that subsection; and in applying this subsection account shall be taken of the treatment under Case I of Sch. D of a person who appropriates land as trading stock.

(8) If all or any part of the gain accruing to any person is derived from value, or an opportunity of realising a gain, provided directly or indirectly, by some other person, whether or not put at the disposal of the first-mentioned person, subs. (3) (b) of this section shall apply to the gain, or that part of it, with the substitution of that other person for the person by whom the gain was realised.

(9) This section shall not apply to a gain accruing to an individual which by virtue of ss. 101 to 105 of the Capital Gains Act 1979 (private residences) is exempt from capital

gains tax, or which would be so exempt but for the provisions of s. 103 (3) of that Act (residence acquired partly with a view to making a gain).

(10) Where there is a disposal of shares in:—

(a) a company which holds land as trading stock, or

(b) a company which owns directly or indirectly 90% or more of the ordinary share capital of another company which holds land as trading stock,

and all the land so held is disposed of in the normal course of its trade by the company which held it, and so as to procure that all opportunity of profit in respect of the land arises to that company, then this section shall not by virtue of subs. (2) (i) apply to any gain to the holder of shares as being a gain on property deriving value from that land (but without prejudice to any liability under para. (ii) of the said subs. (2)).

(11) Where a person who considers that para. (a) or para. (c) of subs. (2) of this section may apply as respects a gain of a capital nature which that person has obtained from the disposal of land, or which he would obtain from a proposed disposal of land, supplies to the inspector to whom he makes his return of income written particulars showing how the gain has arisen or would arise:—

(a) the inspector shall, within thirty days from his receipt of the particulars, notify that person whether or not he is satisfied that, in the circumstances as described in the particulars, the gain will not, or would not, be chargeable to tax on that person under this section, and

(b) if the inspector notifies that person that he is so satisfied the gain shall not be chargeable on that person under this section:

Provided that if the particulars given under this section with respect to the gain are not such as to make full and accurate disclosure of all facts and considerations relating thereto which are material to be known to the inspector, any notification given by the inspector under this subsection shall be void.

(12) In this section:—

(a) references to the land include references to all or any part of the land, and "land" includes buildings, and any estate or interest in land or buildings;

(b) references to property deriving its value from land include:—

(i) any shareholding in a company, or any partnership interest, or any interest in settled property, deriving its value directly or indirectly from land, and

(ii) any option, consent or embargo affecting the disposition of land,

and for the purposes of this section any question whether a person is connected with another shall be determined in accordance with s. 533 of this Act.

(13) This section shall apply to all persons, whether resident in the UK or not, if all or any part of the land in question is situated in the UK.

(14) This section shall not apply to any gain realised before 15 April 1969.

Section 489 reads as follows:—

489 Sale of income and land transactions (ss. 487 and 488): supplemental

(1) This section has effect to supplement ss. 487 and 488 above (in this section called "the principal sections").

(2) In applying the principal sections and this section account shall be taken of any method, however indirect, by which:—

(a) any property or right is transferred or transmitted, or

(b) the value of any property or right is enhanced or diminished,

and accordingly the occasion of the transfer or transmission of any property or right, however indirect, and the occasion when the value of any property or right is enhanced, may be an occasion when, under the principal sections, tax becomes chargeable.

(3) Subsection (2) above applies in particular:—

(a) to sales, contracts and other transactions made otherwise than for full consideration or for more than full consideration, and

(b) to any method by which any property or right, or the control of any property or right, is transferred or transmitted by assigning share capital or other rights in a company or any partnership or interest in settled property, and

(c) to the creation of any option or consent or embargo affecting the disposition of any property or right, and to the consideration given for the option, or for the giving of the consent or the release of the embargo, and

(d) to the disposal of any property or right on the winding up, dissolution or termination of any company, partnership or trust.

(4) In ascertaining for the said purposes the intentions of any persons, the objects and powers of any company, partners or trustees, as set out in any memorandum, articles of association or other document, shall not be conclusive.

(5) In order to ascertain whether and to what extent the value of any property or right is derived from any other property or right, value may be traced through any number of companies, partnerships and trusts, and the property held by any company, partnership or trust shall be attributed to the shareholders, partners or beneficiaries at each stage in such manner as is appropriate in the circumstances.

(6) In applying the principal sections and this section:—

(a) any expenditure or receipt or consideration or other amount may be apportioned by such method as is just and reasonable in the circumstances,

(b) all such valuations shall be made as are appropriate to give effect to the principal sections.

(7) For the purposes of the principal sections and this section (and in particular for the purpose of the reference in s. 487 above to an individual putting some other person in a position to enjoy income or receipts) partners, or the trustees of settled property, or personal representatives, may be regarded as persons distinct from the individuals or other persons who are for the time being partners or trustees or personal representatives.

(8) Where a person is assessed to tax under either of the principal sections, with this section, in respect of consideration receivable by another person:—

(a) he shall be entitled to recover from that other person any part of that tax which he has paid, and

(b) if any part of that tax remains unpaid at the expiration of six months from the date when it became due and payable, it shall be recoverable from that other person as though he were the person assessed, but without prejudice to the right to recover it from the person actually assessed,

and for the purposes of para. (a) above the Board or an inspector shall on request furnish a certificate specifying the amount of income in respect of which tax has been paid, and the amount of tax so paid; and the certificate shall be conclusive evidence of any facts stated therein.

For the purposes of this subsection any income which a person is treated as having by virtue of the principal sections shall, subject to s. 529 of this Act, be treated as the highest part of his income.

(9) If it appears to the Board that any person entitled to any consideration or other amount taxable under the principal sections is not resident in the UK, the Board may direct that s. 53 of this Act (payments not out of profits or gains brought into charge to income tax) shall apply to any payment forming part of that amount as if it were an annual payment charged with tax under Case III of Sch. D, but without prejudice to the final determination of the liability of that person, including any liability under subs. (8) (b) above.

(10) The principal sections have effect subject to Part XVI of this Act and to any other provision of the Tax Acts deeming income to belong to a particular person.

(11) Where under s. 488 (2) (c) above any person is charged to tax on the realisation of a gain, and the computation of the gain proceeded on the footing that the land or some other property was appropriated at any time as trading stock, that land or other property shall be treated on that footing also for the purposes of s. 122 of the Capital Gains Tax Act 1979 . . . (capital gains: property becoming or ceasing to be stock in trade).

(12) Where under s. 487 (1) (b) or 488 (8) above the person charged to tax is a person other than the person for whom the capital amount was obtained or the person by whom the gain was realised, and the tax has been paid, then, for the purposes of ss. 31 and 33 of the Capital Gains Tax Act 1979 (profits taxable as income to be excluded from tax

on capital gains), the person for whom the capital amount was obtained or the person by whom the gain was realised shall be regarded as having been charged to that tax.

(13) For the purposes of the principal sections and this section:—
"capital amount" means any amount, in money or money's worth, which, apart from the principal sections, does not fall to be included in any computation of income for purposes of the Tax Acts, and other expressions including the word "capital" shall be construed accordingly,
"company" includes any body corporate,
"share" includes stock,
and for the said purposes any amount in money or money's worth shall not be regarded as having become receivable by some person until that person can effectively enjoy or dispose of it.

7.3 The provisions in detail

Whilst the heading to TA 1970, s. 488 refers to artificial transactions in land, subs. (1) states that the purpose of the section is to prevent the avoidance of tax by persons concerned with land or the development of land. It will, therefore, apply to bona fide commercial transactions where the avoidance of tax can be shown. Before the section can be invoked three conditions must be satisfied:—

(a) there must be a transaction in land;
(b) there must be a gain of a capital nature from the disposal of land; and
(c) the gain must be realised by a person falling within TA 1970, s. 488 (2) (i) or (ii).

7.3.1 Transactions in land

The first condition is set out in the form of three alternatives (TA 1970, s. 488 (2) (a), (b) and (c)) any one of which will bring the section into effect. Alternatives (a) and (b) are very similar.

It is important to note that (a) and (b) will only be satisfied where the sole or main object is to realise a gain from the disposal of land. This provision is intended to cover the situation where a man sells land for £50,000 a week prior to buying it for £20,000 as in *Johnston v Heath* (1970) 46 TC 463. This is a subjective test and one which puts the onus on the Revenue to satisfy. In relation to TA 1970, s. 170 (hobby farmers' losses) and TA 1970, s. 460 (transactions in securities) the Revenue have not been conspicuously successful but it must be conceded that whenever a person acquires land they invariably hope that it will rise in value. This would seem to suggest that the Revenue are not likely to encounter as much difficulty in applying TA 1970, s. 488 as they have had with TA 1970, ss. 170 and 460. If this is correct, the scope of TA 1970, s. 488 could be very wide.

For instance, suppose a taxpayer initially acquired a factory for use in his business and after several years of operating the factory at a loss he decided to build a supermarket. If the supermarket is sold on completion, how easy or otherwise would it be for the Revenue to establish that the sole or main object of building the supermarket was to realise a gain? Whilst each case will turn on its own unique facts the following principles will be applied to those facts. One of the first points the Inland Revenue will check are the powers in the company's memorandum and articles of association. TA 1970, s. 489 (4) formalises what was already common practice in connection with these documents, by stating that the intentions, objects and powers contained in these documents are not conclusive evidence of these matters. The most important factor is likely to be the commercial realities underlying the disposal. If the company had to build and sell the supermarket to survive it is clear that the main object of developing the land was to realise a gain and so the disposal will be within TA 1970, s. 488 (2) (c). However, if before selling the supermarket, the firm raised sufficient medium or long term funds to ensure the continuity of the business and there was a 'healthy' interval between raising the funds and selling the supermarket it would be very difficult for the Revenue to show that the disposal was necessary to ensure the continuity of the business. It has also been suggested that the requirement actually to obtain longer term funds may not be necessary if the business could show that, in the absence of the funds from the development, it could have raised the requisite funds from an outside source. Whilst this question will be debatable in many circumstances, it will be easier for the larger firm to resist the Revenue's argument than the smaller firm. This is because the impact on the balance sheet of the smaller company is likely to be greater than on the balance sheet of the larger company. A more subtle point is that the larger firm, with a more diversified portfolio of assets, is likely to find it easier to persuade the Inland Revenue that the funds released from a development and used to fund replacement and expansion could have been obtained from outside sources, than the smaller firm. In both cases the funds released from the development may be necessary to ensure the long run viability of each business, but the tax treatment of the funds released may well differ.

7.3.2 Gain of a capital nature

The second condition is that there must be a gain of a capital nature and readers are referred to **7.2** above, TA 1970, s. 488 (4). A disposal of land will cover anything beyond a non-binding gentleman's agreement relating to its disposal. Further, the distinction between the contract and the conveyance will not be important as the section is concerned with realised gains. The payment of the consideration will therefore be of crucial importance; where payment has been made of money or in the form of other consideration, this will be sufficient to satisfy the section's need for a disposal, whatever the state might otherwise be of the transaction.

The sale of a majority shareholding in a company with a substantial portfolio of land would clearly be within this subsection, as would the sale of land owned by a joint venture. It follows that minority shareholdings would not be within this definition but the position would be less clear where several minority shareholders (whose holdings amounted to a majority) sold their holdings, either on the same date or within a very short time interval of each other. What is also unclear from this definition is whether it would cover the sale of an investment in an associated company, as defined for financial reporting purposes and not within the meaning of TA 1970, s. 302 (1) whose main asset was land. The term 'associated company', for financial reporting purposes, is defined in Statement of Standard Accounting Practice 1, Accounting Standards Committee, January 1971 as a shareholding in excess of 20% but less than 50% where the company owning the shares also takes part in the management of the associate. If the term 'control' is narrowly construed it will only apply to shareholdings which carry powers in excess of those normally attributable to such shareholdings. Widely construed it would cover both the sale of an investment in an associated company, and where several minority shareholders (whose combined holdings were in excess of 50%) sold their shares within a short interval of each other.

7.3.3 Who will be within the term 'person', TA 1970, s. 488 (2) (i) and (ii)

It seems to be generally agreed that the word 'developed' is not likely to be given the same meaning as that in the planning legislation. It would seem to refer to all alterations and would include building and conversion work which changes the nature of the property. It would exclude minor repairs and plans for developing a site, including the making of an application for planning permission (*Taylor v Good* [1974] STC 148).

In applying subs. (2), any number of transactions may be regarded as constituting a single arrangement or scheme, if either a common purpose can be discovered, or there is sufficient evidence of a common purpose. What will constitute sufficient evidence has not yet been established by any working practices of the Revenue but it is hoped that a strict interpretation will be given to this subsection, as it may cover transactions not originally intended by the legislation. It has been suggested that this section would cover the sale by a UK resident of a piece of land to a non-resident trust at market value prior to planning permission. If the trust sold the land at a substantial profit after planning permission had been granted the gain could only be taxed on the basis that it was a trading gain. However, as a result of this section the Revenue are able to raise an assessment on the person who provided the opportunity to realise the gain.

The scope of TA 1970, s. 488 (2) (i) and (ii) is further widened by TA 1970, s. 489 (2) and (3). The all-embracing nature of these provisions is restricted by TA 1970, s. 488 (10). This exemption applies where there is a disposal of shares in a company which:—

(a) holds land as trading stock; or
(b) owns directly or indirectly 90% or more of the ordinary share capital of another company which holds land as trading stock.

The effect of this provision is that where land is sold in the normal course of trading and all the profit in respect of that land arises to a company within either (a) or (b), the gain which might accrue to the holder of the shares as being a gain on property deriving value from that land will not be treated as within the principal charging subsection (subs. (2)). This is a restricted exemption and only applies to cases where a person is holding or developing land and not where this is a part of a scheme or arrangement.

7.4 Procedural matters

7.4.1 Introduction

This question gives rise to three issues. These are firstly, the persons who may be assessable to tax under this section, secondly, the computation of the gain and thirdly, the power of the Revenue to obtain information in relation to TA 1970, ss. 487 or 488 transactions.

7.4.2 Persons assessable

TA 1970, s. 488 (3) provides that the gain shall be treated as income of the year in which the gain is realised and chargeable to tax under Sch. D, Case VI. Subject to subs. (8) this gain will be assessed on the person who realises the gain. The latter subsection is much wider and provides that where the gain accrues to one person and the opportunity to realise the gain, either directly or indirectly, is provided by some other person, the assessment will be raised on that other person.

It is obvious that where a person directly realises a gain which is assessable to tax under TA 1970, s. 488 he is responsible for the tax liability. Where the consideration has been received by another person, the first mentioned person is entitled to recover from that other person the tax that is attributable to the consideration received by that other person (TA 1970, s. 489 (8)). If the tax remains unpaid for six months it is recoverable from that other person, but this is without prejudice to the right of the Revenue to recover the outstanding amount from the person actually assessed.

The above analysis has made no reference to the questions of whether TA 1970, s. 488 is confined to land in the UK and whether a person must be resident before the section can be invoked. In this context subs. (13) states that the section shall apply to all persons, irrespective of residency in the UK, if all or any part of the land in question is situated in the UK.

There are two possible interpretations of this section:—

(a) it is intended to be a geographical limitation only in so far as non-residents are concerned as it would not be possible to collect the tax in respect of overseas land;
(b) it only applies to UK land and does not apply in the case of land situated overseas.

In most cases the second view is correct. Three reasons can be advanced to support this proposition:—

(a) The 'source' doctrine. The essence of this doctrine is that tax legislation will only be effective to the extent that it covers either property or persons within the jurisdiction.
(b) Other statutes dealing with land transactions have restricted their scope to land situated in the UK, see s. 38 (1) Finance Act 1974.
(c) The second interpretation seems to accord more closely with the natural meaning of the statute, which is the normal rule for interpreting a statute.

This writer is of the view that (b) and (c) are far from convincing. The most compelling reason from a pragmatic viewpoint is (a). No foreign court would recognise a claim by the Inland Revenue over land under its jurisdiction. However, the position is not clear, where, for instance, a UK controlled company owns land overseas and all the other conditions set out in TA 1970, s. 488 are present. There would seem to be no reason why s. 488 could not be invoked against the company, or in the last resort, the UK resident shareholder.

7.4.3 Computation of the gain

The relevant section (TA 1970, s. 488 (6)) is not very helpful. It merely states that it should be just and reasonable in the circumstances and should take into account what is obtained for the land and only allow such expenses as are attributable to the land that has been sold. This general rule is subject to four exceptions. These are:—

(a) where a freehold is acquired and the reversion is retained, account should be taken of the way in which the person's profits have been computed for Sch. D, Case I purposes (TA 1970, s. 488 (6) (a) and *Hughes v B G Utting & Co* (1940) 23 TC 174);
(b) premiums on leases which have already been assessed to tax under Sch. A (only the balance is assessable under TA 1970, s. 488 (6) (b));
(c) the gain attributable to the period prior to the intention to develop the land was formed (TA 1970, s. 488 (7));
(d) a sale of shares in a company which holds land as trading stock, whether directly or indirectly through a subsidiary.

Problems are likely to occur in the last two cases. In case (c) it will be very difficult to establish in any unequivocal sense that the main object of developing the land was to realise a gain and when the intention to develop was formed.

Where the Revenue succeed in showing that a person satisfies head (c) and are able to ascertain the time when the requisite intention was formed, the application of subs. (7) is likely to cause difficulties. As stated above this exempts the gain attributable to the period prior to the intention being formed to develop the land and also provides that account shall be taken of the treatment under Sch. D, Case I where a person appropriates land to trading stock.

CGTA 1979, s. 122 states that appropriations to trading stock are to be treated as a sale at market value. CGTA 1979, s. 150 defines market value in terms of the price the asset might reasonably fetch on the open market. This gain is subject to capital gains tax and the agreed market value will be the base cost of the TA 1970, s. 488 computation. This begs the question as to what is meant by market value in the context of land and without planning consent – is it current use value, or must an element of 'hope value' be added which reflects the likelihood of planning consent being granted? The latter accords more closely with the terms of CGTA 1979, s. 150 referred to above. There is a third possibility – the value of the land with planning consent. In most cases this would give rise to a substantial gain and unless land prices moved significantly during the period of the development most of the gain would be taxed as a capital gain. This would seem contrary to the purpose of this section and so in practice is unlikely to be acceptable.

In the case of (d) 'a sale of shares in a company which holds land as trading stock', suppose A and B are the sole shareholders of such a company and sell their shares to C. The gains could be (and are likely to be) taxable under TA 1970, s. 488. If the company then sells all the land it seems that A and B would be able to reclaim the tax paid in respect of their shares. But what will be the position if land is sold after the six year time period referred to in TMA 1970, ss. 33 and 34. Will the shareholders be able to reclaim the tax paid under TA 1970, s. 488 and secondly, will they then have to pay capital gains tax?

7.4.4 Power to obtain information

Under TA 1970, s. 490, the Board of Inland Revenue, or an inspector, may by notice in writing require any person to furnish them within such time as the Board or the inspector direct (but not less than 30 days) such particulars as they think necessary for the purposes of TA 1970, s. 488. The particulars which a person must furnish under TA 1970, s. 488 (see TA 1970, s. 490 (2)) include details of:—

(a) transactions or arrangements in which he is or was acting on behalf of others; and

(b) transactions or arrangements which in the opinion of the Board or the inspector should properly be investigated in pursuance of TA 1970, s. 488. This applies even though, in the opinion of the person to whom the notice is given, no liability to tax will arise under TA 1970, s. 488; and

(c) whether the person who has been served with the notice has taken or is taking any, and if so what, part in any, and if so what, transactions or arrangements of a description specified in the notice.

A solicitor shall not be deemed for the purpose of (c) to have taken part in any transactions or arrangements by reason only that he has given professional advice to a client in that connection. In relation to anything done by him on behalf of a client he shall not be compellable, except with the consent of his client, to do more than state that he is or was acting on behalf of a client and to supply details of his client's name and address.

TA 1970, s. 490 has recently been the subject of litigation (*Essex v IRC* [1980] STC 378). The Court of Appeal held:—

(a) the word 'particulars' in the context of a notice was to be construed as synonymous with information and not limited to details of specific transactions or arrangements. It followed that the power conferred on the Commissioners or the inspector by TA 1970, s. 490 (1) was wide enough to require information not related to specific transactions or arrangements; and

(b) the fact that certain terms in the notice were not precisely defined did not render it void and of no effect. The precision of expression was not necessary in a statutory notice which did no more than require the recipient to answer to the best of his information, knowledge and belief.

It is clear from this judgment that the statute has conferred very wide discretionary information powers on the Revenue and the wide interpretation given to this anti-avoidance section by the Court of Appeal accords with judicial policy in relation to anti-avoidance sections.

7.5 Case law

It was stated in **7.1** that two cases have been litigated under TA 1970, s. 488. The cases are *Yuill v Wilson* [1980] STC 460 and *Winterton v Edwards* [1980] STC 206.

7.5.1 *Yuill v Wilson* [1980] STC 460

In *Yuill v Wilson* the taxpayer was a director and chairman of a prosperous building firm ('Y Ltd') in which he, together with English trustees of a trust for the benefit of his family, held a controlling interest. Y Ltd owned two pieces of land which it sold to P Ltd and D Ltd, respectively. The shares in those companies were also owned by the taxpayer and the trustees of the family trust.

In September 1972 the taxpayer formed a settlement in Guernsey for his family and appointed Guernsey residents as trustees. The trustees of this settlement then formed two companies, C Ltd and M Ltd, the shares of which were held by the trustees on trust for the settlement. In December 1972 C Ltd bought for £45,000 the land which had been sold by Y Ltd to P Ltd. This was followed in January 1973 by the acquisition by M Ltd for £81,000 of the land D Ltd had purchased from Y Ltd.

It was common ground that both prices represented the full undeveloped market value of the land. Planning permission had been refused for the land sold to C Ltd, but an appeal was contemplated by Y. It was thought that planning permission might be granted in respect of the land sold to M Ltd. The land sold to C Ltd was 'fen land' and that sold to M Ltd was 'quarry land' (hereinafter these two terms will be used in the text where appropriate to describe the land owned by these two companies).

The acquisitions by C Ltd and M Ltd were for the sole or main purpose of realising a gain from their disposal. In January 1974 the trustees sold the shares in C Ltd and M Ltd to a Guernsey trust company, whose shares were held on trust by the same trustees for overseas beneficiaries. Whilst it was agreed that the Yuill family were not beneficiaries of the trust, there would be nothing to stop a beneficiary of the trust from subsequently benefiting members of the Yuill family. In other words it was not established whether there was some arrangement, however tacit, ultimately to benefit the Yuill family.

In the events which happened planning permission was granted for the land owned by C Ltd, the fen land, one week after the sale of the shares in C Ltd and M Ltd by the trustees. Subsequently in March 1974 C Ltd sold the land to Y Ltd for £700,000 and M Ltd sold the quarry land to Y Ltd for £648,000. The taxpayer, Yuill, was assessed to income tax under Sch. D, Case VI, for the fiscal year 1973–74. The basis of the assessment was that gains of a capital nature had accrued to C Ltd and M Ltd from the disposal of the land and the taxpayer was substituted for these two companies under TA 1970, s. 488 (2).

Before the General Commissioners it was held that the transactions had been carried out pursuant to an arrangement or scheme in which the taxpayer, C Ltd and M Ltd were all concerned and that although the taxpayer was not a party to any of the transactions he had provided C Ltd and M Ltd with an opportunity of realising a gain and so was within TA 1970, s. 488 (8). The taxpayer appealed on the ground that the relevant transactions were at market value and consequently TA 1970, s. 488 had no application. In the High Court, Templeman J held that for TA 1970, s. 488 to be brought into operation it was not the price given for the opportunity to realise the gain but the motive of the person providing the opportunity to realise the gain. If the motive was avoidance of tax the transactions were within TA 1970, s. 488 even though the transactions were at market value. The High Court then went on to uphold the findings of the Commissioners.

The findings of the Commissioners and the High Court were taken to the Court of Appeal, together with the question of whether the full amount of the consideration should be brought into the computation of the gain, even though most of it was contingent on the land in question not being nationalised within a specified period and that during this period a large proportion of the consideration had to be deposited with a third party.

The Court of Appeal agreed with the findings of the High Court that s. 488 could be applied even though the transfer had been at market value where the motive of the transfer was the avoidance of tax. They also agreed with the taxpayer that contingent consideration (the deposit with the third party) did not have to be brought into the calculation of the gain until the consideration became payable. The Court also made some interesting findings on the construction to be given to TA 1970, s. 488 (8).

In the leading judgment, Buckley LJ considered in some detail the meaning of the expression 'indirectly provided'. He thought that possession of legal capacity to transfer the opportunity was not a prerequisite of subs. (8) and recognised that a person might have de facto power to transfer the opportunity to another person. This wider construction was justified on the grounds that any other conclusion would frustrate the purpose of the section. This comes very close to saying that the substance of the transaction must be examined rather than the form and seems contrary to the dicta expressed in *Duke of Westminster v IRC* ((1935) 19 TC 490), and reiterated in *Floor v Davis* [1979] STC 379.

However, his Lordship did concede that such a construction was penal in character. The consequence of this was to render a person liable to tax who would not have been had the evasive action not been taken and the gain been realised by the person who had provided the opportunity of realising it. As such it was important that all the necessary facts should be explicitly and clearly found by the tribunal of fact, i.e. the commissioners. In his view this condition had not been met and so he thought the matter should be sent back to the commissioners to make such findings of fact, given his judgment and what further evidence might be put forward. This a surprising decision, given the findings of the commissioners as reported. Goff LJ in his judgment also considered the meaning of subs. (8). In the context of discussing both subs. (8) and the particular words 'whether or not put at the disposal of the first-mentioned person', he stated:—

> 'I find it very difficult to appreciate precisely what those last-mentioned words were intended to cover. In the case of value I can well see that a gain may be derived by one person from value provided by another, whether directly or indirectly, without that value being put at the disposal of the first-mentioned person; for example, if A pays money to B as consideration for the grant of an option to C. As at present advised, however, I find it very difficult to see how one can derive a gain from an opportunity provided by another, without that opportunity being put at the disposal of the first-mentioned person. I do not think it matters, however, at all events for present purposes, since the words do not exclude any case which would otherwise fall within the subsection, for it is to apply whether or not the value or opportunity be put at the disposal of the person making the gain, and the words do not seem to me to throw any light one way or another on the meaning of the words "an opportunity of realising a gain", provided directly or indirectly by some other person.'

In the House of Lords it was held:—

(a) The disposal of the land at market value to C Ltd and M Ltd did not prevent the application of TA 1970, s. 488 to the transactions.

(b) The commissioners' finding that the taxpayer 'either directly or through his companies and with the help of Guernsey trustees obtained for those companies a gain which fell within TA 1970, s. 488' necessarily implied finding that the taxpayer provided C Ltd and M Ltd with the opportunity of realising a gain within TA 1970, s. 488 (8). The remittal of the case by the Court of Appeal to the commissioners was therefore unnecessary and erroneous.

(c) Gains realised by another person involved consideration having 'become receivable' by that other person within TA 1970, s. 489 (13). Gains which could not be effectively enjoyed or disposed of could not be regarded as 'realised'. In computing the gains of C Ltd and M Ltd for the fiscal year 1973–74 the sums they were required to deposit were not to be taken into account. In addition the cost of the respective pieces of land and the expenses of sale were not to be spread over the years in which the companies might have realised the total sale price.

From this discussion it is clear that:—

(a) a transaction will be within TA 1970, s. 488 (2) even though it is at market value where the motive is to avoid tax;
(b) TA 1970, s. 488 (8) will be construed widely and as Goff LJ's speech indicates, its scope is very uncertain.

7.5.2 *Winterton v Edwards* [1980] STC 266

The second case, *Winterton v Edwards*, has only been heard at first instance, and is complicated by the fact that the relevant transactions form part of a wider and provocative tax scheme. The two taxpayers in the case were shareholders in a group of property dealing companies. Winterton ('W') held 4½% of the shares in the group and Byfield ('B') 5%; the remaining shares were owned by a Mr. Lyon ('L').

In 1970 W and B found out that L had embarked on some property development schemes on his own account but had used the facilities of the group to further his own private schemes. It was then agreed that L should pay the group for the services they had rendered, and that W and B should receive 4½% and 5% respectively of the profit on the development. Letters dated 1 May 1970 and 28 February 1971 confirmed the taxpayers' interests in each property and that the appropriate proportion of the proceeds of sale or other disposal would be held by L on trust for W and B absolutely. W and B were not parties to the sale of the sites in March 1971 and the proceeds of the disposal were received in three instalments, in January and September 1971 and February 1972. The Revenue assessed the capital sums received by W and B under TA 1970, s. 488 (2) and charged them in respect of 1970–71. The taxpayers appealed on four grounds:—

(a) They were not parties to the transactions and had no legal interest in the land within TA 1970, s. 488 (2).
(b) If they had such an interest they had acquired it by way of gift from L and not with the object of realising a gain from its disposition because they were not in a position to dispose of it.

(c) If the schemes fell within TA 1970, s. 488 the gains should be treated as those of L under TA 1970, s. 488 (8).
(d) In any event the assessments for 1970–71 should only be on the sum actually received.

The General Commissioners confirmed the assessments. On appeal to the High Court, Slade J held that:—

(a) The transactions were within TA 1970, s. 488 and the taxpayers were 'concerned in' them within TA 1970, s. 488 (a) (ii).
(b) Although most of the gains were actually received in 1971–72 it could not be said that those gains were not realised by them in 1970–71.
(c) L should not be substituted for the taxpayers.

As regards the first finding, the judge found that:—

(i) The commissioners had found that the land had been acquired by L with the sole or main object of realising a gain within TA 1970, s. 488 (2) (a).
(ii) The taxpayers were 'concerned in' the schemes within TA 1970, s. 488 (2) (ii) as it had been agreed between them and L that they should respectively receive 5% and 4½% of the sale proceeds and this had been confirmed in the letters dated 1 May 1970 and 28 February 1971.
(iii) The scheme 'enabled a gain to be realised' by the taxpayers.

The reasoning behind the second finding was to the effect that the letters referred to in (ii) above gave the taxpayers very clear rights and there was nothing which prevented them from effectively enjoying or disposing of their rights in the sale proceeds of the land. The third finding was based on the evidence before the commissioners and the fact that the taxpayers had received their interests in the land some time before the schemes were implemented. There was therefore no justification for shifting the burden of taxation to L.

7.5.3 *Chilcott v IRC*

In this case the taxpayers owned all the shares in a company, K Ltd, whose only asset was a virtually unsaleable property. When it became apparent that planning permission would be granted to develop the property K Ltd and M Ltd entered into the following transactions:—

(a) by an agreement dated 18 December 1972 M Ltd agreed to purchase the property from K Ltd in consideration for shares in M Ltd;

(b) on the same day the taxpayers agreed to sell all their shares in K Ltd to the TH Group in consideration for cash or fully paid shares in M Ltd or for shares in any other agreed company. This agreement was conditional on the sale of the property to M Ltd.

Subsequently in February 1973 the property was sold to M Ltd and the taxpayers were allotted the shares in M Ltd which K Ltd had acquired when the property had been sold to M Ltd. The Special Commissioners upheld the taxpayers' appeal against assessments to income tax under TA 1970, s. 488 on the disposal of their shares in K Ltd to the TH Group.

Vinelott J held that where a transaction is brought within s. 488 (2) (i) this also brings it within the exception within subs. (10). Where the gain arises from a disposal of shares that is to be treated as a gain obtained from the sale of land because the share disposal was part of an arrangement or scheme (subs. (2) (ii)) by which the property in the land or control over it was disposed of by the person holding the land (K Ltd) within the meaning of subs. (4), it must follow that the disposal of the shares must be treated as a disposal of shares in a company which at the material time held the land as trading stock within subs. (10). But in more simple and perhaps more robust terms, the transactions were not within s. 488 as the section is designed to cover the situation where a gain of a capital nature is realised by a developer or dealer and not where shares in a company holding land as trading stock are sold and the sale is conditional on the company selling the land in the normal course of its trade at full value. In practice this will not involve any complex points of law but a detailed consideration of all the relevant facts.

7.6 Conclusions

With regard to the earlier provision enacted in FA 1969, which subsequently became TA 1970, s. 488, it was said, shortly after its introduction, that this section seemed in parts designed to terrorise by its obscurity. Ten years later this comment is still applicable. Whilst the above analysis has shown that this obscurity has given rise to a number of, as yet, unanswered questions, the Inland Revenue practice until recently was to use the section sparingly.

Instead, the Revenue sought to tax these transactions under Sch. D, Case I.

From the taxpayer's point of view such an assessment is usually preferable to one under TA 1970, s. 488. However, this may not be so if the taxpayer has unrelieved Case VI losses, either brought forward or for the year in which the TA 1970, s. 488 assessment is raised. The significance of a TA 1970, s. 488 assessment is that it is treated as investment income under Case VI and so gives rise to a liability to the investment income surcharge. Losses under Sch. D, Case I in respect of the taxpayer's other activities are unaffected by this treatment.

From the Revenue's point of view it is often easier and more acceptable to the taxpayer's professional adviser to raise a Sch. D, Case I assessment rather than a Sch. D, Case VI assessment under TA 1970, s. 488. It is likely that the Revenue will continue this policy and only raise assessments under TA 1970, s. 488 where the facts are exceptional and these form part of a sophisticated tax avoidance scheme.

Unfortunately, the two recent cases will not be particularly helpful to those interpreting this section. Most of the issues raised were peripheral to the general application of the section and until more cases come before the courts, the scope of the section must remain uncertain. This uncertainty could be improved by improving the clearance mechanisms. In contemplating transactions which might be within this section it is unusual for the taxpayer's advisers to obtain clearance under TA 1970, s. 488 (11) and successful clearances have been something of a rarity. This reluctance can be attributed to the absence of a special department to handle applications, unlike clearances under TA 1970, s. 460 and as a result the process tends to be cumbersome and very slow moving. It is suggested that much of the uncertainty to which this section gives rise could be removed by having a clearance mechanism similar to TA 1970, s. 460.

8 Sale and leaseback transactions

8.1 Introduction

This chapter will examine the taxation treatment of sale and leaseback transactions. These provisions are contained in TA 1970, ss. 491–495 and FA 1972, s. 80. TA 1970, s. 491 and FA 1972, s. 80 cover the sale and leaseback of land. TA 1970, ss. 492–495 cover the sale and leaseback of all other assets. Whilst the provisions are similar there are a number of important differences. The first part of the chapter will review and discuss the provisions as they relate to land; the second part will discuss and review the provisions covering assets other than land.

8.2 Part 1. Land transactions: TA 1970, s. 491 and FA 1972, s. 80

8.2.1 Introduction

For most of the period since the end of the Second World War land values have consistently increased. Whilst investment in land has been and still is a sound investment it 'ties up' capital that could be used by industrial enterprises to expand their business. In the 1950s as a result of:—

(a) the need by industry and commerce for capital; and
(b) the increasing awareness by financial institutions of the investment potential of land,

it became quite common for capital to be raised by industry by what is known as 'sale and leaseback arrangements'. These worked as follows:—

(a) a business would sell all or some of the freehold land (and in some cases the buildings on the land) it owned to a financial institution for a capital sum;

(b) the institution would grant a long lease back to the business;
(c) the rental payments would be wholly deductible against trading profits and the capital sum, if received prior to 6 April 1965, would not be taxable; after that date corporation tax was payable on the chargeable gain.

In some cases the tax advantages were exploited by increasing both the capital sum and the rent payable under the lease. In the case of a trader the rental payments could be challenged on general principles, that is, the payments were not wholly and exclusively for the purposes of the trade but partly to realise a capital sum, TA 1970, s. 130. These were the grounds on which the following cases were decided: *IRC v Land Securities Investment Trust Ltd* (1969) 45 TC 495 and *Littlewoods Mail Order Stores v IRC* (1969) 45 TC 519.

TA 1970, s. 491 extends s. 130 by disallowing sums in excess of a commercial rent.

8.2.2 TA 1970, s. 491

TA 1970, section 491 reads as follows:—

491 Land sold and leased back: limitation on tax reliefs

(1) If land or any estate or interest in land is transferred from one person to another and:—
(a) as a result of a lease of the land or any part of the land granted at that time or subsequently by the transferee to the transferor, or
(b) as a result of any other transaction or series of transactions affecting the land or any estate or interest in the land,

the transferor, or any person who is associated with the transferor, becomes liable at the time of the transfer or subsequently to pay any rent under a lease of the land or any part of the land, this section shall apply to all rent due under the lease from the transferor, or from any person who is associated with the transferor.

(2) If land or any estate or interest in land is transferred from one person to another, and, as a result of any transaction or series of transactions affecting the land or any estate or interest in the land, the transferor, or any person who is associated with the transferor, becomes liable at the time of the transfer or subsequently to make any payment

(other than rent under a lease) for which tax relief of any of the kinds listed in subs. (13) below is available, being a payment by way of rentcharge on the land or any part of the land or a payment in any way connected with the land, this section shall apply to all such payments under the rentcharge or other transaction due from the transferor, or from any person who is associated with the transferor.

(3) The references in subss. (1) and (2) of this section to the transfer of an estate or interest in land include references to:—

(a) the granting of a lease or any other transaction involving the creation of a new estate or interest in the land,

(b) the transfer of the lessee's interest under a lease by surrender or forfeiture of the lease, and

(c) any transaction or series of transactions affecting land, or an estate or interest in land, such that some person is the owner, or one of the owners, before and after the carrying out of the transaction or transactions, but another person becomes or ceases to become one of the owners,

and in relation to any such transaction or series of transactions any person who is an owner before the carrying out of the transaction or transactions, and is not the sole owner thereafter, shall be regarded for the purposes of this section as a transferor.

(4) A deduction by way of tax relief which is one of the kinds to which this section applies, being a deduction in respect of rent or of any other payment to which this section applies, shall not exceed the commercial rent for the period for which the rent or other payment is made of the land in respect of which that payment is made.

(5) If under subs. (4) of this section part of a payment which would otherwise be allowable as a deduction by way of tax relief of one of the kinds to which this section applies is not so allowable, and one or more subsequent payments are made by the transferor, or a person who is associated with the transferor, under the lease or other transaction, that part of the first-mentioned payment may be carried forward and treated for the purposes of any such deduction by way of tax relief as if it were made at

the time when the next of those subsequent payments was made, and so made for the period for which that subsequent payment was made.

(6) For the purposes of subs. (4) of this section:—

(a) if more than one payment is made for the same period the payments shall be taken together,

(b) if payments are made for periods which overlap, the payments shall be apportioned, and the apportioned payments which belong to the common part of the overlapping periods shall be taken together,

(c) the preceding references to payments include references to parts of payments which under subs. (5) of this section are treated as if made at a time subsequent to that at which they were made, and to the extent that a part of a payment so carried forward under subs. (5) of this section is not so allowable as a deduction by way of tax relief, it may again be carried forward under subs. (5) of this section,

(d) so much of any payment as is in respect of services or the use of assets or rates usually borne by the tenant shall be excluded, and in determining the amount to be so excluded provisions in any lease or agreement fixing the payments or parts of payments which are in respect of services or the use of assets may be overridden.

(7) A payment made for a period all of which falls more than one year after the payment is made shall be treated for the purposes of this section as made for that period of one year beginning with the date on which the payment was made, and a payment for a period part of which falls after the end of that year shall be treated for those purposes as if a corresponding part of the payment was made for that year (and no part for any later period).

(8) For the purpose of making a comparison under subs. (4) of this section between a payment consisting of rent under a lease (in this subsection referred to as "the actual lease"), or such payments taken together, and the commercial rent of the land, "commercial rent" shall mean the rent which might be expected to be paid under a lease of the land negotiated in the open market at the time when the actual lease was created, being a lease which is of the same duration as the actual lease, which is, as

respects liability for maintenance and repairs, subject to the terms and conditions of the actual lease and which provides for rent payable at uniform intervals and:—

(a) at a uniform rate, or

(b) if the rent payable under the actual lease is rent at a progressive rate (and such that the amount of rent payable for any year is never less than the amount payable for any previous year), a rent which progresses by gradations proportionate to those provided by the actual lease.

(9) For the purpose of making a comparison under subs. (4) of this section between a payment which does not consist of rent under a lease (or such a payment taken together with other payments) and the commercial rent of the land, "commercial rent" shall mean the rent which might be expected to be paid under a tenant's repairing lease negotiated in the open market at the time when the transaction was effected under which the payment or payments became due, being:—

(a) where the period over which payments are to be made under that transaction is not less than 200 years, or the obligation to make such payments is perpetual, a lease for 200 years, and

(b) where that period is less than 200 years, a lease which is of the same duration as that period.

(10) In this section references to rent under a lease include references to rent which the person entitled to the lease is under subs. (2) or (3) of s. 83, or under s. 134, of this Act (allowance to person paying a premium taxed as income) treated, for any purpose, as paying in respect of land comprised in the lease, and such rent shall be treated for the purposes of this section as having been paid from day to day as it has become due.

(11) For the purposes of this section the following persons shall be deemed to be associated with one another, that is:—

(a) the transferor in any such transaction as is described in subs. (1) or subs. (2) of this section, and the transferor in another such transaction, if those two persons are acting in concert, or if the two transactions are in any way reciprocal, and any person who is an associate of either of those associated transferors;

(b) any two or more bodies corporate participating in, or incorporated for the purposes of, a scheme for the reconstruction of any body or bodies corporate or for the amalgamation of any two or more bodies corporate;

(c) any persons who are associates as defined in s. 494 (10) below.

(12) In this section:—

(a) "asset" means any description of property or rights other than land or an interest in land,

(b) "lease" includes an underlease, sublease or any tenancy or licence, and any agreement for a lease, underlease, sublease or tenancy or licence and, in the case of land outside the UK, any interest corresponding to a lease as so defined; and, in relation to such land, expressions in this section relating to interests in land and their disposition shall be construed accordingly,

(c) "rent" includes any payment made under a lease as so defined,

(d) "tenant's repairing lease" means a lease where the lessee is under an obligation to maintain and repair the whole, or substantially the whole, of the premises comprised in the lease.

(13) The kinds of deductions by way of tax relief to which this section applies are as follows:—

(a) a deduction in computing profits or gains chargeable under Sch. A allowable by virtue of ss. 71 to 77 of, and Sch. 2 to, this Act,

(b) a deduction in computing profits or gains or losses of a trade, profession or vocation for the purposes of tax,

(c) a deduction in computing profits or gains chargeable under Case VI of Sch. D, or in computing any loss for which relief is allowable under s. 176 or s. 179 of this Act (Case VI losses),

(d) allowance of a payment under s. 304 or 305 of this Act (management expenses),

(e) a deduction from emoluments to be assessed under Sch. E made in pursuance of s. 189 (1) of this Act (necessary expenses), or allowable in computing losses in an employment for tax purposes,

(f) a deduction allowable for tax purposes in computing profits or gains or losses arising from woodlands.

(14) This section shall not apply if the transfer described in subs. (1) or subs. (2) above was on or before 14 April 1964.

8.2.3 The scope of the provisions

Before TA 1970, s. 491 (4) can be invoked the conditions set out in either subs. (1) or (2) must be present. Subsection (1) covers where:—

(a) the transferee grants a lease to the transferor; or

(b) as a result of any other transaction or transactions relating to the land, or any estate or interest in the land,

rent is payable under a lease of the land or any part of the land by the transferor, or someone associated with the transferor.

Subsection (2) is much wider and covers where land or any estate or interest in land is transferred from one person to another and there is no leaseback of the land, but the transferor or someone connected with the transferor becomes liable either at the time of the transfer, or subsequently, to make a payment other than rent for which tax relief is available under one of the following headings:—

(a) Sch. A;

(b) Sch. D, Case I or II;

(c) Sch. D, Case VI;

(d) Management expenses;

(e) Sch. E expenses.

Payment in this context includes a rent charge and any other payment connected with the land.

Not surprisingly the terms 'transfer of an estate' and 'interest in land' are defined widely in subs. (3) to include:—

(a) the granting of a lease or any other transaction involving the creation of a new estate or interest in the land;

(b) the transfer of the lessee's interest under a lease by surrender or forfeiture of the lease; and

(c) any transaction where a person is the owner or one of the owners before and after the transaction but someone else becomes or ceases to be one of the owners and if the owner before the transaction is not the sole owner after the transaction he is to be treated as a transferor.

Where a payment is disallowed it can be carried forward and is treated as having been paid in the year relief is claimed. There is no time limit to carrying forward disallowed payments but where relief is claimed for a particular period another payment under the lease or transaction must be payable for that period.

In determining the quantum of allowable expenditure the following factors must be taken into account:—

(a) where more than one payment is made for the same period the payments will be aggregated;
(b) if payments relate to periods which overlap, the payments will be apportioned and where the apportioned payments belong to a common part of the overlapping periods they will be aggregated;
(c) any payment in respect of services, or for the use of assets other than land, or rates, which are usually borne by the tenant are excluded;
(d) where the payment is made for a period all of which falls more than one year after the payment is made it is treated as if made for that period of one year commencing with the date of payment;
(e) where a payment covers a period in excess of twelve months it is treated as a payment for twelve months commencing with the date of payment.

Commercial rent is defined in terms of the market rent which could be obtained from letting the property:—

(a) for the same period as the actual lease; and
(b) on the same terms and conditions as regards liability for maintenance and repairs as the actual lease; and
(c) at a rent payable at quarterly intervals and is either payable at a uniform rate or, where the lease provides for rent reviews, at a rent which increases at the same rate as that incorporated in the actual lease.

Where the payments do not consist of rent reserved under a lease the commercial rent is defined as the open market rent under a tenant's repairing lease, after taking into account when the payments fall due as follows:—

(a) where the time period over which the payments are to be made is more than 200 years, or the obligation to make such payments is perpetual, a lease for 200 years; and
(b) where the time period is less than 200 years, a lease of the same duration as the period over which the payments are to be made.

In summary, the effect of these very detailed provisions is to disallow the non-commercial element in the rent payable under the lease but to tax the recipient in full on the rent payable.

8.2.4 FA 1972, s. 80: Land sold and leased back: taxation of consideration received

Introduction

In the last twenty years there has been a marked increase in rental values; this trend has been exploited by lessees under leases which provided for a fixed rent. The absence of a rent review clause means that shortly after the lease takes effect the commercial rent for a lease of the same term will be in excess of the fixed rent. This situation was exploited as follows. The lessee for a capital sum would surrender his lease to the landlord and at the same time be granted a new lease at an increased rent. The capital sum would only be taxed at 30% and if increased rent payable under the new lease was commercial then it would be an allowable deduction in the computation of the lessee's profits. To counter this abuse the above section was introduced to tax a proportion of the capital as income.

8.2.5 FA 1972, s. 80: The statutory provisions

FA 1972, s. 80 reads as follows:—

> **80 Land sold and leased back: taxation of consideration received**
>
> (1) If, in any case where a person (in this section referred to as "the lessee") who is a lessee of land under a lease having not more than 50 years to run (in this section referred to as "the original lease") is entitled in respect of the rent under the lease to a deduction by way of tax relief of a kind to which s. 491 of the Taxes Act applies (land sold and leased back: limitation on tax reliefs):—
>
> (a) the lessee assigns the original lease to another person, or surrenders it to his landlord, for a consideration which apart from this section would not be taxable otherwise than as capital in the hands of the lessee, and
>
> (b) there is granted or assigned to the lessee another lease (in this section referred to as "the new lease") of or including the whole or any part of the land which was the subject of the original lease for a term not exceeding 15 years,
>
> then, subject to the following provisions of this section, the provisions of the Taxes Act providing for deductions or allowances by way of tax relief in respect of payments

of rent shall apply in relation to the rent under the new lease, and for the purposes of the Tax Acts a proportion of the consideration received by the lessee shall be treated not as a capital receipt but in accordance with subs. (3) below.

(2) For the purposes of this section:—

(a) if the aggregate of the rent payable under the new lease in respect of any rental period ending on a date falling before the 15th anniversary of the date on which the term of the new lease begins is greater than the aggregate of the rent payable under the new lease in respect of the period of equal duration beginning on the day following that date, then unless the term of the new lease would be treated as ending on an earlier date by virtue of para. (b) below, that term shall be treated as ending on that date, and

(b) if under the terms of the new lease either the lessor or the lessee has power to determine the new lease at a time before the expiry of the term for which it was granted or the lessee has power to vary his obligations under the new lease so as to reduce the rent which he would otherwise have to pay or in any other manner beneficial to him, then, unless the term of the new lease would be treated as ending on an earlier date by virtue of para. (a) above, that term shall be treated as ending on the earliest date with effect from which, in exercise of that power, the lessor or the lessee could determine the new lease or, as the case may be, the lessee could so vary his obligations;

and in any case where a rentcharge payable by the lessee is secured on the whole or any part of the property which is the subject of the new lease, the rent payable under the new lease shall be treated for the purposes of paras. (a) and (b) above as equal to the aggregate of the rentcharge and the rent payable under the terms of that lease.

(3) Subject to the following provisions of this section, the proportion of the consideration received by the lessee as mentioned in subs. (1) above, or of any instalment thereof, which for the purposes of the Tax Acts is to be treated not as a capital receipt but in accordance with this subsection shall be determined by the formula:—

$$\frac{16 - n}{15}$$

where "n" is the term of the new lease expressed in years or, if that term is less than a year, where "n" is 1; and that proportion shall be treated for the purposes of those Acts:—

(a) as a receipt of a trade, profession or vocation, if the rent payable by the lessee under the new lease is allowable as a deduction in computing profits or gains or losses of a trade, profession or vocation for the purposes of tax and if the consideration is received by the lessee in the course of that trade, profession or vocation, and

(b) in any other case, as a profit or gain chargeable under Case VI of Sch. D.

(4) In any case where the property which is the subject of the new lease does not include the whole of the property which was the subject of the original lease, the consideration received by the lessee shall be treated for the purposes of subs. (3) above as reduced to that portion thereof which is reasonably attributable to such part of the property which was the subject of the original lease as consists of, or is included in, the property which is the subject of the new lease.

(5) Schedule 3 to the Taxes Act (relief for individuals in respect of premiums taxable under Schs. D and A) shall have effect for the purpose of giving relief, on a claim being made in that behalf, from any increase in an individual's liability to income tax which is attributable to any amount being treated, by virtue of subs. (3) above, as an income receipt for a single year of assessment rather than as a series of such receipts during the term of the new lease; and in the application of that Schedule by virtue of this subsection, for the definitions of "chargeable sum" and "relevant period" there shall be substituted the following definitions:—

"chargeable sum" means the amount in respect of which, by virtue of subs. (3) above, the claimant is chargeable for income tax for the year of assessment;

"relevant period", in relation to any chargeable sum, means the term of the new lease.

(6) Where, by agreement with his landlord, the lessee varies the terms of the original lease in such a manner that, in return for such a consideration as is specified in subs. (1) (a)

above, the lessee undertakes to pay, during a period ending not later than 15 years after the date on which the consideration, or if the consideration is paid in instalments, the last instalment thereof, is paid to the lessee, a rent greater than that payable under the original lease, he shall be treated for the purposes of this section as having surrendered the original lease for that consideration and as having been granted a new lease for a term not exceeding 15 years but otherwise on the terms of the original lease as so varied.

(7) References in this section to the lessee (other than in subs. (1) (a) above) include references to a person who is a partner or associate of the lessee or an associate of a partner of the lessee; and for the purposes of this section the expression "associate" shall be construed in accordance with s. 494 (10) of the Taxes Act.

(8) Subject to subs. (7) above, expressions used in this section have the meanings assigned to them by s. 90 of the Taxes Act (interpretation of Part III), and in subs. (2) (a) above "rental period" means a period in respect of which a payment of rent falls to be made, and for the purposes of that subsection, in a case where the rental period is a quarter or a month, each such period shall be treated as of equal duration.

(9) The preceding provisions of this section shall not apply if the lessee had, before 22 June 1971, a right enforceable at law or in equity to the grant of the new lease, but in any case where, apart from this subsection, those provisions would apply, no part of the rent paid under the new lease shall be treated as a payment of capital, and the provisions of the Taxes Act providing for deductions or allowances by way of tax relief in respect of payments of rent shall apply accordingly.

8.2.6 The scope of FA 1972, s. 80

This section will only apply where all the following conditions are present:—

(a) the duration of the lease is less than 50 years;

(b) the lessee is entitled to tax relief in respect of the rent reserved under the lease;

(c) the lessee assigns the original lease to another person or surrenders it to his landlord for a consideration which would otherwise not be taxed as income;

(d) the lessee is assigned or granted a new lease of the whole or any part of the land which was the subject of the original lease for a term less than or equal to 15 years.

Where these conditions are present a proportion of the capital sum received by the lessee is treated as income. The relevant proportion is prescribed by the formula set out below:—

$$\frac{16 - n}{15}$$

where n = the term of the new lease expressed in years, where $n < 1$, n is deemed to be equal to one.

For example, suppose the lessee received £15,000 in consideration of the landlord granting a new 10 year lease. The proportion taxable as income would be:—

$$£15{,}000 \times \frac{16 - 10}{15} = £6{,}000$$

Where the rent payable under the new lease is deductible under Sch. D, Case I or II the proportion is also taxed under Sch. D, Case I or II. In any other case the proportion is treated as a Sch. D, Case VI receipt.

Where the property comprised in the new lease is less than the property subject to the old lease the capital sum taxed as income is reduced on a pro rata basis. For example, suppose the lessee receives £60,000 for the surrender of a 20 year lease and takes back a 6 year lease of half the premises which were subject to the original lease. The amount that would be treated as income of the lessee would be:—

$$\tfrac{1}{2} \times £60{,}000 \times \frac{16 - 6}{15} = £20{,}000$$

Where the capital sum is received by an individual 'top-slicing' relief is available (see TA 1970, Sch. 3) but subject to the modification set out in s. 80 (5). In the first case, where a consideration of £15,000 was received and the term of the new lease is ten years, the rate of tax on the capital receipt is found by adding to the individual's total income for the year in which the consideration is received the capital sum divided by the length of the new lease, i.e.

$$\frac{15{,}000}{10} = £1{,}500$$

This sum is treated as the 'top-slice' of the individual's income and the rate of tax applicable to this sum calculated accordingly. The rate calculated on this sum is then applied to the whole of the capital received.

In applying these rules two further points must be borne in mind. These cover where:—

(a) the currency of the lease is more than 15 years and the rent payable for the first 15 years is more than that payable after that period;

(b) either the lessor or lessee has power to determine the new lease prior to the expiration of the lease or the lessee can vary his obligations under the lease for his own benefit.

Where (a) is in point, the lease is treated as being one for 15 years. In relation to (b) the lease is treated as ending on the earliest date the lease can be determined, or on the date the lessee can vary his obligation.

The rules described above will also apply where the lessee makes an *arrangement* with the landlord to vary the terms of the lease. Where the variation involves the lessee receiving a capital sum for varying the terms of his lease and the lessee agrees to pay a higher rent for a period of less than 15 years, the lessee will be treated as having been granted a new lease for a term not exceeding 15 years but otherwise on the same terms as the original lease. The capital sum will be taxed in accordance with the rules discussed above.

8.2.7 Conclusions

The difficulties encountered in applying the legislation have arisen as follows:—

(a) Section 491. The difficulty of determining a commercial rent as no two persons' view of what constitutes a commercial rent will be the same and in some cases can vary substantially. It is difficult to see how the uncertainty created by the legislation could be resolved as the question is a factual one and is largely dependent on the evidence of reputable professional people, who often differ in their opinions.

(b) Section 80. This section is badly drafted and has been relatively easy to avoid. Problems have occurred where the original lease is surrendered to the landlord who subsequently demolishes the existing premises and builds a tower block on the site of the old premises and then grants a lease to the original lessee of a floor which was airspace before the rebuilding.

8.3 Part 2. Other assets: TA 1970, ss. 492, 493, 494 and 495

8.3.1 Introduction

The abuse which gave rise to these subsections is very similar to the sale and leaseback of land. A trader would sell an asset which he used in his business for a capital sum and would then lease the asset from the purchaser on terms which provided for a high rental in the early years of the lease and a nominal sum in the later years. This exercise could then be repeated every few years by the lessee selling his interest to a third party and taking a sub-lease from the third party on the same footing as the original lease. If the capital sum was received prior to 15 April 1964 no tax was payable on the capital sum and the rentals, as fully deductible expenses, reduced taxable profits during the period of the high rental. Section 492 attacks such devices by charging the capital sum to tax under Sch. D, Case VI and is complemented by s. 493, which is cast in similar terms to s. 491 and disallows the rental element in excess of a commercial rent. Section 494 is a procedural section and defines the scope and operation of s. 492. Section 495 covers the situation where leased assets are subject to hire-purchase agreements and contains similar provisions to those contained in s. 493.

8.3.2 TA 1970, ss. 492 and 494: The statutory provisions

TA 1970, ss. 492 and 494 read as follows:—

492 Assets leased to traders and others

(1) Subject to s. 493 below, where:—

(a) a deduction by way of tax relief which is of one of the kinds listed in subs. (3) below is allowable in respect of a payment made under a lease of an asset of any description, and

(b) before, at or after the time when the payment is made, either:—

(i) the person who made the payment has obtained or obtains a capital sum in respect of the lessee's interest in the lease, or

(ii) the lessor's interest in the lease, or any other interest in the asset, has belonged to an associate of the person who made the payment, and that associate has obtained a capital sum in respect of that interest,

the person obtaining that sum shall be charged under Case VI of Sch. D for the chargeable period in which the sum is obtained with tax on an amount equal to the amount of the payment in respect of which tax relief is so allowed:

Provided that the total amount on which he is assessed by reference to the capital sum shall not exceed the amount of the capital sum.

(2) Subsection (1) above shall not apply to payments under a lease created on or before 14 April 1964.

(3) The kinds of deductions by way of tax relief to which subs. (1) above applies are as follows:—

(a) a deduction in computing profits or gains or losses of a trade, profession or vocation for the purposes of tax,

(b) a deduction in computing profits or gains chargeable under Case VI of Sch. D, or in computing any loss for which relief is allowable under s. 176 or s. 179 of this Act (Case VI losses),

(c) allowance of a payment under s. 304 or 305 of this Act (management expenses),

(d) a deduction from emoluments to be assessed under Sch. E made in pursuance of s. 189 (1) of this Act (necessary expenses), or allowable in computing losses in an employment for tax purposes,

(e) a deduction allowable for tax purposes in computing profits or gains or losses arising from woodlands.

(4) Where the deduction by way of tax relief mentioned in subs. (1) (a) of this section is a deduction in computing, for income tax purposes, profits or gains or losses of a trade, profession or vocation, or arising from woodlands, and any part of the payments made under the lease by the person obtaining the capital sum is a payment in respect of which a deduction is not allowed for the reason that the whole or any part of the period in which the payment would fall to be allowed is not a period on the profits or gains of which income tax falls to be computed in respect of the trade, profession or vocation, for the reference in the proviso to the said subs. (1) to the amount of the capital sum there shall be substituted a reference to that amount after deducting the amount of the payment in respect of which a deduction is not allowed for that reason.

(5) So far as in respect of a capital sum any part of a payment allowed as a deduction by way of tax relief of a kind to which this section applies is taken into account in making an assessment under subs. (1) of this section, that part of the payment shall be left out of account in determining whether any and if so what amount should be assessed by reference to any other capital sum; and the order in which this subsection is applied shall be the order in which the capital sums are obtained.

(6) In this section and ss. 493, 494 and 495 below:—
"asset" means any description of property or rights other than land or an interest in land,
"capital sum" means any sum of money, or any money's worth, except so far as it or any part of it is to be treated for the purposes of tax as a receipt to be taken into account in computing the profits or gains or losses of a trade, profession or vocation, or profits or gains or losses arising from woodlands, or is, apart from this section, chargeable under Case VI of Sch. D, and
"lease", in relation to an asset, means any kind of agreement or arrangement under which payments are made for the use of, or otherwise in respect of, an asset, and includes, in particular, any agreement or arrangement all or any of the payments under which represent instalments of, or payments towards, a purchase price.

(7) There shall be made all such adjustments of tax, whether by way of making assessments or by repayment of tax, as are required after the making of any such payment as is described in subs. (1) of this section to give effect to the charge under that subsection in respect of a sum obtained before the making of the payment.

(8) Notwithstanding anything in the Tax Acts limiting the time within which an assessment may be made or a claim for relief may be admitted any such adjustment may be made, by making an assessment or otherwise, at any time not more than six years from the end of the chargeable period in which the payment was made.

(9) This section shall not apply if the capital sum obtained in respect of the lessee's interest in a lease constituting a hire-purchase agreement for machinery or plant is a sum which is required to be brought into account as the whole

or part of the disposal value of the machinery or plant under s. 45 (2) of the Finance Act 1971.

494 Leased assets: supplemental

(1) References in s. 492 above (in this section called "the principal section") to a sum obtained in respect of the lessee's interest in a lease of an asset, or in respect of any other interest in an asset include:—

(a) in the case of a lessee's interest, references to sums representing the consideration in money or money's worth obtained on a surrender of the rights to the lessor, or on an assignment of the lease, or on creating a sublease or any other interest out of the lease, and

(b) references to any insurance moneys payable in respect of the asset, so far as payable to the owner of the interest in the asset.

(2) Such references also include references to sums representing money or money's worth obtained by the person entitled to the interest by a transaction or series of transactions disposing of the asset, or of an interest in the asset, and in particular transactions which comprise arrangements under which the rights of the lessee under a lease of the asset are merged in any way with the rights of the lessor, or with any other rights as respects the asset, so far as the money or money's worth so obtained is attributable to the rights of the lessee under the lease.

(3) References in the principal section to sums obtained in respect of any interest in an asset include references to money or money's worth so obtained in any transaction (including a transaction of the kind described in the preceding provisions of this section) by way of consideration received by a person who is an associate of the person entitled to the interest in the asset.

(4) If an interest in the asset is disposed of by any person to a person who is his associate, the person disposing of the interest shall (unless in fact he obtains a greater sum) be treated for the purposes of the principal section as having obtained in respect of the interest:—

(a) the value of the interest in the open market, or

(b) the value of the interest to the person to whom it is, in effect, transferred,

whichever is the greater.

(5) For the purposes of subss. (3) and (4) above a disposition may be direct or indirect and may be effected by any such transaction as is described in subs. (2) above.

(6) For the purposes of the principal section, this section and s. 495 below, any sum obtained by persons carrying on a trade, profession or vocation in partnership in respect of an interest in an asset which is and continues to be used for the purposes of the trade, profession or vocation shall be regarded as apportionable between them in the shares in which they are then entitled to the profits of the trade, profession or vocation.

(7) Subject to subs. (6) above, for those purposes a sum obtained by persons jointly entitled to an interest in an asset shall be apportionable according to their respective interests in the rights.

(8) For the said purposes, any payment in respect of which a deduction is allowable by way of tax relief which is made by persons carrying on a trade, profession or vocation in partnership shall be apportioned in such manner as may be just.

(9) Where under this section any sum or payment falls to be apportioned and, at the time of the apportionment, it appears that it is material as respects the liability to tax (for whatever period) of two or more persons, any question which arises as to the manner in which the sum or payment is to be apportioned shall be determined, for the purposes of the tax of all those persons:—

(a) in a case where the same body of General Commissioners have jurisdiction with respect to all those persons, by those Commissioners, unless all those persons agree that it shall be determined by the Special Commissioners,

(b) in a case where different bodies of Commissioners have jurisdiction with respect to those persons, by such of those bodies as the Board may direct, unless all those persons agree that it shall be determined by the Special Commissioners, and

(c) in any other case, by the Special Commissioners,

and any such Commissioners shall determine the question in like manner as if it were an appeal:

Provided that all the said persons shall be entitled to appear and be heard by the Commissioners who are to make the determination or to make representations to them in writing.

(10) For the purposes of this section and in construing the expressions "associate" and "associated" in the principal section and this section, the following persons shall be deemed to be associated with each other, that is to say:—

(a) any individual and that individual's husband or wife, and any relative, or husband or wife of a relative, of that individual or of that individual's husband or wife ("relative" meaning for this purpose brother, sister, ancestor or lineal descendant);

(b) any person in his capacity of trustee of a settlement and any individual who in relation to the settlement is a settlor, and any person associated with that individual ("settlement" and "settlor" having for this purpose the meanings assigned to them by s. 444 (2) of this Act);

(c) any person and a body of persons of which that person, or persons associated with him, or that person and persons associated with him, has or have control;

(d) any two or more bodies of persons associated with the same person by virtue of para. (c) above;

(e) in relation to a disposal by joint owners, the joint owners and any person associated with any of them.

In this subsection "body of persons" includes a partnership and "control" has the meaning assigned to it by s. 534 of this Act.

8.3.3 The scope of TA 1970, ss. 492 and 494

8.3.4 TA 1970, s. 492

TA 1970, s. 492 is not dissimilar to FA 1970, s. 80 and covers where a lessee has claimed a tax deduction in respect of lease payments for an asset and in consideration has received a capital sum. This sum will be taxed as follows. The lease payments on which tax relief is claimed will be charged to tax under Sch. D, Case VI until in aggregate the assessments equal the capital sum received. In this context tax relief covers:—

(a) a deduction in computing profits and losses of a trade, profession or vocation;

(b) a deduction against Sch. D, Case VI profits or gains or losses;
(c) management expenses;
(d) a deduction from emoluments under TA 1970, s. 189;
(e) a deduction in computing profits or gains or losses from woodlands.

In the case of (a) and (e) above, where the trade or management of the woodlands has not been carried on for the whole of the chargeable period and a proportion of the rent is disallowed, the person in receipt of the capital sum will be assessed on the sum received after deducting the rental disallowed.

Where more than one capital sum is received the rental payments are to be taken in the same order as the capital sums received. Assessments can be made at any time within 6 years from the end of the year in which a payment was made and so tax is limited to the aggregate of 6 years' payments. Where the capital sum is received prior to the payments under the lease an assessment in respect of this sum can be adjusted at a later date to take into account subsequent events. An exemption is provided where the capital sum received by the lessee represents part or whole of the disposal proceeds to be brought into account under FA 1971, s. 45 (2); this section covers the sale proceeds of plant and machinery subject to a hire purchase or lease agreement.

EXAMPLE 1

X Ltd took a lease of plant from Y Ltd at a rent of £10,000 for a period of 4 years and thereafter at a nominal rent of £1 per annum. The lease was signed on 1 April 1980 and on 31 March 1982 X Ltd sold the lease for £24,000. A Case VI assessment would be raised on X Ltd on the sum of the payments on which tax relief had been allowed, i.e. £20,000 (£10,000 + £10,000).

EXAMPLE 2

X Ltd took a lease of plant from Y Ltd as from 1 April 1976 at a rent of £10,000 for 3 years and subsequently, £50 per year. On 31 December 1977 X Ltd sublet the plant to Z Ltd at a rent of £6,000 per annum for 4 years and thereafter at £200 per annum a machine valued at £8,000. At 31 December 1978 Y Ltd wished to make use of the plant and agreed to pay X Ltd £14,000 for cancellation of its interest in the lease. At that date Z Ltd also agreed to surrender the sub-lease it held from X Ltd and in consideration received £3,000 from X Ltd and equipment from Y Ltd valued at £5,000. These transactions will give rise to the following Case VI assessments:—

X Ltd

Rent paid	*£000*
Year ending 31.3.77	10.0
Year ending 31.3.78	10.0
Nine months to 31.12.78	7.5
	27.5

Case VI assessments

1977–78: Value of machine	8.0
1978–79: Capital sum received	14.0
	22.0

Z Ltd

Rent paid	
Year ending 31.12.78	6.0

Case VI assessment 1978–79		*£000*
Capital sum from X Ltd	3.0	
Value of machine from Y Ltd	5.0	
	8.0	
Total capital receipts		8.0
Rent paid		6.0
		2.0
	6.0	

8.3.5 TA 1970, s. 494

This section covers the scope of s. 494. Readers will have noted in **8.3.2** that the section can be broken down into two parts, i.e. subss. (1)–(5) and (10) define the terms used in s. 492 and subss. (6)–(9) relate to procedural matters.

Subsections (1) and (2) define in more detail references in s. 492 to a sum obtained in respect of the lessee's interest in a lease of an asset, or in respect of any other interest in an asset. Subsections (1) (a) and (b) provide that it shall include:—

(a) in the case of the lessee's interest, references to sums representing the consideration in money or money's worth obtained on the surrender of the rights to the lessor, or on an assignment of the lease, or on creating a sublease or any other interest out of the lease, and

(b) references to any insurance moneys payable in respect of the asset, so far as payable to the owner of the interest in the asset.

This is further extended by subs. (2) which provides that:—

> 'Such references also include . . . sums representing money or money's worth obtained by the person entitled to the interest by a transaction or series of transactions disposing of the asset, or of an interest in the asset, and in particular transactions which comprise arrangements under which the rights of the lessee under a lease of the asset are merged in any way with the rights of the lessor, or with any other rights as respects the asset, so far as the money or money's worth so obtained is attributable to the rights of the lessee under the lease.'

These very broad provisions extend the scope of the section to transactions where an asset is disposed of or an interest in it is disposed of and would include a merger of a lessee's and lessor's interest. Where an associate of a person entitled to an interest in an asset received a capital sum these are brought within the ambit of s. 494 by subs. (3). Where an interest in an asset is sold by a person to an associate of that person subs. (4) enables the Revenue to substitute for the sum received, unless that is greater, the market value of the interest, or the value to the transferee, whichever is greater.

Subsections (6)–(9) cover the apportionment of capital sums received or sums paid for an interest in an asset where the sum is paid or received by a partnership, or by joint owners. In the case of a partnership the sum is to be apportioned according to the partners' respective profit shares; in the case of joint owners, according their respective interests in the asset or assets. Where a deduction falls due in respect of rental payments the deduction is to be apportioned in such a manner as may be just. Where this gives rise to a dispute and the tax relief is material subs. (9) provides:—

> (a) '. . . where the same body of General Commissioners have jurisdiction with respect to all those persons, by those Commissioners, unless all those persons agree that it shall be determined by the Special Commissioners;
>
> (b) . . . where different bodies of Commissioners have jurisdiction with respect to those persons, by such of those bodies as the Board may direct, unless all those persons

agree that it shall be determined by the Special Commissioners; and

(c) in any other case, by the Special Commissioners.'

The Commissioners shall determine the question as if it were an appeal and the various parties are entitled to appear and be heard by the Commissioners or to make representations to them in writing.

8.3.6 TA 1970, s. 493: The statutory provisions

TA 1970, s. 493 reads as follows:—

493 Leased assets: special cases

(1) This section shall apply, and s. 492 above shall not apply, to payments:—
- (a) which are allowable by way of deductions in computing the profits or gains or losses of a trade, and
- (b) which are made under a lease of an asset which at any time before the creation of the lease was used for the purposes:—
  - (i) of that trade, or
  - (ii) of another trade carried on by the person who at that time or later was carrying on the first mentioned trade,

and when so used, was owned by the person carrying on the trade in which it was being used.

(2) Subject to this section, the deduction allowable in computing the profits or gains or losses of the trade for the purposes of tax as respects any such payment shall not exceed the commercial rent of the asset for the period for which the payment was made.

(3) If under subs. (2) of this section part of a payment which would otherwise be allowable as a deduction is not so allowable, and one or more subsequent payments are made by the same person under the same lease, that part of the first-mentioned payment may be carried forward and treated for the purposes of computing the profits or gains or losses of the trade for the purposes of tax as if it were made at the time when the next of those subsequent payments was made, and so made for the period for which that subsequent payment was made.

(4) For the purposes of subs. (2) of this section:—

(a) if more than one payment is made for the same period the payments shall be taken together,

(b) if payments are made for periods which overlap, the payments shall be apportioned, and the apportioned payments which belong to the common part of the overlapping periods shall be taken together,

(c) the preceding references to payments include references to parts of payments which under subs. (3) of this section are treated as if made at a time subsequent to that at which they were made,

and to the extent that a part of a payment carried forward under subs. (3) of this section is not allowable as a deduction it may again be carried forward under the said subs. (3).

(5) A payment made for a period all of which falls more than one year after the payment is made shall be treated for the purposes of this section as made for that period of one year beginning with the date on which the payment is made, and a payment for a period part of which falls after the end of that year shall be treated for those purposes as if a corresponding part of the payment was made for that year (and no part for any later period).

(6) For the purpose of making a comparison under subs. (2) of this section between a payment, or payments taken together, and the commercial rent of the asset, "commercial rent" shall mean the rent which might at the relevant time be expected to be paid under a lease of the asset for the remainder of the anticipated normal working life of the asset, being a rent payable at uniform intervals and at a uniform rate which would afford a reasonable return for its market value at the relevant time, having regard to the terms and conditions of the lease, and in this subsection:—

"anticipated normal working life" means, in the case of any asset, the period which might be expected, when the asset is first put into use, to be going to elapse before it is finally put out of use as being unfit for further use, it being assumed that the asset is going to be used in the normal manner and to the normal extent, and is going to be so used throughout that period, and

"the relevant time" means the time when the lease was created under which the payment was made with which the commercial rent is to be compared:

Provided that if the asset is used at the same time partly for the purposes of the trade and partly for other purposes the commercial rent as defined in this subsection shall be determined by reference to what would be paid for such a partial use of the asset.

(7) This section shall not apply in relation to payments made under a lease created on or before 14 April 1964.

(8) In this section references to the person carrying on a trade are references to the person carrying on the trade for the time being, and where at any time a person succeeds to a trade which until that time was carried on by another person, and by virtue of s. 154 or s. 251 (1) of this Act the trade is to be treated as discontinued, the trade shall, nonetheless, be treated as the same trade for the purposes of this section.

(9) In this section references to a trade include references to a profession or vocation.

8.3.7 The scope of TA 1970, s. 493

This section is similar to TA 1970, s. 491 which covers the taxation treatment of sale and leaseback of land transactions. This section restricts the deductibility of lease payments. Only those sums which represent a commercial rent can be deducted in computing the profits or losses of a trader where the asset was used for the purpose of his trade prior to the creation of the lease. Where part of a rental payment is disallowed it can be carried forward to subsequent periods and is treated as if it had been paid in the later period. The same commercial criterion is also applied to later periods where these include payments brought forward and payments made during the later period. Subsection (4) prescribes how payments are to be apportioned where the periods they cover overlap and where several payments are made during a period.

There are also provisions which re-allocate payments where the leaseback hiring agreement provides for the rental to be spread over the period of the hire but provides that whilst the rental hire should be paid in earlier years it should also cover later years. Subsection (5) provides that where a payment is made for a period, all of which commences more than a year after payment is made, it is treated as if made for a period commencing on the date of the payment. Suppose a payment is made on 1 April 1980 for a period commencing 1 June 1981 it would be treated as if made for a period commencing on 1 April 1980. As a corollary, where a payment for a period, part of which falls after the end of that year, in the above example after 31 March 1981, it is to be treated as if paid for that year and not for any later period.

Subsection (8) covers a business which is transferred from one person to another and the latter succeeds to the business discontinued by the former: in such cases the trade will be treated as being the same trade as that of the predecessor.

EXAMPLE

A Ltd owns a machine which originally cost £10,000; on 1 September 1978 he sells the machine to a dealer for £6,000, subject to a leaseback agreement from the dealer for a period of 8 years at a rent of £5,000 payable on 1 September 1978, £2,400 on 1 July 1980, £2,200 on 1 July 1981 and thereafter annually at the rate of £1 per annum. The working life of the asset is assessed at 8 years. The market value of the machine at 1.9.78 is £7,000 and a reasonable commercial rent would be £1,000 per annum.

A Ltd has a 31 August accounting period. The amount deductible in the accounts of A Ltd would be as follows:—

	£000	*Rent paid* *£000*		*Allowable* *£000*
Paid 1.9.78		5.0		
Deductible y/e 31.8.79	1.0			1.0
Deductible y/e 31.8.80	1.0	2.0		1.0
		3.0		
Paid 1.7.80		2.4		
		5.4		
Paid 1.7.81		2.2		
		7.6		
Deductible y/e 31.8.81		1.0		1.0
		6.6		
Deductible y/e 31.8.82		1.0		1.0
		5.6		
4 years rent to 31.8.86		–		
		5.6		
Deductible for the 4 y/e 31.8.86		4.0		4.0
Total Disallowed		1.6	Allowed	8.0

8.3.8 TA 1970, s. 495: The statutory provisions

TA 1970, s. 495 reads as follows:—

495 Leased assets subject to hire-purchase agreements

(1) In the application of s. 492 above (in this section called "the principal section") to a lease which constitutes a hire purchase agreement, for the reference in the proviso to subs. (1) of that section to the amount of the capital sum there shall, where that capital sum was obtained in respect of the lessee's interest in the lease constituting the hire-purchase agreement, be substituted references to the amount of the capital sum (adjusted, if necessary, under subs. (4) of the principal section) after deducting any capital expenditure which was incurred by the person obtaining the capital sum in providing the lessee's interest and which is, for capital allowance purposes, still unallowed at the time when the assignment or other transaction takes place in respect of which the capital sum is obtained.

(2) In subs. (1) above "capital expenditure incurred by the person obtaining the capital sum in providing the lessee's interest" means:—

(a) so much of any payment made under the lease by the person obtaining the capital sum (or, where the capital sum was obtained by the personal representatives of a deceased person, so made by that deceased person) as is not a payment in respect of which a deduction is allowable by way of tax relief which is one of the kinds listed in subs. (3) of the principal section, plus

(b) where the lessee's interest was assigned to the person obtaining the capital sum, any capital payment made by that person as consideration for the assignment.

(3) In subs. (1) above the reference to the amount of capital expenditure which is, for capital allowance purposes, still unallowed at the said time shall be construed as a reference to the amount of the capital expenditure after deducting any amount which, under s. 41 of the Capital Allowances Act 1968 (definition of "expenditure unallowed" for purposes of capital allowances for machinery and plant), would be deductible in ascertaining as at that time the amount still unallowed of expenditure incurred by the said person in providing the leased asset.

(4) If the amount to be deducted in pursuance of subs. (1) above exceeds the amount of the capital sum from which it is to be deducted, no charge shall arise under subs. (1) of the principal section in respect of the capital sum.

(5) If the capital sum represents the consideration for part only of the lessee's interest in the lease which constitutes a hire-purchase agreement, the amount to be deducted under subs. (1) above shall be such proportion of the capital expenditure which is still unallowed as is reasonable having regard to the degree to which the capital expenditure has contributed to the value of what is disposed of in return for the capital sum.

(6) If more than one capital sum is, or is to be regarded as, obtained by the same person in respect of the lessee's interest in the lease which constitutes a hire-purchase agreement, then, so far as in respect of one of those capital sums any deduction is made in respect of capital expenditure in pursuance of subs. (1) above that capital expenditure shall be left out of account in applying subss. (1) and (4) above to any other such capital sum; and the order in which this subsection is applied shall be the order in which the capital sums are obtained.

(7) In this section "hire-purchase agreement" has the meaning given by s. 1 of the Hire-Purchase Act 1965.

In Scotland for the preceding definition there shall be substituted the following definition:—
"hire-purchase agreement" means any contract, in whatsoever terms it may be expressed, whereby goods are taken on hire by one person from another person in consideration of periodical payments to be made by the first mentioned person to the other person with an option to the first mentioned person to become the buyer of the goods.

8.3.9 The scope of TA 1970, s. 495

This section covers the situation where assets are the subject of a lease which takes the form of a hire-purchase arrangement (this has the same meaning as s. 1 of the Hire Purchase Act 1965). Where a lessee receives a capital sum from selling his interest in the lease he will be taxed on the capital sum after deducting any capital expenditure he has incurred in acquiring the interest in the asset. This deduction will only be available where the asset is not yet written off for tax purposes. Unallowed capital expenditure is to be construed in accordance with s. 41 Capital Allowances Act 1968 and where the sum to be deducted exceeds the capital sum received no charge to tax will arise. If the capital sum received by the lessee represents part only of the consideration the deduction from the capital sum will be on a pro rata basis. Where more than one capital sum is received in respect of a lease and a deduction for unallowed capital expenditure has been given against one of the capital sums, it is to be disregarded in applying the above provisions to any other capital sum. The capital expenditure is to be deducted from the capital sums in the order in which they are received.

EXAMPLE

X Ltd entered into a hire-purchase agreement to purchase a piece of plant and machinery on the following terms:—

(a) 4 annual instalments of £6,000; and
(b) a final instalment of £500.

The first payment is to be made on 1 April 1978 and annually thereafter. It is ascertained that the 4 instalments represent capital of £5,000 and the balance of £1,000 represents interest: the final instalment represents interest. Suppose that the first year allowance is not claimed for the accounting period to 30.6.78 and that X Ltd sells its interest in the agreement for £25,000 on 29 June 1980.

	£000
1 April 78 Cost of machine	20
Y/E 30.6.78 No allowance falls due	–
	20
Y/E 30.6.79 – 25%	5
Written down value at 30.6.79	15

The balancing charge is not £10,000 (£25,000 – £15,000); an assessment under s. 495 (1) will be made as follows:—

	£000	£000
Capital sum received		25
Deduct Capital expenditure incurred		
1.4.78	5	
1.4.79	5	
1.4.80	5	
	15	
Less Capital allowances	5	10
Sch. D, Case VI		15

8.4 Conclusions

The provisions as they relate to other assets are more widely drawn than those relating to land. In practice it is not difficult to avoid the latter provisions as they and particularly FA 1972, s. 80 are badly drafted. Furthermore, it is these provisions which the practitioner is more likely to meet as the sale and leaseback of land is more common than the sale and leaseback of other assets, such as plant and machinery. The reason is self evident for land is more acceptable as a security than plant and machinery as it tends to appreciate in value over time in contrast to the latter which tends to fall in value. The practitioner should not consider the two sections covering land transactions in isolation. It could be that transactions falling within FA 1972, s. 80 might also be within TA 1970, s. 488. As we have seen the scope of the provisions is very wide and the professional adviser should take great care when advising on land transactions to ensure that all three sections are taken into account. There is no equivalent problem in relation to the sale and leaseback of other assets. Indeed, such transactions are now somewhat of a rarity.

9 Miscellaneous tax avoidance legislation

9.1 TA 1970, s. 487: Sale by an individual of income derived from his personal activities

9.1.1 The abuse

In the late 1960s it became common for higher rate taxpayers, whose income was to a large extent dependent on their personal activities, to incorporate themselves and to subsequently sell their shares in the company by 'floating it on the market'. The advantage of the scheme was that it converted earned income, then taxed at rates up to 83%, to capital gains, which when realised were, and still are, only taxed at 30%. This became known as the 'constellation scheme' and a variety of performers are known to have taken advantage of these schemes and include such famous names as Engelbert Humperdinck, Tom Jones and David Hemmings. The legislation is directed at such schemes and the Revenue to date have shown very little interest in applying it to other professions such as accountants, solicitors and estate agents, who often use service companies to promote some or all of their activities. However, there has been talk in the press that the Football League will allow footballers to 'incorporate' and hire their services to football clubs. If allowed this will 'shelter' some of the footballers' income and in this author's view, make them vulnerable to attack under TA 1970, s. 487.

9.1.2 The legislation – TA 1970, s. 487

TA 1970, s. 487 reads as follows:—

487 Sale by individual of income derived from his personal activities

(1) Subject to subs. (5) below, this section has effect where:—
(a) transactions or arrangements are effected or made to exploit the earning capacity of an individual in any

occupation by putting some other person in a position to enjoy all or any part of the profits or gains or other income, or of the receipts, derived from the individual's activities in that occupation, or anything derived directly or indirectly from any such income or receipts, and

(b) as part of, or in connection with, or in consequence of, the transactions or arrangements any capital amount is obtained by the individual for himself or for any other person, and

(c) the main object, or one of the main objects, of the transactions or arrangements was the avoidance or reduction of liability to income tax.

(2) Any such capital amount shall for all the purposes of the Income Tax Acts be treated as being earned income of the individual which arises when the capital amount is receivable, and which is chargeable to tax under Case VI of Sch. D.

(3) In this section:—

(a) references to any occupation are references to any activities of any of the kinds pursued in any profession or vocation, irrespective of whether the individual is engaged in a profession or vocation, or is employed by or holds office under some other person, and

(b) references in subs. (1) above to income or receipts include references to payments for any description of copyright or licence or franchise or other right deriving its value from the activities, including past activities, of the individual.

(4) This section shall not apply to a capital amount obtained from the disposal:—

(a) of assets (including any goodwill) of a profession or vocation, or of a share in a partnership which is carrying on a profession or vocation, or

(b) of shares in a company,

so far as the value of what is disposed of, at the time of disposal, is attributable to the value of the profession or vocation as a going concern, or as the case may be to the value of the company's business, as a going concern:

Provided that if the value of the profession, vocation or business as a going concern is derived to a material extent from prospective income or receipts derived directly or indirectly from the individual's activities in the occupation, and for which, when all capital amounts are disregarded, the individual will not have received full consideration, whether as a partner in a partnership or as an employee or otherwise, this subsection shall not exempt the part of the capital amount so derived.

In this subsection references to the company's business include references to the business of any other company in which it holds shares directly or indirectly.

(5) This subsection has effect where on any occasion an individual obtains a capital amount consisting of any property or right which derives substantially the whole of its value from the activities of the individual, or (as in the case where the individual acquires a stock option and subsequently exercises the stock option) there are two or more occasions on which an individual obtains a capital amount consisting of any such property or right.

Tax under this section shall not be charged on any such occasion, but, without prejudice to the generality of the provisions of this section or s. 489 below, tax under this section shall be charged on the occasion when the capital amount, or any such capital amount, is sold or otherwise realised, and shall be so charged by reference to the proceeds of sale or the realised value.

(6) For the purposes of subs. (1) (b) above the cases where an individual obtains any capital amount for some other person include cases where the individual has put some other person in a position to receive the capital amount by providing that other person with something of value derived, directly or indirectly, from the individual's activities in the occupation.

(7) This section shall apply to all persons, whether resident in the UK or not, if the occupation of the individual is carried on wholly or partly in the UK.

(8) This section shall not apply as respects a capital amount receivable before 15 April 1969.

9.1.3 The scope of the provisions

Before the section can be invoked three conditions must be satisfied:—

(a) transactions or arrangements are made to exploit the earning power of an individual in any occupation by putting some other person (e.g. a limited company) in a position to enjoy all or any part of the profits or gains . . . derived from the individual's activities;
(b) as a result of these arrangements a capital sum is obtained by the individual either for himself or for any other person;
(c) the main object, or one of the main objects of the transactions or arrangements, was the avoidance or reduction of liability to income tax.

Income or receipts, for the purposes of subs. (1), includes copyright, licence and franchise payments and other rights deriving their value from the activities of the individual and so trading activities are outside the scope of the legislation.

Subsection (4) provides an exemption in the case of a bona fide sale of a profession or vocation, irrespective of what form the sale takes, e.g. sale of assets owned by a partnership or a sale of shares in a company. The exemption is limited to cases where the purchase price is attributable to the value of the profession or vocation as a going concern, or where applicable, the value of the company's business as a going concern. This would not cover a variant of the constellation scheme in the guise of a partnership. The individual would take a small proportion of the profit and a large share of the assets when the partnership was dissolved. This possibility is nullified in the penultimate paragraph of subs. (4) which restricts the exemption to cases where the individual has been fully remunerated for his services. Where the individual does not satisfy this condition part of the capital sum will be taxed as income. This sum will represent the capitalised value of the difference between the sum he should have charged for his services and the sum that was charged.

Subsection (5) is defined in all embracing but non-exhaustive terms. However, tax will only be charged when the capital amount, or sum representing the capital amount, is sold or otherwise realised. In the circumstances it is surprising that the latter is not defined.

The possible scope of the legislation in this author's view has been underestimated and could cover the following bona fide commercial transactions:—

(a) X, Y and Z are partners who take in another partner A and under the terms of the partnership deed A is required to pay a premium. Unless the old partners receive full consideration for their duties the Revenue may seek to tax the premium as a capital sum under s. 487.

The author thinks the Revenue would have great difficulty in persuading a tribunal that income tax avoidance was the main purpose of such a transaction but it remains a possibility. Such a burden would be extremely onerous in anything other than a blatant tax avoidance arrangement.

(b) X in the partnership referred to above now wishes to retire but the partnership want to retain him as a consultant after his retirement. If he does not receive full consideration for the services he renders any capital sum he receives on his retirement could be taxed under s. 487. This author thinks this danger is more apparent than real, for the same reason as was stated above in connection with (a).

(c) The Revenue would also have difficulties, for the same reasons, in raising an assessment where one of the partners accepted a smaller profit share in consideration of a larger capital sum on dissolution.

9.2 TA 1970, s. 496: Transactions associated with loans or credits

9.2.1 The abuse

In recent years the eligibility of interest for relief against income tax has become restricted to certain quite tightly prescribed purposes. To overcome these restrictions lenders disguised interest payments on loans by requiring the borrower to repay the interest and capital in the form of either an annuity or as an annual payment (i.e. other than in the form of interest). The following section was enacted to counter this abuse.

9.2.2 The legislation – TA 1970, s. 496

Section 496 reads as follows:—

496 Transactions associated with loans or credit

(1) This section applies as respects any transaction effected with reference to the lending of money or the giving of credit, or the varying of the terms on which money is lent or credit is given, or which is effected with a view to enabling or facilitating any such arrangement concerning the lending of money or the giving of credit.

This subsection has effect whether the transaction is effected between the lender or creditor and the borrower or debtor, or between either of them and a person connected with the other or between a person connected with one and a person connected with the other.

(2) If the transaction provides for the payment of any annuity or other annual payment, not being interest, being a payment chargeable to tax under Case III of Sch. D, the payment shall be treated for all the purposes of the Tax Acts as if it were a payment of annual interest.

(3) If the transaction is one by which the owner of any securities or other property carrying a right to income agrees to sell or transfer the property, and by the same or any collateral agreement:—

(a) the purchaser or transferee, or a person connected with him, agrees that at a later date he will sell or transfer the same or any other property to the first-mentioned person, or a person connected with him, or

(b) the first-mentioned person, or a person connected with him, acquires an option which he subsequently exercises, to buy or acquire the same or any other property from the said purchaser or transferee or a person connected with him,

then, without prejudice to the liability of any other person, the first-mentioned person shall be chargeable to tax under Case VI of Sch. D on an amount equal to any income which arises from the first-mentioned property at any time before the repayment of the loan or the termination of the credit.

(4) If under the transaction a person assigns, surrenders or otherwise agrees to waive or forgo income arising from any property (without a sale or transfer of the property) then, without prejudice to the liability of any other person, he shall be chargeable to tax under Case VI of Sch. D on a sum equal to the amount of income assigned, surrendered, waived or forgone.

(5) If credit is given for the purchase price of any property, and the rights attaching to the property are such that, during the subsistence of the debt, the purchaser's rights to income from the property are suspended or restricted, he shall be treated for the purposes of subs. (4) above as if he had surrendered a right to income of an amount equivalent

to the income which he has in effect forgone by obtaining the credit.

(6) The amount of any income payable subject to deduction of income tax . . . shall be taken for the purposes of subs. (4) above as the amount before deduction of that tax.

(7) References in this section to connected persons shall be construed in accordance with s. 533 of this Act.

9.2.3 The scope of the provisions

In summary, before the annuity or annual payment can be treated as annual interest for the purpose of income tax and corporation tax the following conditions must be satisfied:—

(a) money is lent, or credit is given, or the terms of these facilities are varied; and
(b) the transaction is effected with a view to 'enabling or facilitating' (a); and
(c) whether the transaction is effected between the lender or creditor and the borrower or debtor, or between either of them and a person connected with the other or between a person connected with one and a person connected with the other.

Subsection (3) covers where:—

(a) the owner of any income-yielding asset agrees to sell or transfer the asset and by the same or collateral agreement the purchaser, transferee or connected person agrees to sell the original or other assets to the owner or connected person; or
(b) the owner or connected person acquires an option which he subsequently exercises to buy or acquire the same or other assets from the purchaser, transferee or connected person,

the owner will be assessed to tax under Sch. D, Case VI on the income from the property before the loan is repaid or terminated.

This subsection is further extended by subs. (4) to include the situation where a person assigns, surrenders or agrees to waive or forgo income from any asset of which he continues to be the legal and beneficial owner. To cover more sophisticated arrangements, such as where assets are acquired but completion is delayed and during the period between acquisition and completion the purchaser's rights to income from the assets are either restricted or suspended, the debtor will be treated as if he had surrendered a right to the amount of income which arises during that period. This subsection is intended to cover the following types of transactions, namely a sale of shares in a company with deferred rights or the acquisition of property, which is subject to a rackrent lease, where the purchaser forgoes his right to the rent for a period which may or may not be related to the period between acquisition and completion.

In summary, the comprehensive nature of this subsection effectively frustrates the devices for avoiding the restrictions on the deductibility of interest and especially FA 1972, s. 75 (2) and taxes the seller on income which arises during the period between the date the asset is sold and the date it is subsequently repurchased.

9.3 Stock relief: FA 1976, Sch. 5, paras. 22 and 23

9.3.1 Introduction

Obviously relief for the increase in stock values over an accounting period is at the very least a valuable deferral and if stock values are maintained for 6 years the deferral becomes a permanent tax saving (FA 1976, Sch. 5, para. 26 (3)). It is obvious that this legislation could be abused unless the Revenue were given sufficient countervailing power. This power is contained in FA 1976, Sch. 5, paras. 22 and 23.

9.3.2 The legislation – FA 1976, Sch. 5, paras. 22 and 23

22. (a) Where any arrangements have been effected by a person carrying on a trade, or by him and other persons acting together, such as, in particular, the following:—

(i) any acquisition or disposal of trading stock otherwise than in the normal course of the trade in question; or

(ii) any change in the normal pattern or method of carrying on the trade; or

(iii) any change in the date to which the accounts of the trade are made up; or

(iv) any increase in the value of a person's trading stock which is associated with a decrease in the trading stock of another person connected with him (within the meaning of TA 1970, s. 533 (5) or (6)),

and it appears that the sole or main benefit which, but for this paragraph, might have been expected to accrue to that person was the obtaining or the reduction of the amount of a charge under this Schedule, an adjustment shall be made under this paragraph.

(b) The adjustment is to substitute, for the purposes of this Schedule, for any opening or closing value of trading stock in any period of account which appears to have been affected by the arrangements, the value which it appears there would have been had those arrangements not been made.

23. (a) For the purpose of this Schedule in ascertaining the entitlement of a person to relief, or his liability to a charge, in respect of any period of account:—

(i) in a case where at any time during the twelve months preceding the beginning of that period of account he was not carrying on the trade in question; or

(ii) in a case where during that period of account there was a major alteration in the conduct of the trade in question which resulted in an exceptional increase in his trading stock,

he shall be treated as having at the beginning of that period of account trading stock of such value as may be attributed in accordance with this paragraph.

(b) If for any of the purposes of this Schedule there falls to be ascertained the value of any trading stock at a date other than the beginning or end of a period of account and when no value was in fact determined, that value shall be such as may be attributed in accordance with this paragraph.

(c) The value to be attributed is such value as is reasonable and just having regard to all the relevant circumstances of the case, and in particular:—

(i) to the opening and closing values of trading stock of the trade for that period of account;

(ii) to movements during that period of account in the costs of items of a kind comprised in the person's trading stock during the period; and

(iii) to changes during that period in the volume of the trade carried on by that person.

9.3.3 The scope of the provisions

These provisions enable the Revenue to substitute a stock value other than that shown in the company's tax computation. The most important point about these two provisions is that the question of whether a transaction or transactions is, or are, within para. 22 is a factual one and so findings of the Special Commissioners in this area will be absolutely crucial. It follows that when a business is increasing its level of stock it should conduct a thorough factual analysis as to the reasons. Apart from the taxation aspects it may well have beneficial managerial effects. For instance, as a result of the analysis it might be found that stocks are higher than they otherwise should be.

Paragraph 23 is purely procedural. In practice the Revenue have agreed to most suggestions put forward by advisers. Whilst the Revenue have internal guidelines they seem prepared to modify these to take into account industry factors.

To date these two paragraphs have not given rise to any litigation. The Revenue's practice in interpreting these two paragraphs has been remarkably liberal. One suspects that this is not because of any hitherto unknown benevolence on the part of the Revenue, but the hard economic fact that stock values are an important determinant of short-term employment.

9.3.4 The new stock relief

The new form of stock relief, based on the opening value of stock and an all-stock index, will be effective for any accounting period which ends on or includes 14 November 1980. FA 1981, Sch. 9, paras. 22–24 contains very similar provisions and as these are so similar to the previous provisions it was felt unnecessary to consider them further.

9.4 Particular schemes

9.4.1 Introduction

Until recently individuals earning over £20,000 were subject to high rates of personal tax in excess of 50%. This gave rise to a thriving tax avoidance industry and each tax year a different tax scheme would be 'marketed'. Inevitably this took the form of the creation of a deduction against income followed by a non-taxable receipt. Inevitably these schemes attracted the attention of the Government and each year legislation would be enacted to counter the scheme then in operation. This section will cover the following schemes:—

(a) the advanced-interest arrangement;
(b) the reverse-annuity;
(c) the individual/company capital allowance arrangements;
(d) the commodity carry-over scheme;
(e) leasing;
(f) films.

9.4.2 The advanced-interest arrangement

This arrangement is currently being considered by the Special Commissioners and, in essence, took the following form. A taxpayer would borrow a large sum of money on which he was immediately charged interest. The loan would be from a bank and as soon as the interest was charged it would be eligible for tax relief. The promoter of the arrangement would then arrange for the taxpayer to novate the loan to a third party. The novation would be at a lower figure than the original loan plus the interest; whilst the interest charged on the loan would be deductible the gain on the loan novation would not be taxable. It is perhaps easier to understand this arrangement by working through an example:—

Step 1 Taxpayer borrows £100,000 and is immediately charged interest of £15,000.

Step 2 The loan (including the rolled-up interest) is then novated for, say, £112,000.

The effect of these two transactions is that the taxpayer is £3,000 out of pocket and this represents the promoter's charge. There were a number of variations of this scheme; these variants were not radically different from the scheme outlined above. These schemes were effectively stopped by FA 1976, s. 38.

9.4.3 FA 1976, s. 38

Section 38 reads as follows:—

38 Restriction of relief for payments of interest

(1) Relief shall not be given to any person under any provisions of the Tax Acts in respect of any payment of interest if a scheme has been effected or arrangements have been made (whether before or after the time when the payment is made) such that the sole or main benefit that might be expected to accrue to that person from the transaction

under which the interest is paid was the obtaining of a reduction in tax liability by means of such relief as aforesaid.

(2) In this section "relief" means relief by way of deduction in computing profits or gains or deduction or set off against income or total profits.

(3) Where the relief is claimed by virtue of s. 259 (6) of the Taxes Act (group relief) any question under this section as to what benefit might be expected to accrue from the transaction in question shall be determined by reference to the claimant company and the surrendering company taken together.

(4) This section applies
(a) where the payment is after 8 June 1976; and
(b) as respect relief:—
(i) under s. 248 or 259 (6) of the Taxes Act in relation to the total profits for an accounting period beginning after that date or for any part falling after that date of an accounting period beginning earlier; or
(ii) under s. 75 of the Finance Act 1972 in relation to income for the part of the year 1976–77 falling after that date,
where the payment is on or before that date.

(5) For the purposes of subs. (4) (b) above:—
(a) the total profits for part of an accounting period shall be so much of the total profits for the whole period (reduced by any relief otherwise than in respect of the payment or payments in question) as is apportioned to that part;
(b) the income for part of a year of assessment shall be so much of the income for the whole year (reduced by any relief otherwise than as aforesaid and otherwise than under Chapter II of Part I of the Taxes Act) as is apportioned to that part;
and any apportionment for the purposes of this subsection shall be made on a time basis.

Before turning to the reverse-annuity scheme, reference should be made to the criterion to be applied to these payments – that is, the words 'sole or main benefit etc'. As with TA 1970, ss. 460 and 488 the question arises as to whether the test is subjective or objective. This matter will be discussed in more detail in the final chapter.

9.4.4 The reverse-annuity scheme

As with most schemes there were a number of variants. Basically the scheme worked as follows. In consideration of receiving a capital sum from a charity the taxpayer would covenant to make a series of annual payments to the charity. The annual payment would be an allowable deduction for higher rate tax purposes and the income tax deducted from the annual payment under TA 1970, s. 53 could be reclaimed by the charity from the Inland Revenue. The capital sum received by the taxpayer at the commencement of the scheme was usually deposited with a bank and used to make the subsequent annual payments. One of these cases, *IRC v Plummer* [1979] STC 793, has been fought very bitterly all the way to the House of Lords where the taxpayer was ultimately successful. In a majority decision it was held that:—

(a) Per Lord Wilberforce, Lord Fraser of Tullybelton and Lord Keith, Viscount Dilhorne dissenting. The general rule that an annuity purchased with capital was income of the recipient applied to the facts of this case, as the legal form of the documents comprising the various transactions could not be disregarded.
(b) Per Lord Wilberforce, Viscount Dilhorne, Lord Fraser of Tullybelton and Lord Keith. The annual payments were to be treated as having been made wholly out of profits or gains brought into charge to tax within TA 1970, s. 52 (1), even though the source of the payments was not the taxpayer's taxed income but the capital sum deposited with the bank. Relief could be obtained under s. 52 (1) if the payment was less than or equal to the taxpayer's income.
(c) Per Lord Wilberforce, Viscount Dilhorne, Lord Fraser of Tullybelton and Lord Keith. The annual payments were made for 'valuable and sufficient consideration' within TA 1970, s. 434 (1). Furthermore, they also found that the expected tax benefits had to be taken into account in making the evaluation of whether the consideration was sufficient.
(d) Viscount Dilhorne and Lord Diplock dissenting. The annual payments did not fall to be treated as the taxpayer's income under TA 1970, s. 457 (1) because the word 'settlement' in s. 454 (3) applied only to transactions with an element of bounty and not to bona fide commercial transactions. As there was no element of bounty in the transactions it was not a 'settlement' within s. 457 (1).

To counter such schemes s. 48 of the Finance Act 1977 was enacted.

9.4.5 Finance Act 1977, s. 48

FA 1977, s. 48 reads as follows:—

48 Annual payments for non-taxable consideration

(1) Any payment to which this subsection applies shall be made without deduction of income tax, shall not be allowed as a deduction in computing the income or total income of the person by whom it is made and shall not be a charge on income for the purposes of corporation tax.

(2) Subject to the following provisions of this section, subs. (1) above applies to any payment which:—
- (a) is an annuity or other annual payment charged with tax under Case III of Sch. D, not being interest; and
- (b) is made under a liability incurred for consideration in money or money's worth all or any of which is not required to be brought into account in computing for the purposes of income tax or corporation tax the income of the person making the payment.

(3) Subsection (1) above does not apply to:—
- (a) any payment which in the hands of the recipient is income falling within s. 457 (1) (a) or (c) or (2) of the Taxes Act (partnership agreements, transfers of businesses and maintenance agreements);
- (b) any payment made to an individual under a liability incurred in consideration of his surrendering, assigning or releasing an interest in settled property to or in favour of a person having a subsequent interest;
- (c) any annuity granted in the ordinary course of a business of granting annuities; or
- (d) any annuity charged on an interest in settled property and granted at any time before 30 March 1977 by an individual to a company whose business at that time consisted wholly or mainly in the acquisition of interests in settled property or which was at that time carrying on life assurance business in the UK.

(4) In the application of this section to Scotland the references in subs. (3) above to settled property shall be construed as references to property held in trust.

(5) Subsection (1) above does not apply to any payment made on or before 29 March 1977 but applies to a payment made

after that date irrespective of when the liability to make it was incurred.

Before turning to the next scheme two points should be mentioned:—

(a) taxpayers who entered into the scheme on the same or similar footing to the facts in *IRC v Plummer* are, it is understood, having great difficulty in obtaining their refunds. In fact it is thought that the taxpayers may have to fight the Revenue in the courts on the same basis as in *IRC v Plummer* before a refund is made; and

(b) the scheme still exists, albeit in a more refined basis by seeking to take advantage of subs. (3) (b).

The questions raised by (a) above obviously give rise to constitutional questions and will be discussed in more detail in the concluding chapter. The post *IRC v Plummer* arrangement referred to in (b) has not been resolved. To date it is thought that only one of the cases has been heard by the Special Commissioners, but with no result as yet.

9.4.6 Individual/company capital allowance arrangements

In common with the two schemes outlined above there were also a number of variants of this scheme. An individual and a company would form a leasing partnership. Profit would be shared on, say, a 50:50 basis and losses on, say, a 90:10 basis. The scheme worked as follows. A partnership would purchase a piece of plant machinery which would be leased to a trading company. If there were no other transactions during the period, 9/10 of the losses of the partnership would be attributed to the individual. Shortly after the end of the fiscal year he would assign his interest in the partnership to the company for a capital sum. The capital sum would not be taxable as it would be equal to, or nearly equal to, the capital contributed by the individual. The lease rentals were not taxable in the hands of the company, as inevitably it was based overseas. FA 1976, s. 41 nullifies these schemes.

9.4.7 Finance Act 1976, s. 41

FA 1976, s. 41 reads as follows:—

(1) Relief shall not be given to an individual under s. 168 of the Taxes Act (set-off against general income) by reference

to a first-year allowance made to him in respect of expenditure incurred on the provision of machinery or plant for leasing in the course of a trade if:—

(a) at the time when the expenditure was incurred the trade was carried on by him in partnership with a company (with or without other partners); or

(b) a scheme had been effected or arrangements have been made (whether before or after that time) with a view to the trade being carried on by him as aforesaid.

(2) Relief shall not be given to an individual under the said s. 168 by reference to a first-year allowance if:—

(a) the allowance is made in connection with:—

(i) a trade which at the time when the expenditure was incurred was carried on by him in partnership or which has subsequently been carried on by him in partnership or transferred to a person who was connected with him within the meaning of s. 533 of the Taxes Act; or

(ii) an asset which after that time has been transferred by him to a person who was connected with him as aforesaid or, at a price lower than that which it would have fetched if sold in the open market, to any other person; and

(b) a scheme has been effected or arrangements have been made (whether before or after that time) such that the sole or main benefit that might be expected to accrue to the individual from the transaction under which the expenditure was incurred was the obtaining of a reduction in tax liability by means of such relief as aforesaid.

(3) Where relief has been given in a case to which subs. (1) or (2) above applies it shall be withdrawn by the making of an assessment under Case VI of Sch. D.

(4) For the purposes of subs. (1) above letting a ship on charter shall be regarded as leasing it if, apart from this provision, it would not be so regarded.

(5) In this section "first-year allowance" means a first-year allowance under Chapter I of Part III of the Finance Act 1971, "trade" includes any activity in connection with which a first-year allowance can be given and any expression defined in s. 50 of the said Act of 1971 has the meaning given in that section.

(6) This section applies to relief under the proviso to s. 71 (1) of the Capital Allowances Act 1968 as it applies to relief under the said s. 168.

(7) Subsections (1) and (2) above apply where the expenditure in respect of which the allowance is made to the individual in question was incurred by him after the commencement date and otherwise than under a contract entered into by him on or before that date; and "the commencement date" is, in relation to subs. (1), 15 December 1975 and, in relation to subs. (2), 6 April 1976.

The reference to s. 71 (1) of the Capital Allowances Act 1968 is where an allowance is given by way of discharge or repayment of tax. This relief principally arises in connection with agricultural buildings and other works. It should be noted that the section does not apply to a partnership between individuals, providing the sole or main benefit . . . etc was not the obtaining of a reduction in tax liability. Again it is noticeable that the legislation is couched in terms of the 'sole or main benefit'.

9.4.8 Commodity carry-over schemes

This arrangement was so widely publicised that retrospective legislation was introduced to nullify the tax advantages to which the scheme gave rise. The substance of the scheme was similar to the capital allowance scheme discussed above. A taxpayer would enter into a partnership with an offshore company and set up a trade as dealers in commodity futures. It is possible, by various devices, but one known to this author as the 'butterfly straddle', to realise a loss in one period and to subsequently realise a gain of a similar magnitude in a later period. If in the earlier period losses are shared by the taxpayer as to 90% and an offshore limited company as to 10% and the partnership invested £150,000 in such a straddle the individual would be entitled to loss relief of £135,000, the sum he would have contributed to the partnership. After the fiscal year it inevitably followed that he would resign and his original capital contribution (£135,000) or a sum close to that figure would be repaid. The other side of the butterfly, the unrealised gain, would be realised but if it was realised after the individual retired from the partnership, the realised gain would accrue to the offshore company. It is likely that such a company would have organised things such that no tax would arise on the realised gain. The effect of the scheme is therefore to give the taxpayer loss relief under TA 1970,

s. 168 and no tax liability on the capital repaid by the company partner. Finance Act 1978, s. 31 effectively counters these arrangements.

9.4.9 Finance Act 1978, s. 31

Section 31 reads as follows:—

> (1) Relief shall not be given to any person under s. 168 or 177 (2) of the Taxes Act or s. 30 above (set-off of trading losses against general income) in respect of a loss sustained in a trade of dealing in commodity futures if:—
> (a) the loss was sustained in a trade carried on in partnership and that person or one or more of the other partners was a company; and
> (b) a scheme has been effected or arrangements have been made (whether by the partnership agreement or otherwise) such that the sole or main benefit that might be expected to accrue to that person from his interest in the partnership was the obtaining of a reduction in tax liability by means of such relief as aforesaid.
>
> (2) Where relief has been given in a case to which this section applies it shall be withdrawn by the making of an assessment under Case VI of Sch. D.
>
> (3) This section applies whether the loss was sustained before or after the passing of this Act but not where the scheme was effected or the arrangements were made wholly before 6 April 1976.

The only point to note is the criteria which brings this section into operation, 'the sole or main benefit' test. This has already been alluded to above. This now seems to be the standard weapon used by the Revenue to counter tax avoidance schemes. It could also affect innocent commercial transactions.

9.4.10 Leasing

These schemes took two forms:—

(a) purely deferral: tax in such cases could be saved if income was diverted from one period (when it would be highly taxed) to another period (when it would be taxed at a lower rate);

(b) husband and wife partnerships: the husband would enter into a partnership with his wife on a 90:10 basis (10% husband and 90% wife). Capital expenditure would be incurred in the first year, against which the 100% first year allowance would be claimed. This could be offset against the husband's income under TA 1970, s. 169. In the second and subsequent years nine-tenths of the income from the leases would be treated as the wife's earned income and a significant tax saving could be effected by the wife claiming separate treatment of her earnings.

Schemes such as (b) above were very common and in many cases were accepted by the Revenue, although a few were heard by the Special Commissioners but from press reports it appears that in most cases the taxpayers were successful with their appeals. It was felt by the Government that the subsidy to the taxpayer was too expensive in relation to the beneficial employment effects and as a result legislation was introduced to nullify the generous capital allowances that could be claimed by individuals (including partnerships) who carried on the trade of leasing.

FA 1980, s. 70 now provides as follows:—

70 Leasing by individuals

(1) There shall be disregarded for the purposes of s. 169 of the Taxes Act (set-off against general income) any allowances made to an individual under Chapter I of Part III of the Finance Act 1971 in respect of expenditure incurred on the provision of machinery or plant for leasing in the course of a trade unless:—

(a) the trade is carried on by him for a continuous period of at least six months in, or beginning or ending in, the year of loss as defined in that section; and

(b) he devotes substantially the whole of his time to carrying it on throughout that year or if it is set up or permanently discontinued (or both) in that year, for a continuous period of at least six months beginning or ending in that year.

(2) Subsection (1) above shall apply also to expenditure incurred by an individual on the provision for the purposes of a trade carried on by him of an asset which is not to be leased if payments in the nature of royalties or licence fees are to accrue from rights granted by him in connection with that asset.

(3) In the proviso to s. 48 (4) of the said Act of 1971 (allowances in respect of expenditure on machinery or plant let otherwise than in the course of a trade):—
(a) after the words "Provided that" there shall be inserted the words "the proviso to subs. (1) of the said s. 71 shall not apply to an allowance made by virtue of s. 46 (1) above and"; and
(b) for the words "the proviso to subs. (1) of the said s. 71 or, as the case may be, subs. (4) of the said s. 74" there shall be substituted the words "subs. (3) of the said s. 74".

(4) Where relief has been given in a case to which this section applies it shall be withdrawn by the making of an assessment under Case VI of Sch. D.

(5) References in this section to the carrying on of a trade by an individual are to his carrying it on either alone or in partnership.

(6) This section is without prejudice to s. 41 of the Finance Act 1976.

The only comment to which this section gives rise is the meaning to be attributed to the words 'he devotes substantially the whole of his time'. It is felt by most people that a commonsense interpretation will be followed and the section will be interpreted as one would expect, namely that an individual must spend most of his time in the leasing trade before he can claim any relief under TA 1970, s. 169. Shortly after the 1980 budget it was suggested that it could be argued that wives, with no other occupation, might satisfy this requirement in relation to the few hours they might spend dealing with their leasing activities. This it is submitted is wrong. It could hardly be argued that the wife, in such circumstances, spent substantially the whole of her time in the leasing trade. Time in this context must be viewed against the background of a working week. Clearly the wife would not be within FA 1980, s. 70 (1) (b).

9.4.11 Films and tapes

In recent years tax planners have become aware of the potential planning opportunities inherent in the production of films and tapes. This arises from the peculiar nature of the industry. Most of the expenditure on the production of a film negative or master tape is incurred some time before the receipt of any income. Clearly by judicious use of accounting periods expenditure on the film or tape can be apportioned to one accounting period and the receipts attributed to another. If the film is produced by a partnership which has access to bank finance it is possible to apportion to an individual partner, in the accounting period the film or tape is produced, losses in excess of his capital contribution. In the subsequent period he can either:—

(a) retire and hope that the Revenue allow the apportioned losses against his other income; or
(b) continue in the partnership; and either,
(c) offset the apportioned losses against his income of the year in which they were incurred; and then
(d) carry forward any unutilised losses against future income from the partnership.

In August 1979 the Revenue issued a statement of practice on the treatment of expenditure on producing films and certain other assets, such as tapes. Paragraphs 3 and 4 of this statement read as follows:—

> 3. The Inland Revenue has been reviewing the position and agrees that film production expenses can qualify for capital allowances. In future therefore capital allowance claims for film production expenditure will be accepted, provided the master-print of the film can properly be regarded as a capital asset in the business. In practice a master-print would be regarded as meeting this condition if it is retained by the production company and has an anticipated potential life of not less than 2 years.
> 4. Similar considerations apply to some other types of expenditure on producing assets, e.g. capital expenditure incurred in producing the master copy of records and tapes. Capital allowance claims for such expenditure will be allowed on the same basis.

This statement gave rise to a number of film arrangements, some of which were highly publicised and provided 'gearing' in the region of 5:1. One suspects that as a result of the publicity the Government were forced to introduce legislation. This is contained in the section which covers leasing arrangements and readers are referred to **9.4.10** for the provisions which provide that where first year allowances are claimed on such assets no loss relief under TA 1970, s. 169 shall be given.

It should be pointed out that this legislation does not affect film schemes where, instead of claiming first year allowances, the cost of the film is immediately written off in the profit and loss account. The other point is whether a limited partner can obtain loss relief in excess of his capital contribution. The majority view is that he can if there is a commercial likelihood of the film being a success and that his decision to retire or remain in the partnership is based on commercial principles.

9.5 Conclusions

This section has reviewed mainly anti-avoidance legislation which has been enacted to nullify specific schemes. The exception was in the case of stock relief where the provisions are of general application. The legislation that has been reviewed has been of a restorative, rather penal nature. This may not be the case in the future. What is clear from this review is that as soon as a scheme attracts press publicity the Government are forced to act quickly and legislate. The danger of rapidly enacted legislation is that it may have adverse consequences not originally envisaged for quite innocent commercial transactions. In practice this probably means that tax-efficient arrangements which are not widely 'marketed' and abused will go largely unchallenged in the courts by the Revenue but provocative schemes which are marketed are almost certain to go to the House of Lords. Further it now seems common in relation to such schemes that the Revenue are less than cooperative in trying to resolve the issues to which the schemes give rise, either during the course of litigation or subsequently as a result of a House of Lords' decision in a case, which for most purposes is identical. This certainly seems to be the experience of participants in the 'reverse-annuity *Plummer* scheme' as it has come to be known. This should be a salutary warning to those entering such schemes and should put them on notice that they can expect 'guerilla' tactics to be employed by the Revenue.

10 Statutory interpretation

10.1 Introduction

The aim of this chapter is to give guidance to the professional adviser on a number of issues to which the legislation reviewed in the previous chapters gives rise. In a specific context, the rules applied by the judiciary in interpreting fiscal statutes will be discussed in order to provide guidance to the adviser in cases where the words in a statute have not yet been the subject of litigation. In practice advisers are also asked whether a decision on a point of interpretation is correct; this subject will be covered in the context of the *Vestey* decision [1980] STC 10, HL. In this case reference was also made to the role of extra-statutory concessions and this subject will be discussed in the same section. In a more general context, advisers are frequently called upon to give advice in connection with arrangements where a number of sequential transactions, occurring at varying time intervals, are in contemplation. This necessitates considering the attitude of the courts to such arrangements where there is an element of tax avoidance and the two arguments which have been put forward with increasing sophistication by the Revenue and known as 'the sham doctrine' and 'the substance and form argument' and the recent *Ramsay* decision [1981] STC 174 HL. Obviously these topics are interrelated and so it will not be possible or useful to discuss them in isolation.

10.2 The normal rules of statutory interpretation

10.2.1 The basic rules

Where there is any ambiguity in the legislation the benefit of the doubt should generally be given to the taxpayer, *Scott v Russell* (1945) 30 TC 375, Viscount Simonds at 424, and *Kanjee Naranjee v*

I T Comrs [1965] AC 1238, PC. This principle has been cut down where a provision gives relief from a section which clearly imposes liability, *Littman v Barron* (1951) 2 All ER 393 at 398 per Cohen LJ, affirmed sub nom *Barron v Littman* (1953) 33 TC 373. In deciding whether there is any ambiguity in the statute three rules have been developed by the judiciary for the purpose of interpreting statutes. These are the 'literal rule', the 'golden rule' and the 'mischief rule'.

As a general rule all statutes will be presumed to use words in their popular sense, unless the context otherwise requires, *Clerical, Medical and General Life Assurance Society v Carter* (1889) 22 QBD 444 at 448 per Lord Eacher, MR. This means that the words of a statute will be given their ordinary grammatical meaning. Where the literal rule gives rise to a wholly unrealistic result the golden rule has been applied. This rule was first enunciated by Lord Wensleydale in *Grey v Pearson* (1857) 6 HLC 61 at 106. Where this rule is applied the ordinary sense of the words is modified to avoid absurdity or inconsistency, but no further. The third rule, known as the mischief rule, is derived from a famous case in the sixteenth century, *Heydon's Case* (1584) 3 Co Rep 7a. The Barons of the Exchequer held that:—

> '. . . for the sure and true interpretation of all statutes in general four things are to be discerned and considered: (1) what was the common law before the passing of the Act; (2) what was the mischief and defect for which the common law did not provide; (3) what remedy the Parliament later resolved and appointed to cure the disease of the Commonwealth; (4) the true reason of the remedy.
>
> And then the office of all the judges is always to make such construction as shall suppress the mischief and advance the remedy, and to suppress subtle invention and evasions for the continuance of the mischief.'

Where this rule is applied the object and purpose of the Act is considered and specifically, the context and setting in which the words are placed, together with the design of the whole statute. Lord Denning, who as we shall see is a well known crusader against the tax avoider, would attempt to examine anti-avoidance legislation by looking at the avoidance scheme first. This comes very close to applying the mischief rule, see *Escoigne Properties Ltd v IRC* [1958] AC 549 at 565 and *Shop and Store Developments v IRC* [1966] Ch 108 at 130. Whilst this method of interpreting a statute is not usually adopted by other members of the judiciary it should be pointed out that where legislation is drafted in very wide terms such as FA 1960, s. 28, now TA 1970, s. 460 (transactions designed to avoid tax) the judiciary have been given statutory authority to look at the transactions as a whole, which can come very close to adopting the mischief rule. The question of the courts' attitude to s. 460 cases will be discussed in more detail in a subsequent paragraph; the intention in this paragraph is merely to highlight a section of the Income and Corporation Taxes Act 1970 which endorses the use of the mischief rule by the judiciary.

In applying the above rules the judiciary should also take into account the fact that a statute is designed to be workable and construed so as to secure that object, unless there is some omission or other direction that makes this end unattainable. When interpreting an expression used in a statute the courts should find out what the legislature really meant by the expression, without necessarily attributing to it a precise technical definition. In *R v I T General Comrs for the City of London, ex parte Gibbs* (1942) 24 TC 221 at 255 it was held that the court can only look at the statute, it cannot refer to the speeches in Parliament which preceded the passing of the statute. Where there is ambiguity as to the meaning of an expression the court can adopt a construction most likely to carry out the general intention of Parliament, per Lord Macmillan in *Perry v Astor* (1935) 19 TC 255 at 288. Where there is no ambiguity the court has no choice but to give the words the clear meaning they bear.

The principles discussed above have been admirably summarised by Lord Donovan in *Mangin v IRC* [1971] AC 739 at 746.

> 'First, the words are to be given their ordinary meaning. They are not to be given some other meaning simply because their object is to frustrate legitimate tax avoidance devices. . . . Secondly, . . . one has to look at what is clearly said. There is no room for an intendment. There is no equity about a tax. There is no presumption as to tax. Nothing is to be read in, nothing is to be implied. One can only look fairly at the language used. . . . Thirdly, the object of the construction of a statute being to ascertain the will of the legislature it may be presumed that neither injustice or absurdity was intended. If, therefore, a literal interpretation would produce such a result, and the language admits of an interpretation which would avoid it, then such an interpretation may be adopted. Fourthly, the history of an enactment and the reasons which led to its being passed may be used as an aid to its construction.'

10.2.2 Statutory interpretation of earlier Acts with later Acts

It is usual for the annual Finance Act to provide that the sections which relate to income tax be 'construed as one with the Income Tax Acts'. One of the questions that can arise is how far an ambiguity in one Act can be resolved by reference to other Finance Acts. Where the latest in a series of Acts dealing with the same subject matter is being construed considerable emphasis should be placed on any scheme which can be seen clearly from the legislation, per Lord Simonds in *Fendoch Investment Trust Co v IRC* (1945) 27 TC 53 at 68. This should also be followed in the case of amendments.

Different considerations apply when an earlier Act is ambiguous and reference is made to the ambiguous point in a later statute. If the later Act purports to amend or declare the meaning of an earlier Act it is clear that the later Act prevails. Where an earlier Act states one thing and a later Act, by inference or otherwise, indicates that the legislators misapprehend the law as it then prevailed the earlier Act must be construed without reference to the later Act, per Lord Buckmaster in *Ormond Investment Co Ltd v Betts* (1928) 13 TC 400 at 428. Where the provision in the earlier Act is ambiguous and is open to two perfectly clear or plain constructions, or contains a phrase capable of diverse meanings, reference is then made to the later Act to resolve it. *The Camille and Henry Dreyfus Foundation Inc v IRC* (1955) 36 TC 126.

A later Act will be totally disregarded if it is drafted differently from an earlier Act, per Megarry J, *C and J Clark Ltd v IRC* [1973] STC 299 at 308.

This rule is modified in two cases:—

(a) where a later Act gives rise to a doubt as to the extent of an earlier Act which imposes a penalty, the later Act can be invoked by the taxpayer to show that the Crown has not discharged the onus of proving that the subject is liable to the penalty, *Ormond Investment Co Ltd v Betts* (1928) 13 TC 400 at 428;

(b) where an earlier Act has been judicially construed prior to the passing of a later Act and the Act adopts that construction it is not open to a higher court to reverse the earlier judicial construction.

By similar reasoning where a phrase in an earlier Act has received judicial pronouncement, the same phrase in a later Act must be assumed to bear that construction, unless a contrary meaning is stated, *Barras v Aberdeen Steam Trawling and Fishing Co Ltd* [1933]

AC 402. However, this does not mean that all previous decisions of the judiciary as to the meaning of general terms in a taxing Act will be treated as sacrosanct once they have been repeated in a subsequent Act, *Ostime v Australian Mutual Provident Society* (1959) 38 TC 492 at 519 and in practice has had little effect, see *Re Earl Fitzwilliam's Agreement* [1950] 1 All ER 191.

10.3 The implications of the *Vestey* case [1980] STC 10, HL

10.3.1 Introduction

Whilst this case has already been discussed in some detail in Chapter 3 it also gave rise to a number of other issues. In the House of Lords there was considerable discussion by all the Law Lords of two questions, firstly the circumstances that must be present before a previous decision will be reconsidered and secondly the status of extra-statutory concessions was discussed at some length by Lord Edmund-Davies. In this section I propose to review the various speeches as they relate to these issues and to discuss their implications for practice. The major speeches were by Lord Wilberforce, Viscount Dilhorne and Lord Edmund-Davies.

10.3.2 The status of 'earlier' decisions of the House of Lords

Lord Wilberforce thought that the Practice Direction (1966) 3 All ER 77 enabling the Law Lords to reverse previous decisions of the House should be used sparingly and be governed by stated principles. Whilst this may suggest some inflexibility he qualified this by saying that where the facts of a particular case could not be brought precisely within these principles this would not necessarily be fatal. The doctrine of precedent and certainty of interest usually dictated that once a decision had been reached it had to be applied subsequently to new and unforeseen circumstances. In this particular case he thought that to follow the previous decision would create serious administrative and constitutional problems. Quite what he meant by the latter is not enumerated in his judgment. Presumably, in the context of the case, he meant that the Revenue's practice, having no basis in law, was an abuse of the rule of law, a basic feature of our unwritten constitution.

Viscount Dilhorne analysed this question by examining the decision in *Jones v Secretary of State for Social Services* [1972] 1 All ER

145. In this case the decision of the House of Lords in *Minister of Social Security v Amalgamated Engineering Union* [1967] 1 All ER 210 ('*Dowling*'s case') was challenged. It was decided by a committee of seven, four of whom held that the case had been wrongly decided but four of whom that it should not be reversed. Lord Reid was of the view that a decision should only be reconsidered where some broad issue of policy was involved and only exceptionally where the issue turned on the construction of statutes and documents. This was because much depended on the particular person's approach. A meticulous examination of the language might give a different answer to one where more attention had been paid to the apparent object of the statute. He thought that a decision to reverse *Dowling* would encourage litigation and impair the underlying certainty of the law. Lord Morris thought it wholly inappropriate not to treat *Dowling*'s case as binding authority as it concerned statutory interpretation. Lord Pearson felt that the view expressed in *Dowling* was tenable and that if it was reversed it might lead to a third case which restored the first decision. Lord Simonds was of the view that on a matter of statutory construction the taxpayer would have to show that a previous construction was clearly wrong and causing administrative difficulties or individual injustice. In summary, a decision will only be reconsidered if some policy issue is involved or the circumstances are otherwise exceptional.

Where a decision had been reconsidered Viscount Dilhorne expressed the view that the possibility of the House re-examining it again was very remote.

The only other case where this question has been considered was in *Fitzleet Estates Ltd v Cherry* [1977] STC 397. In that case it was held that a previous decision would only be reconsidered where there had been a material change in circumstances since the previous case, such as that which occurred in *Miliangos v George Frank (Textiles) Ltd* [1973] 3 All ER 801, where the monetary basis of international trade changed from fixed exchange rates to floating exchange rates. It was not sufficient that doubts were expressed by a minority in an earlier case: a narrow decision would therefore be followed unless there was something of more substance than mere doubt.

10.3.3 Extra-statutory concessions

Lord Edmund-Davies's judgment is of considerable interest for the pertinent comments he made in connection with the executive's claim to make extra-statutory concessions. He pointed out that it was difficult to reconcile this with the view expressed by Lord Loreburn in *Drummond v Collins* (1915) 6 TC 525 at 539, that if the person comes within the letter of the law, he must be taxed irrespective of how unequitable the tax is. He pointed out that they had come into existence without any legal authority and that judicial comment regarding extra-statutory concessions had been mixed. Donovan LJ had observed, *FS Securities Ltd v IRC* (1963) 41 TC 666 at 683, that the income tax code was difficult to administer and practical considerations justified some departure from the strict law for the common convenience of both the Revenue and the taxpayer. In *Bates v IRC* (1966) 44 TC 225 at 268, Lord Upjohn expressed the view that such concessions had arisen because the commissioners, realising the result of applying the legislation strictly, worked out more equitable ways of operating it. However, he was unable to understand their legal basis. In the following year in *Korner v IRC* (1969) 45 TC 287 at 297 he commented favourably on an unpublished concession. Against this the views of Lord Radcliffe were noted. In *IRC v Frere* (1964) 42 TC 125 at 154 he stated that he never understood how extra-statutory concessions came into operation, given that Parliament could and does adjust the income tax code every year. In *IRC v Bates* (1966) 44 TC 225, referred to above, Lord Wilberforce had also said that administrative moderation was no substitute for legislative clarity and precision. In line with these observations Scott LJ stated in *Absalom v Talbot* (1943) 26 TC 166 at 181 that no judicial countenance could or ought to be given to extra-legal concessions, despite the fact that in many cases they avoided undue hardship. In his view it followed that their mere existence was indicative that the legislation was defective.

10.4 The attitude of the courts

The earliest reported case where a strict approach was taken to the interpretation of a fiscal statute was in *Partington v Attorney-General* and in particular, the speech of Lord Cairns, (1869) LR 4 HL 100 at 122.

> '. . . If the person sought to be taxed comes within the letter of the law he must be taxed, however great the hardship may appear to the judicial mind to be. On the other hand, if the

> Crown seeking to recover the tax, cannot bring the subject within the letter of the law, the subject is free, however apparently within the spirit of the law the case might otherwise appear to be. In other words, if there be admissible, in any statute, what is called an equitable construction, certainly such a construction is not admissible in a taxing statute, where you can simply adhere to the words of the statute.'

Similar words were expressed by Rowlett J in *Cape Brandy Syndicate v IRC* (1920) 12 TC 358 at 366.

The implications of these speeches were extended by Lord Clyde's famous speech in *Ayreshire Pullman Motor Services and Ritchie v IRC* (1929) 14 TC 754 at 763:—

> 'No man in this country is under the smallest obligation, moral or other, so to arrange his legal relations to his business or to his property as to enable the Inland Revenue to put the largest possible shovel into his stores. The Inland Revenue is not slow – and quite rightly – to take every advantage which is open to it under the taxing statutes for the purpose of depleting the taxpayer's pocket. And the taxpayer is, in like manner, entitled to be astute to prevent, so far as he honestly can, the depletion of his means by the Revenue.'

Some commentators have interpreted this as judicial countenance of tax avoidance; in this author's view this is an optimistic assessment. Lord Clyde's speech seems to be saying two things. Firstly, morality is irrelevant in interpretating fiscal statutes and secondly tax avoidance is a game of chess between the taxpayer and the Revenue. What Lord Clyde left unanswered was how far legislation should go to counter a loophole. For instance, there is no reference to the acceptability or otherwise of widely drawn anti-avoidance legislation.

As we have seen in the chapter which examined TA 1970, s. 478, tax avoidance arrangements, quite naturally, attracted the hostility of the courts during the war. Examples of this have already been cited but perhaps the most robust manifestation of this was the speech by Lord Greene MR in *Lord Howard de Walden v IRC* (1941) 25 TC 121 at 134.

> 'It scarcely lies in the mouth of the taxpayer who plays with fire to complain of burnt fingers.'

This hostility was followed by a boom in devices known as 'dividend stripping' and 'bond washing' which were subsequently enacted against. During this period there was also a boom in property prices and substantial capital gains were realised which prior to 1965 were not taxed at all. More recently very sophisticated arrangements have come before the courts, such as *Ransom v Higgs* [1974] STC 539, where gains from the sale of land were realised, albeit by a very circuitous route. This led to what is now TA 1970, s. 488. Since the 1950s three trends can be discerned:—

(a) the mixed views of the judiciary towards tax-avoidance schemes until recently;
(b) the abandonment of the traditional rules of statutory interpretation in cases where TA 1970, s. 460 has been in point;
(c) the recent hostility of the Court of Appeal and now the House of Lords to avoidance schemes.

Examples of (a) are:—

(i) Lord Denning's dissenting minority speech in *J P Harrison (Watford) Ltd v Griffiths* (1962) 40 TC 281 at 300.

'. . . I do not believe there is any rule of law which requires the Commissioners to disregard the object of the transaction or its result. . . . the Commissioners were entitled to see these people as they really are, prospectors digging for wealth in the subterranean passages of the Revenue, searching for tax repayments. They are not simple traders dealing in stocks and shares.'

(ii) This should be contrasted with Lord Simon of Glaisdale's speech in *Ransom v Higgs* [1974] STC 539 at 559:—

'But for the courts to try to stretch the law to meet hard cases (whether the hardship appears to bear on the individual taxpayer or on the general body of taxpayers as represented by the Inland Revenue) is not merely to make bad law but to run the risk of subverting the rule of the law itself.'

He then quoted Lord Tomlin's speech in *Duke of Westminster v IRC* (1936) 19 TC 490 at 520 where he cites *Heydon*'s Case (1584) 3 Co Rep 7a, on the danger of substituting 'the uncertain and crooked cord of discretion for the golden and straight metwand of the law.'

Similar sentiments were echoed recently by Ackner LJ in *Berry v Warnett* [1980] STC 631, CA 630 at 640.

Examples of (b) are:—

(i) Lord Reid in *Greenberg v IRC* (1971) 47 TC 240 at 272.

> 'I must confess that I do not like being forced step by step to a conclusion of this kind. . . . We seem to have travelled a long way from the general and salutary rule that the subject is not to be taxed except by plain words. But I must recognise that plain words are seldom adequate to anticipate and forestall the multiplicity of ingenious schemes which are consistently being devised to evade taxation. Parliament is very properly determined to prevent this kind of tax evasion, and if the courts find it impossible to give very wide meanings to general phrases the only alternative may be for Parliament to do as some other countries have done and introduce legislation of a more sweeping character, which will put the ordinary well-intentioned person at much greater risk than is created by a wide interpretation of such provisions as those which we are now considering.'

A similar view was put forward by Lord Wilberforce in *IRC v Joiner* [1975] STC 657 at 662.

(ii) Lord Wilberforce has also stated that the section is not without limits, *IRC v Parker* (1965) 43 TC 396 at 440:—

> 'We must take the Act as we find it and endeavour to see what it fairly covers. But we need not be surprised if it turns out that the attack is confined to a limited section of the front.'

Similar comments, albeit at first instance only, have been expressed by Browne-Wilkinson J in *Anysz v IRC* [1978] STC 296 at 318 and Slade J in *IRC v Garvin* [1979] STC 98, Ch.D.

Limits to this method of interpretation and in particular Lord Reid's speech in *Greenberg*, have also been expressed by Buckley LJ in a majority speech, in the Court of Appeal in *IRC v Garvin* [1980] STC 295 at 301, CA:—

> '. . . a court should officiously strive to construe a section in its widest possible significance in order to give it the widest possible operation but that one must look for the meaning evidently intended by the language used bearing in mind the objects of the section, and apply that section accordingly without giving either the taxpayer or the Revenue the benefit of any doubt or ambiguity.'

Examples of (c) are illustrated in the next three sections, see **10.5** The sham doctrine; **10.6** The form and substance doctrine and **10.7** *Eilbeck v Rawling Ramsay (WT) v IRC* [1981] STC 174, HL.

10.5 The sham doctrine

This doctrine is frequently cited by the Revenue where a taxpayer has entered into a series of highly artificial transactions in order to create a loss or avoid an assessment to tax. A recent example of this was the case of *Eilbeck v Rawling* [1980] STC 192, CA. A capital gains tax loss was manufactured by the use a reversionary interest and an advancement from a settlement. All the various transactions were pre-arranged and carried out with what the courts have described as military precision.

The 'sham doctrine' has arisen as a result of a number of hire-purchase and bills of sale cases. See, for example, *Yorkshire Railway Wagon Co v Maclure* (1882) 21 Ch.D. 309; *Madell v Thomas & Co* [1891] 1 QB 230 and the cases cited in *Stoneleigh Finance Ltd v Phillips* [1965] 1 All ER 513. Despite frequent judicial references to the doctrine its extent has remained uncertain and illusive. In the Oxford English Dictionary a sham is defined as:—

> 'something that is intended to be taken for something else, or that is not what it purports to be; a spurious imitation, a counterfeit . . . something not genuine or true.'

The judicial definition has extended this to include what might be called a 'cloak', which in effect conceals the true nature of the transactions. One such definition was put forward by Diplock LJ in *Snook v London and West Riding Investments Ltd* [1967] 1 All ER 518 at 528.

> '. . . if it has any meaning in law, it means acts done or documents executed by the parties to the 'sham' which are intended by them to give to third parties or to the court the appearance of creating between the parties legal rights and obligations different from the actual legal rights and obligations (if any) which the parties intend to create.'

Where the transaction is neither a fraud nor a nullity the legal characteristics of a sham are more difficult to recognise. The dicta of Diplock LJ indicate that a transaction will be regarded as a sham if it is intended by the parties to have a different legal effect from that which appears on the documents. For instance, suppose two parties agree that a loan should be made by one party to the other secured on certain property, but the documents are dressed up as a sale and hire-purchase agreement. The transaction may, depending on the facts, be regarded as a sham. For the transaction to be treated as a sham it seems that two tests must be satisfied. Firstly there must be an intention on the part of the parties to mislead and secondly there must be an element of incompleteness or deceit, see *Yorkshire Railway Wagon Co v Maclure* (1882) 21 Ch.D. 309.

In practice it is the second condition that prevents the Revenue from successfully invoking this doctrine, even where the transactions are part of a highly artificial tax scheme. It follows that where a transaction or document is genuine and creates the legal rights and obligations intended by the parties, it cannot be set aside as a sham, however artificial or commercially unjustifiable the transactions. This means that contracts and agreements must be validly entered into and executed, payments actually made and board meetings properly held etc.

As a result of the narrowness in scope of the doctrine the Revenue rarely seek to maintain the 'sham' argument in cases which come before the courts (see *Black Nominees Ltd v Nicol* (1975) 50 TC 229 at 250), although in recent cases before the Special Commissioners the Revenue have been putting forward 'the sham doctrine' in a more sophisticated form and in conjunction with the 'form and substance' argument which will be discussed in **10.6**. This recent version has been recently upheld before the Commissioners but until these cases reach the courts the scope of this new line of argument must remain uncertain.

10.6 The form and substance doctrine

10.6.1 Introduction

This argument usually takes the following form, namely that although the individual transactions are outside the scope of the statute, the various transactions taken together as a scheme can be brought within the statute on the basis that they represent the situation posited by the statute. In other words, the courts can ignore the legal effect of the transactions and substitute the substance of the transactions taken together.

The doctrine was finally established in the now famous and often cited *Duke of Westminster* case (1935) 19 TC 490. In that case the Duke of Westminster had executed deeds of covenant in favour of his employees; the covenanted payments were equal to their wages and it was understood, but without any legal obligation, that the employees would accept the payments under the covenant in lieu of wages. By a majority of four to one, the House of Lords rejected the claim by the Revenue to disallow the payments under the covenant as a surtax deduction on the grounds that whilst the payments had the legal character of annuities in substance they were payments for services. Perhaps the clearest statement of this doctrine can be found in the speech of Lord Russell, *Duke of Westminster v IRC* (1935) 19 TC 490 at 524:—

> 'The commissioners and Mr Justice Finlay took the opposite view on the ground that, as they said, looking at the substance of the thing the payments were payments of wages. This simply means that the true legal position is disregarded and a different legal right and liability substituted in the place of the legal right and liability which the parties have created. I confess that I view with disfavour the doctrine that in taxation cases the subject is to be taxed if, in accordance with a court's view of what it considers the substance of the transaction, the court thinks that the case falls within the contemplation or spirit of the statute. The subject is not taxable by inference or by analogy, but only by the plain words of a statute applicable to the facts and circumstances of his case. . . . If all that is meant by the doctrine is that having once ascertained the legal rights of the parties you may disregard mere nomenclature and decide the question of taxability or non-taxability in accordance with the legal rights, well and good. . . . If, on the other hand, the doctrine means that you may brush aside deeds, disregard the legal rights and liabilities arising under a contract between parties and decide the question of taxability or non-taxability upon the footing of the rights and liabilities of the parties being different from what in law they are, then I entirely dissent from such a doctrine.'

These principles have been affirmed in a number of recent tax avoidance schemes and in particular by Lord Wilberforce in *IRC v Europa Oil (NZ) Ltd* [1971] AC 760 at 771, PC.

Other instances of support for this view are:—

(a) Buckley LJ in *Newstead v Frost* [1979] STC 45 at 53, CA.
(b) Sir John Pennycuick in *Floor v Davis* [1978] STC 436 at 441, CA.

(c) Walton J in *Burman v Hedges and Butler Ltd* [1979] STC 136 at 147, Ch.D.

Before turning to the more subtle arguments the Revenue have put forward in an attempt to 'blur' the distinction between the two terms it is necessary to explore their scope in more detail.

10.6.2 Form

This refers to the legal rights and obligations created by the transaction or document. This means that however the transaction might be dressed up this will not necessarily be decisive of its form, although inevitably it will be of considerable evidential value.

10.6.3 Substance

This term is used confusingly in two contexts:—

(a) Where a particular financial result can be obtained in two or more ways, one will result in tax being payable and the other in no tax being payable. If the latter method is adopted, following *Duke of Westminster v IRC* (1935) 19 TC 490 and *IRC v Wesleyan & General Assurance Society* (1948) 30 TC 11, the Revenue will not be able to extract the tax that would have been payable had the first method been adopted.

(b) A narrower meaning: whether looking at the various transactions and documents as a whole it is legitimate to look at the net result rather than viewing each part of the scheme separately and in isolation.

In practice this distinction is often a matter of degree and in recent years the courts have been mainly concerned with (b). Lord Wilberforce in *Ransom v Higgs* (1974) 50 TC 1 said that the court were entitled to look at all the transactions together where there was evidence that each step was dependent on the others in deciding whether the taxpayer was trading. He had also taken this view in *IRC v Europa Oil (NZ) Ltd* [1971] AC 760 at 771, PC but Lord Donovan and Viscount Dilhorne dissented strongly from this view and held that the legal rights and obligations had to be taken in isolation and not together.

The view of Lord Wilberforce has also been followed in *Black Nominees Ltd v Nicol* (1975) 50 TC 229, a complicated tax avoidance scheme devised by the advisers of actress Julie Christie. Templeman J, as he then was, held that the transactions entered into by the various participants could not be viewed in isolation without regard to the consequences of the other transactions. The scheme as a whole had to be considered as each step was dependent on the others being carried out. Templeman LJ is well known for his negative attitude towards tax avoidance schemes, see *W T Ramsay Ltd v IRC* [1979] STC 582, CA and *Eilbeck v Rawling* [1980] STC 192, CA.

This view was also supported by Scarman LJ at 590. Templeman LJ also reiterated a similar view in *Eilbeck v Rawling* [1980] STC 192 at 202, CA:—

> '. . . one single circular contract or a series of interdependent contracts which revolves one property in a circle cannot be divided into separate transactions in order to determine the effect of the contract or series.'
>
> 'A circular contract which requires one asset to be revolved in a circle must be judged by the difference (if any) between the position of each party at the start and at the finish of the contract.'

Until the recent decision in the *Ramsay* case these views were not held by the House of Lords and particularly Lord Wilberforce in *IRC v Plummer* [1979] STC 793 at 797:—

> 'The plan now involved was explained by the brokers in great detail and its intended accomplishment set out, with time-tables, in almost military precision. This (as I ventured to suggest in *IRC v Church Comrs for England* (1976) STC 339) entitles and requires us to look at the plan as a whole. It does not entitle us to disregard the legal form and nature of the transactions carried out.'

In a more recent case, *Chinn v Collins* [1981] STC 1, HL, he modified this 'robust' approach slightly; where there is a pre-arranged pre-drafted tax avoidance scheme the court are entitled to look at the plan as a whole without disregarding the legal form and nature of the various transactions.

In summary, until the *Ramsay* decision, the present Court of Appeal was more ready than the House of Lords to look at a scheme as a whole where there are various inter-related transactions, either explicitly or implicitly dependent on each other. The recent *Ramsay* decision will now be considered in some detail.

10.7 *Eilbeck v Rawling; W T Ramsay Ltd v IRC* [1981] STC 174, HL

These two appeals were heard together as they both involved the question as to whether tax avoidance schemes involving a number of separate transactions, none of which were a sham, should be considered as one transaction comprising a number of what might be called sub-transactions or as two separate groups of transactions. If the former view were accepted the taxpayer's capital loss would be the difference between his position at the start of the scheme with his position at the end of the scheme. In practical terms this would mean that his capital loss would be restricted to the professional fees paid to the promoters of the scheme. If the other view were accepted the scheme would produce a deductible capital loss and a compensating non-taxable capital gain. Rather surprisingly a unanimous House of Lords accepted the former and so, it is argued, sounded the death knoll to 'the tax avoidance industry'.

The main speeches were by Lords Wilberforce and Fraser of Tullybelton. The salient points of Lord Wilberforce's speech are set out below.

(a) Each scheme consisted of a number of steps to be carried out according to a timetable, involving documents to be executed and payments to be made, in both cases with rapid succession.
(b) Once the scheme was in motion it would not be arrested at any stage. In the *Eilbeck* case this followed from the contractual nature of the arrangements whereas in the *Ramsay* case there was an expectation that the scheme would be fully implemented.
(c) Although considerable sums of money were involved at the various stages in the scheme the taxpayer did not have to put his hand in his pocket. The money was provided by a loan from a finance house and was secured by a charge on the asset which formed part of the scheme. When the various transactions were completed the loan was repaid and in some cases there was doubt as to whether any money existed at all.
(d) The purpose of the scheme was the avoidance of tax.
(e) The principle established in the *Duke of Westminster* case (1936) 19 TC 490 should not be over-stated or over-extended. It does not compel the court to look at a document or a transaction in blinkers. If a document or transaction is part of a nexus or series of transactions, or a wider transaction intended as a whole, the court can regard it as such. The court should ascertain the legal nature of the transactions and so in appropriate cases it may be

necessary to consider each individual step in a composite transaction intended to be carried through as a whole.

(f) A number of recent cases have illustrated the limitations of the *Duke of Westminster* doctrine.

(i) *Floor v Davis* [1978] STC 436, CA, affd (1979) STC 379, HL.

Eveleigh LJ, in dissenting judgment, upheld the Crown's argument that a sale arrangement comprising of two stages should be considered as an integrated transaction, despite the fact that each sale was genuine. This approach has also been supported by Templeman LJ in his Court of Appeal judgment in *Eilbeck v Rawling* [1980] STC 192, CA and referred to above in **10.6**.

(ii) *IRC v Plummer* [1979] STC 793, HL.

One of the findings by the House of Lords was that the various arrangements could be taken together as a whole. The case was not authority for the proposition that the court in other cases with different findings of fact, may not reach the conclusion that, viewed as a whole, a composite transaction may produce an effect which brings it within a fiscal statute.

(iii) *Chinn v Collins* [1981] STC 1, HL.

Although the separate steps were 'genuine' and had to be accepted under the *Westminster* doctrine the court could, on the basis of the findings made and its own legal analysis, consider the scheme as a whole and was not confined to a step by step examination.

Acceptance that the court is not confined to a single step approach was a logical development of existing authorities and a generalisation of particular decisions.

(g) The taxpayers argued that if the Crown's wide contention was accepted this would necessitate rejecting accepted and established canons of interpretation and it was for Parliament to enact widely drawn provisions to counter tax avoidance schemes. This argument was rejected on the grounds that acceptance of the Crown's contention would not involve a new principle. The court had both the power and duty to determine the nature of these new and sophisticated legal devices and to relate them to existing legislation. The courts were not obliged to stand still, as such a policy might result in loss of tax or prejudicing other taxpayers or Parliamentary congestion or all three. It was felt that any other approach would be a denial rather than an affirmation of the judicial process.

On the basis of the above analysis, he felt it would be wrong to pick out and stop at the one step in the combination which produced the loss, it being entirely dependent on, and merely a reflection of the gain. Taking the scheme as a whole he concluded that there was neither a gain nor a loss.

Lord Fraser of Tullybelton agreed with Lord Wilberforce and stated that the court is entitled and perhaps more significantly, bound to consider the scheme as a whole. On the question of whether this involved departing from a long line of authorities which required the courts to regard the legal form and nature of the various transactions he was of the opinion that his views were not inconsistent with the decision in the *Westminster* case. In that case there was only one transaction and there was no question of it forming part of a larger scheme. He felt that his views were consistent with the decision in *Chinn v Collins* [1981] STC 1 HL and the dissenting opinion of Eveleigh LJ in *Floor v Davis* [1978] STC 436, CA, affd [1979] STC 379, HL.

At first sight the implications of this case for tax planning seem nothing short of disastrous. The implications of the case will take a number of years to work out and in particular the extent to which the decision will be either followed or distinguished. As a result what follows must inevitably be tentative.

It could be argued that this case must be confined to artificial capital gains tax schemes and have no application to income schemes, such as the advanced interest arrangement. Such a restricted view is supported on the following grounds:—

(a) in the case of the capital loss schemes, there is an expectation, often near certainty, that once the scheme is put in motion it will not be arrested until all the transactions have been completed;

(b) by contrast most income schemes are arranged in such a manner that each step is independent of the next step and there is, at least in theory, a higher probability that not all the transactions in the scheme will be completed.

It is submitted that this view is incorrect. Most income schemes are artificial to the extent that the transactions are similar to those in the *Ramsay* case and there is very little likelihood that the scheme will be arrested half way through. It is this author's view that the advanced interest scheme is within the *Ramsay* case principles although the taxpayer is not totally bereft of arguments and particularly if he can show that the arrangements were of a bona fide commercial nature, following *IRC v Plummer* [1979] STC 793. However, given the current attitude of the courts it is very unlikely that the taxpayer will succeed in this case.

The only case where he is likely to succeed is where the taxpayer enters into commercial arrangements with tax advantages which arise at the commencement of the arrangement. For instance, oil and gas shelters and film productions all involve substantial sums of what has come to be known as 'front end' money. The tax advantages are usually exploited by means of a partnership which is able to borrow substantial sums of money. In such cases, a 'real' film is produced or an actual well drilled. It is a commercial decision as to when the taxpayer retires from the partnership but this is usually weighted against the taxpayer so that he retires very shortly after receiving his tax deduction. In this author's view the taxpayer is more likely to obtain his deduction the longer he remains in the partnership and so the taxpayer should give very careful consideration to this question when deciding whether to retire from such a partnership.

10.8 Conclusions

The UK like most other countries has reacted to tax avoidance schemes in a piecemeal manner. However, having said this three trends are readily discernible:—

(a) increasing use in statutes countering tax avoidance schemes of the phrase 'if a scheme has been effected or arrangements have been made . . . such that the *sole or main benefit* might be expected to accrue . . . was the obtaining of a reduction in tax liability;
(b) increasing use of clearance procedures in tax avoidance statutes;
(c) the increasing hostility of the Inland Revenue towards tax avoidance schemes.

The sole or main benefit test was first enacted during the war and subsequently in the now defunct profits tax (FA 1951, s. 32). In *Crown Bedding Co and South Wales Flock Co Ltd v IRC* [1946] 1 All ER 452, CA, it was held that the test was an objective one and this was confirmed in later decisions. However, the term did give rise to considerable dispute as it is capable of a variety of constructions. This test has been enacted in what might be called the general legislation (TA 1970, s. 460 and s. 488) and also the specific legislation (for example, FA 1976, s. 38 and FA 1978, s. 31). Rather surprisingly no cases have been litigated on this point to date and obviously the practitioner will be more concerned about its application in relation to the former than the latter. The difficulty he faces in this situation is that whilst the test is currently objective, if a provocative tax scheme was litigated in the courts the courts might be tempted to find some way of distinguishing the early cases and as a result possibly endanger future bona fide commercial transactions carried out by taxpayers. Whilst this is always a danger and one that admits of no solution, the adviser should always bear this in mind in tendering advice on bona fide commercial transactions with what might be called 'a tax flavour' and falling within either TA 1970, s. 460 or s. 488.

The clearance procedures, whilst growing with the legislation, are potpourri. For instance, in the case of s. 460 transactions application is made to an unusually helpful specialist body in Somerset House. Other sections, for instance, s. 478, have no clearance mechanism as yet, whilst under s. 488 clearance is obtained from the taxpayer's local inspector of taxes. What is not clear from s. 488 is the position where the inspector, within the 30 day limit, does not make a pronouncement: can the inspector subsequently raise s. 488 against the taxpayer? In practice the answer must be yes unless the clearance application was very carefully drafted. Clearance procedures are also appearing in legislation covering other taxes, for instance, CGTA 1979, s. 88. However, the application is made to a different specialist body from that which deals with s. 460 clearances.

The third discernible trend is the increasing hostility of the Inland Revenue in dealing with tax avoidance schemes. An instance of this is said to be the attitude of the Revenue to those taxpayers who participated in the reverse-annuity scheme in *IRC v Plummer* [1979] STC 793, which has been upheld by the House of Lords. It is understood that the Revenue take the view that it can be distinguished from otherwise indistinguishable cases, as the taxpayers entered into almost identical transactions to those of Mr Plummer. Another example of such tactics is to be seen in *IRC v Rossminster Ltd* [1980] STC 42. From press reports it appears that the Revenue are requiring every document to be proved, however trivial its status. This has added extra burdens on both the taxpayer and taxpayers in general, as a result of the extra legal costs incurred by this process. It also appears from these reports that the Revenue are no longer agreeing to fight a test case and apply the result to all taxpayers who participated in the scheme. Indeed one gathers that each taxpayer will have to pursue his case all the way to the House of Lords. However, if several cases went in favour of the taxpayer the Comptroller General might then intervene to stop further litigation in order to avert wasting further public money. Pesumably this tactic is designed to fulfil two functions:—

(a) increase the pressure on the taxpayer to abandon the scheme, and;

(b) discourage taxpayers from entering into schemes in the future. The tactics described above are a recent innovation and appear to change the nature of anti-avoidance legislation from restorative to penal.

The attitude of the Revenue has been supported by certain members of the judiciary and particularly Templeman LJ in the Court of Appeal and now in the House of Lords. Indeed in the Court of Appeal the view has been expressed by Scarman LJ in *W T Ramsay Ltd v IRC* [1979] STC 582 at 590, that he hopes in the near future that the House of Lords will reverse the dictum of the *Duke of Westminster* case. As a result of the recent *Ramsay* decision in the House of Lords the *Duke of Westminster* case will now be of limited application and if the current judicial trend is not halted there is a real danger that the uncertain and crooked cord of discretion will be substituted for the golden and straight method of the law (adapted from Coke, *Heydon's* Case (1584) 3 Co Rep 7a). This would hardly be a satisfactory state of affairs in a society which otherwise gives pre-eminence to the rule of law.

Index